# The Aesthetic of Our Anger

*Anarcho-Punk, Politics and Music*

## EDITED BY MIKE DINES & MATTHEW WORLEY

MINOR COMPOSITIONS 2016

*The Aesthetic of Our Anger. Anarcho-Punk, Politics and Music*
Edited by Mike Dines & Matthew Worley

ISBN 978-1-57027-318-6
Cover design by Haduhi Szukis
Cover image by Savage Pencil
Interior design by Margaret Killjoy

Released by Minor Compositions 2016
Colchester / New York / Port Watson

Minor Compositions is a series of interventions & provocations
drawing from autonomous politics, avant-garde aesthetics, and the
revolutions of everyday life.

Minor Compositions is an imprint of Autonomedia
www.minorcompositions.info | minorcompositions@gmail.com

Distributed by Autonomedia
PO Box 568 Williamsburgh Station
Brooklyn, NY 11211

www.autonomedia.org
info@autonomedia.org

# CONTENTS

# ACKNOWLEDGEMENTS

**THE EDITORS WOULD** like to say thanks to the contributors and to all those involved in the Punk Scholars Network. In particular they would like to thank Alastair Gordon, Russ Bestley and Rich Cross, and Vyvy for their additional comments, edits and proofing. Thanks, too, to George McKay, whose 4word makes a worthy contribution, to Steve Ignorant for agreeing to be interviewed, and to Dick Lucas for his interview and insightful views into the anarcho-scene. Throughout, the support offered by Stevphen Shukaitis and Autonomedia has been exemplary; and we are proud to be associated with such an eminent, independent publisher. The editors would also like to thank those of you that made the movement possible, the musicians, artists, writers and activists. Onwards and Upwards!

*For Sheila Whiteley (1941–2015)*

GEORGE MCKAY

# 4WORD

## AN.OK4U2@32+1984

**THAT FIRST TIME** in Norwich, Crass and Poison
Girls were astonishing, not just to me, but to all the
punks who knew about the gig and had turned up,
the more so because the bands were so casual about it,
wandering around the half-empty hall before and after
playing, wanting us, waiting for us, to talk to them.
They were out front drinking tea – I'd never ever seen
bands doing that at the end of a gig before. Music was
material to them, and they showed that; the performance was an object, clearly delineated, which they
involved themselves in and then exited. Music happened for a while and then it didn't happen. The bands
extended the performance entirely and indefinitely, to
include the pre- and post-show, the setting up of the
PA, the draping of flags and banners and subsequent
transformation of the hall, Crass in their problemat-
ically paramilitary black garb and red armbands, the

GEORGE MCKAY

sexy sexless women. Either way I was totally intimidated, and deeply attracted. Here were people doing exactly what I thought punk should do, be a force.

This was me, an eighteen-year-old punk in 1979, having his anxieties that maybe punk wasn't going to change the world (for the better) after all put on hold for a couple of more years. I'm uncertain how powerfully the sensation lasted. (Occasionally, yes, I can still express that sentence today as: I'm uncertain how powerfully the sensation *has* lasted.) It was the laying out and laying bare of ideals, culture and event presented in a total package that I fell for in that old barn that night. Nine or ten months later, the same bands played a small hall in Suffolk, a benefit gig for local peace groups. There were clashes in the sleepy market town between outsider punks and local bikers, and the bikers circulated around the hall brandishing chains waiting for lone punks to attack.

Plenty of people in the crowd – me included – aren't interested in this at all; we want to see the bands, experience the whole Crass & Poison Girls trip, that sensurround gig of music, TVs, banners, flags, uniforms, wrapped in an unpretentious delivery of the mundane. Disapproving comments are shared as we try to reassure one another, there are sneers at this new mods-and-rockers-style moment, this isn't punk, we're here for a pacifist benefit. The transformed church hall is made a site of extreme rhetoric and cultural production for two hours. But outside …

The open space of an anarcho-punk gig, where subcultural contestation and negotiation could sometimes take place, where self-determination and self-policing could take a while to work through, operated very poorly for me *that* night. Six bikers trapped me alone near the train station in the dark after the gig and taught me an unforgettable lesson about the limits of tolerance and freedom among British youth in the countryside. Welcome to anarcho-punk. Rival tribal rebel revels, indeed.

The late 1970s and early 1980s were an extraordinary period in British social history. There were sustained manifestations of violence from the Northern Ireland troubles, to the Yorkshire Ripper to the Falklands War; there was mass protest from Greenham Common to the Miners' Strike; there were periodic riots sweeping across much of the country, a socially divisive government, mass unemployment and racism. As a teenager moving into early manhood, trying to find my way in the world, it felt like I was in a country falling, or being pulled, apart. All of this was happening under the grand penetrating paranoia of the MAD ('mutually assured destruction') discourse of the nuclear sublime of the late Cold War. When you looked out across Britain then, it was tired, frightening, a bit of a dump. With, okay, some great music. It was something like this version of the British landscape that formed the dark palette of choice for an apocalyptic and dystopian sense of the world that anarcho-punk fiercely, or crudely, or both, depicted and critiqued.

For Matthew Worley the anarcho-punk scene 'served as a nexus for a range of political movements that included anarchism, feminism, anti-militarism, animal rights activism and the early 1980s Stop the City campaigns that fed into the anti-capitalism and anti-globalisation movements' of today.[1] One can look back as well as forward, and see some kinds of origins of anarcho-punk in the communes movement, in the avant-garde happenings of the 1960s counterculture, and in the 1970s free festival movement; this constructs an even more enduring tradition of cultural radicalism, while also resisting a Year Zero reading of punk. The retrospective aspects *within* anarcho-punk are important in themselves, too: cross-generational dialogue, for example, happened within bands, and enriched them with creative tension. So elder activists or counterculturalists like Penny Rimbaud of Crass or Vi Subversa of the Poison Girls would share stage and studio with young punks, and would also extend the cultural reference of the scene by drawing on their past experiences in happenings or avant-garde cabaret.

It was indeed a remarkably rich and vibrant multimedia and cross-cultural social scene, with music at its heart: music recording, production and distribution, live performance, recorded sound, film and video experimentation, clothing/style, visual art and design, graffiti and street art, typography (the Crass font), alternative organisation

---

1     Matthew Worley, "Shot By Both Sides: Punk, Politics, and the End of 'Consensus,'" *Contemporary British History* 26:3 (2012): 333-354.

networks, domestic arrangements, fundraising for campaigns, détour-
nements – all of these featured in an ambitious and encompassing
extension of DIY practice. We can also factor in other notable contributions, ranging from developments in the autonomous social centre, some of it linked with squatting culture, to a zealous commitment among some to animal rights and aspects of food production
and consumption such as vegetarianism and later permaculture, to a
considered exploration of gender politics in song from Poison Girls'
"Underbitch" and "Real Woman" to Crass's "Big Man Big M.A.N."
and *Penis Envy,* to a partial internationalisation of the project's scope.
The latter is traced by Stacy Thompson: anarcho-punk 'spread from
England to Holland and the United States and adopted economic and
aesthetic forms of negation of, and resistance to, commodification
similar to and inspired by Crass.'[2] Although it is not easy to evaluate
and substantiate, it seems clear that anarcho-punk quickly became
a remarkably popular underground music scene, achieved with very
little coverage in the mainstream music press, no advertising, no television appearances, and little radio coverage or interest. (The leading
band, Crass, never played on BBC television's leading weekly pop programme *Top of the Pops,* and recorded only one session for the John
Peel BBC Radio 1 nightly show.) It is estimated that Crass alone sold
two million records during the band's productive existence;[3] '[t]heo-
retically,' wrote one English music magazine retrospectively of their
'phenomenal record sales,' 'their walls should be covered in gold discs.'[4]

Of course, not everyone was convinced. For some anarchists, the
subcultural turn of the movement was a mistake because punk turned
off far more people than it turned on. It seemed to fetishise the chaotic and confrontational; its aggression could be frightening and intimidating. For others, culture *per se* was always secondary to class awareness and economics, and there was great distrust of ex-public school
hippy dropouts from anarcho-punk (as some indeed were) preaching
a move beyond class, away from collective organisation, and apart
from the bulk of the revolutionary left. Musicians who were themselves politically radical – from folk or jazz scenes, for instance – heard

---

2    Stacy Thompson, *Punk Productions: Unfinished Business* (Albany NY: State
     University of New York Press, 2004), 92.

3    Penny Rimbaud, *Shibboleth: My Revolting Life* (Edinburgh: AK Press, 1998), 277.

4    Thompson, *Punk Productions,* 99.

only the crude shouted slogans, naïve lyrics and images, and poor musicianship that expressed to them a lack of imagination. Too cultural for some of the existing left, not cultural enough for others, then.

The sometimes complex aesthetic of anarcho-punk claimed to be predicated on anger, as Crass sloganised on the cover of 1983's *Yes Sir, I Will*, as the band Omega Tribe put it with their 1982 EP release on Crass Records, *Angry Songs,* (as incidentally, punk itself would revisit with something like John Lydon's new autobiography *Anger is an Energy* in 2014), and as this book's very title maintains. But there were other models of anger around anarchism – only a few years earlier in London, after all, the Angry Brigade of clandestine 'urban guerrillas' and stark communiqués had employed political violence in the form of a bombing campaign aimed at engendering armed insurrection. What would be different about this new anarchist anger? It was musical and it had a specific sound – transmitted in part through the sound of the singing voice and its delivery of words ('the anger was in the vocals – raw, unprecedented, primal'[5]), and in the lyrics themselves, not least through the use of swearing. However, the sound needed capturing through the recording process, and much of the success here was down to the innovative approach of Southern Studio's owner and producer John Loder. In Samantha Bennett's view, Loder's achievements would go on to read 'like a "who's who" of 1980s and 1990s underground and alternative music, with a focus on punk, hardcore, post-hardcore, noisecore, grunge and industrial subgenres: Crass, Ministry, Fugazi, Babes in Toyland, Big Black, The Cravats, Rudimentary Peni, Shellac, and Jesus and Mary Chain.'[6]

We should consider further quite how influence and legacy operate. For example, punk, Crass, anarcho-punk and the pacifist end of the anarchist movement were the engines of my own politicisation as a teenager. They gave me frames and questions with which to think about the world, and they gave (or confirmed in) me an attitudinality

5    George Berger, *The Story of Crass* (London: Omnibus, 1998), 116.

6    Samantha Bennett, "Recording the Musical Underworld: John Loder's Southern sonic style" (paper presented at the International Association for the Study of Popular Music (UK & Ireland) biennial conference, University College, Cork, 2014). See also Oliver Sheppard, "The Postpunk Legacy of Crass Records," *Souciant* online magazine, July 9, 2012. Accessed January 21 2015, http://souciant.com/2012/07/the-postpunk-legacy-of-crass-records.

I have never quite lost. I first presented an academic piece about Crass in 1992 – I actually remember being surprised even then, just a few years after the band's end, that no-one else seemed to be paying them any attention. My earliest book as an academic, two decades ago, developed that work into the first in-depth writing about Crass and the position of anarcho-punk in the radical tradition of countercultural practice in Britain.[7] (In fact, that book, *Senseless Acts of Beauty*, had originally been conceived of by me as a book about anarcho-punk.) All my work since then, from jazz to protest to festival to gardening to disability – and lately, to my own surprise, as I get older, returning to punk – has had something or everything of the anarchist and activist in it. I even dedicated one of my books to Penny Rimbaud (he didn't really need it, having dedicated his own autobiography to...himself). Such work is itself a sort of legacy of anarcho-punk, as someone like me, or Crass historian George Berger, or some of the contributors here, have journeyed from the audience to the written page. The thoughtful, provocative, committed essays collected here will further contribute to and interrogate the anarcho-punk movement, its sounds and cultures, its energy and contradictions, its claims, achievements and any lasting importance. They are part of a growing body of writing in the form of band memoirs and collections (such as Rimbaud's *Shibboleth: My Revolting Life* (1998), Ignorant's *The Rest is Propaganda* (2010), Vaucher's *Crass Art and Other Prepostmodernist Monsters 1961-1997* (2012) and Steve Lake's *Zounds Demystified* (2013)), music journalism and popular history, as well as the first academic drafts of new understanding in the form of PhD theses. I am, I will say, surprised that it has taken over three decades for an in-depth set of critical studies of that important cultural and social movement to appear, but also delighted that one finally has. More, please, for the future.

So, in a spirit of anarcho-perversity, I finish this foreword and open up this collection with the wise words of a Victorian Jesuit, the poet-priest Gerard Manley Hopkins: 'piecemeal peace is poor peace; what pure peace allows... the death of it?' I can hear someone like Penny Rimbaud reciting those words, you know, at a poetry reading in a jazz club, say, in a lamentable accusation to our warring political and faith leaders: 'piecemeal peace'/'poor peace'. The unattainable

---

7    George McKay, *Senseless Acts of Beauty: Cultures of Resistance Since the Sixties* (London: Verso, 1996), chapter 3.

ideal, unrealistic even in articulation, of 'pure peace', is something to take still from anarcho-punk, too, I think – even if and precisely because it may be imbued with 'classic "impossiblist" anarchist sentiment.'[8] Is there any other music practice or cultural formation that has such an insistent and relentless core message around pacifism? Within the orthodoxy of militarism which we seem compelled to inhabit in contemporary society, the impossible demand for 'pure peace' needs hearing more than ever. For in the midst of all their shouting, and swearing, and noise, and anger, let us continue to hear and think on this, from our *visionary* anarcho-punks, amidst our daily diet of rumours and alarums of state bombing and religious terror: FIGHT WAR NOT WARS. FIGHT WAR NOT WARS. FIGHT WAR NOT WARS. Now, there is something in that.

---

8    Rich Cross, "'There is no Authority But Yourself': The Individual and the Collective in British Anarcho-Punk," *Music and Politics* 4:2 (Summer 2010).

MIKE DINES

# INTRODUCTION

**THE ENDURING LEGACY** of anarcho-punk underlines its significance in expressing the political and cultural landscape of the 1980s. As a subculture built primarily upon subversion and political malcontent, anarcho-punk was shaped not just by style and music but also by a broad dialogue with the many political and cultural ideas/movements that fed into the scene. From the aesthetic (i.e., the stark and horrifying album covers showing bleak images of war) to the notion of lifestyle (e.g., the Stop the City protests of the mid-1980s and links to so-called 'new-age travellers') anarcho-punk was informed by much that remained on the peripheral.

Indeed, to label anarcho-punk as a subculture which was shaped by those increasingly frustrated and disillusioned by the somewhat commercial nature of 'first wave' punk is somewhat simplistic. To see it as a backlash against the increasing dependence of punk upon the mainstream denigrates it as a means of encompassing the political and cultural landscape of the 1980s. That said anarcho-punk drew upon a number of ideals that many saw to be central to the so-called 'original' or 'authentic' punk ethos of the early to mid-1970s. These included a return to an essential 'anyone-can-do-it' culture of music production and performance, a political and grassroots emphasis upon the means of distribution in terms of zine and record distribution, and the importance of individual personal freedom to experiment with identity and expression. However, anarcho-punk became more than the sum of its parts. To merely contemplate the 'punk' in anarcho-punk tells only part of the story.

Central to this narrative was taking the concept of 'anarchy' not only seriously but also, for some, literally and thus developing ideas which incorporated co-operation and collaboration in order to incite focused political debate and organised subversive activities. These included a heightened awareness of political issues such as feminism, pacifism, and animal rights, as well as the development of local co-operatives where musicians, artists, and like-minded people could meet. Furthermore, anarcho-punk tended not to adhere to any established political creed. Whereas many artists within first wave punk – most notably, perhaps, The Clash – were seen to have an alliance with the Left, anarcho-punk bands advocated a freedom of expression away from what they saw as the constraints of party politics.

It is a context which was echoed by George McKay in *Senseless Acts of Beauty: Cultures of Resistance Since the Sixties* (1996) where a chapter on anarcho-punk is sandwiched between chapters on free festivals and illegal raves. In discussing Crass – the main protagonists of the scene – McKay notes that '[the band] were a radical anarcho-pacifist, anarcha-feminist, vegetarian collective, and the anarchy it espoused was not of the anarchy of the Pistols…but a lifestyle and worldview that developed through a combination of hippy idealism and resistance, punk energy and cheek…'[1] McKay's comments not only illuminate the re-interpretation of the anarchistic, but also the situating of Crass – and anarcho-punk – within the wider protest movement. 'As clothes of punks, new-age travellers, of people at free festivals are a patchwork of styles and views,' he notes, 'so the *bricolage* of Crass is a patchwork of ideas, strategies, voices, beliefs, and so on.'[2]

McKay's locating of anarcho-punk within a broader tradition of insurrection and protest further emphasizes the various cultural and political influences on the scene. That said it is obvious that Crass

---

1   George McKay, *Senseless Acts of Beauty: Cultures of Resistance since the* Sixties (London: Verso, 1996), 75.

2   Ibid., 78.

– formed in 1977 at Dial House in Epping Forest – was the epicenter of British anarcho-punk. This is reflected by Jon Savage who, in referring to the band's *Feeding of the 5000* (1978), notes how it 'was the first of a sequence of media (records, slogans, books, posters, magazines, films, actions and concerts) so complex…and so effective that they sowed the ground for the return of serious anarchism and popularity of CND in the early eighties.'[3]

Rich Cross's article '"The Hippies Now Wear Black": Crass and the Anarcho-Punk Movement, 1977-1984' is a useful addition to this contextualization. Cross looks at anarcho-punk's influence in the various fields of music, fashion and design, art and aesthetics. He notes the complexity of bands such as Crass in asserting 'a belief in politics and punk [as] autonomous, subversive and free from commercial corruption.' Instead, ' [by] embracing the politics of anarchism, anti-militarism and pacifism, Crass worked to popularize the notion of a consciously revolutionary punk rock culture.'[4]

Cross's work provides an essential backdrop to the origins and formation of anarcho-punk. Not only does he look at the links between first-wave punk – the notion of rejecting the mainstream for instance, or the obvious links to anarchism – but Cross also places anarcho-punk in a wider context of the counter-culture. For Crass in particular, inspiration was drawn 'from Ghandian principles, radical philosophy, the aesthetics of the Beat and Bohemian poets, and the words of Rimbaud and Baudelaire, as much as from the formal anarchist tradition.'[5] As reflected in the counter-cultural connotations in his title, Cross underlines the importance of the diverse influences that impacted on both Crass and the anarcho-punk scene.

Political complexities are further discussed in Cross's article '"There Is No Authority But Yourself": The Individual and the Collective in British Anarcho-Punk." Quoting the 'expansion of state power' that for some accompanied the election of Thatcher in the late 1970s, Cross notes that there consisted, in opposition, 'a tangle of what were

---

3    Jon Savage, *England's Dreaming: Sex Pistols and Punk Rock* (London: Faber and Faber, 1991), 584.

4    "The Hippies Now Wear Black," https://thehippiesnowwearblack.files.wordpress.com/2014/05/the_hippies_now_wear_black_11_may_2014.pdf, accessed November 18, 2015.

5    Ibid.

collectively (if inaccurately) deemed as "progressive" ideologies – from old-fashioned Labourism, Trotskyism and radical Leftism, to liberal anti-racism and ethical anti-militarism.'[6] Cross's thoughts are useful in comprehending the political milieu of the time, not only in terms of Thatcherism, but also in the back-drop of political radicalism in the late 1970s and 1980s.

Therefore, if 'anarchist politics...had remained a significant, if incoherent, presence on the UK political fringe,' Cross notes how it was punk rock that provided a stimulus for anarchism's revival. Firstly, through the correlation between first wave punk and the Pistols' "Anarchy in the UK" and then through the emergence of an-archo-punk, 'which identified itself as a "restorative," dissident move-ment within punk: one which aimed to reassert the primacy of punk as an agency of political subversion.'[7] Although anarcho-punk lacked the strategic or ideological concerns of anarchism, bands such as Crass ignited a passionate, visceral response to Thatcherism and the political backdrop of the 1980s.

This is echoed in *The Story of Crass* (2008), George Berger's biog-raphy of the band. If McKay, Cross, and Savage had pinpointed the influence of Crass within a wider context of punk, protest, and the 1980s, then the latter's note that '[Crass] deserve a book to them-selves,'[8] was eventually realized in Berger's account. Instead of mere-ly an indignant subculture, with various links with first wave punk, Berger's work presents Crass – and anarcho-punk – as a re-action to, amongst other things, the politics of Thatcher's Britain in the 1980s. Once again, the reading of *The Story of Crass* highlights the complexi-ties of drawing together a cohesive identity of anarcho-punk.

Berger's account is useful because it illuminates the improvisatory nature of the emergence of the anarcho-scene. It is obvious through-out that Crass were conscious of a movement in which they were the instigators and core agitators. Yet, as events unravelled and the political situation in the 1980s heightened in intensity, it was a move-ment that began to spiral out of their control. In particular, *Yes Sir, I Will* (1983) epitomized the shifting mindset of the band. 'From here

---

6    Rich Cross, "'There Is No Authority But Yourself': The Individual and the Collective in British Anarcho-Punk," *Music & Politics* 4 (2010).

7    Ibid.

8    Savage, *England's Dreaming*, 584.

on in,' notes Berger, 'everything they did was re-active – all artistic output was dictated by external events.'[9] It was also around this time that Crass saw themselves not just as a punk band, but also, in George McKay's words, 'as the confirmation of everything that they feared… [That] there was a grand conspiratorial side of Crass – the system will get you, everything was the system.'[10]

It was Ian Glasper's *The Day the Country Died: The History of Anarcho-Punk 1980-1984* (2006) that consolidated anarcho-punk, drawing together the many bands that were affiliated with the scene. Whilst on the one hand Glasper unconsciously highlighted the overdue nature of recognizing the anarcho, on the other, it captured a key concern that many have in the writing of this present volume: the pigeonholing and therefore, impairing, of anarcho-punk. '…By even trying the label anarcho-punk as "anarcho-punk,"' he notes, 'you seek to leech away much of its power…where, once classified, it can be more easily controlled.'[11]

Glasper's prevailing form of allowing band members a voice in which to describe their own politics and placement within anarcho-punk counteracts this mythology to a degree. *The Day the Country Died* delves into musical and political complexities, providing a space where band-members are given the independence to narrate their own stories and experiences. Those that are sometimes forgotten – such as Barnsley's Kulturkampf, the Wales-based Symbol of Freedom, and London's Anathema – are given a voice alongside Crass, Flux of Pink Indians, and the Subhumans.[12] Indeed, giving a voice to those who were not so prevalent rekindles the grass-roots nature of anarcho-punk and draws attention to complex relationships between music and intent: in stating that output is not necessarily akin to participation or commitment.

9    George Berger, *The Story of Crass* (London: Omnibus Press, 2008), 214.

10   Ibid.

11   Ian Glasper, *The Day the Country Died: A History of Anarcho-Punk 1908-1984* (London: Cherry Red, 2006), 6.

12   Glasper does not, however, explore the influence of Poison Girls. For an excellent introduction to the band, one needs only turn to Rich Cross's, "'Take the Toys from the Boys': Gender, Generation and the Anarchist Intent in the Work of Poison Girls," *Punk & Post-Punk* 3:2 (2015): 117–145

*The Aesthetic of Our Anger* looks to further formalize and inter-rogate anarcho-punk, to examine its origins, its form, and cultural significance. Of the ways in which anarcho-punk emerged from first wave punk, studying those properties which anarcho-punk appropri-ated, as well as discarded, from its predecessor. Indeed, an import-ant part of this volume is to raise questions over the ways in which first wave punk and anarcho-punk used the concepts and ideas sur-rounding the terminology and concept of 'anarchy.' Not least, this will be concerned with how anarcho-punk moved away from using 'anarchy' as mere connotation and 'shock-value,' prioritizing instead a more focused political debate; a step which laid particular empha-sis on personal freedom from the constraints of government legisla-tion. In addition, this volume attempts to bring together the broad dialogue between anarcho-punk and the many political and cultural ideas/movements that fed into it. These include the Stop the City marches of the mid-1980s, the influence of free festivals (especially around Stonehenge) and the subsequent squatting culture and the rise of new-age travellers. The complexity of anarcho-punk lies in its reflexive and kaleidoscopic ability to integrate and appropriate the subversive in an intelligent and effective manner.

One difficulty in presenting an overview of anarcho-punk lies in the precarious joining-up of the musical, artistic, and political as a sense of the subcultural: to delineate a sense of identity and core defi-nition. *The Aesthetic of Our Anger*, therefore, aims to unpack these in-tricacies. The book is structured so as to guide the reader through the many faces of the anarcho-scene. It begins with a contextualization. Through David Solomons's chapter, the reader is given a political and subcultural overview – almost an historical snapshot – of the emer-gence of Crass and the cultural context of Thatcherism and the 1980s. Solomons provides a narrative, pulling upon imagery and analogy to highlight the complexity of the moment and the aesthetic of the band within the wider political landscape. Such a contextualization is essen-tial in understanding anarcho-punk in its entirety.

It is through the work of Ana Raposo and Russ Bestley that the anarcho-aesthetic is examined. The use of symbols as a means of ideo-logical positioning within the wider punk movement is set against the political posturing of the movement. Raposo, in particular, ex-plores disputes over authenticity in the contentious use of imagery by bands such as Crass, the Apostles, and Flux of Pink Indians set against the provocation of Oi! In a timely fashion, Bestley continues the exploration of the political, looking at the migration of the anarchist symbol across the range of punk graphic material. Furthermore, the latter highlights the complex debates between punk and anarchist ideologies: a debate that underlies much of the writing throughout this volume.

Helen Reddington's chapter raises the question of gender. The prominence of women in first wave punk is apparent, not least in bands such as Siouxsie and the Banshees, X-Ray Spex, and the Slits. Reddington continues this narrative, pulling upon the pioneering aesthetic of Poison Girls (and the inimitable Vi Subversa), Ziliah Ashworth (Rubella Ballet), and Lucy Toothpaste (whose zine *Jolt* highlighted the influence of women in the punk movement). Here, Reddington looks at the way in which feminism – and the role of women – is embedded in subcultural praxis, providing scrutiny of engagement of music-making, performance, and female visibility as articulated within the framework of the anarcho-movement.

The following chapters on Stop the City, anarcho-punk zines, and the Bristol squatting scene aim to provide a discourse between anarcho-punk, resistance and lifestyle. Rich Cross's chapter on the Stop the City demonstrations looks at the mobilization of anarcho-punk within a wider context of the radical political expression in the 1980s and its ability to project political practice at a collective level. Cross brings in the influence of fellow protestors' Campaign for Nuclear Disarmament (CND) as a means of highlighting the tension found in anarcho-punk of the means of confrontation and political action. Furthermore, the author provides an analysis of anarcho-punk within a framework of radical currents which run through the protest movement at the time and which draw upon Stop the City's audacious attempt to close down the financial nerve-centre of the City of London.

Matt Grimes's chapter focusses on the role that alternative publications played in the cultural, political, and ideological practices of the anarcho-punk movement. Specifically, Grimes explores how zines disseminated the central ideas of the movement, unpacking ways in which editorials, reviews and articles mediated a shifting notion of 'punk,' and how these 'amateur' publications fit into the paradoxical construction of the scene. Furthermore, the chapter focusses on the visual and textual discourses of anarcho-punk 'zines' and examines how discourses of authenticity, community, and identity were embodied and reinforced by and for their producers and consumers. In doing so, Grimes examines how DIY fan production practices, through the articulation of ideological positions, contributed to the construction of the musical, cultural, and political boundaries of the anarcho-punk movement.

Anarcho-punk, as a 'scene' and 'lifestyle', is further explored in Pete Webb's chapter 'Dirty Squatters, Anarchy, Politics and Smack: A Journey Through Bristol's Squat Punk Milieu.' Here, Webb draws upon the reflections of band members who were involved in and around Bristol, looking at how the musical, artistic, and lyrical reflected the main concerns of individuals at that time. As well as exploring the creativity of Bristol's punks, Webb also explores the destructive elements, highlighting the use of alcoholism and drug abuse and their impact. Reflection upon the subcultural can sometimes lend itself to nostalgia. Using Bristol as a starting point, Webb counters this by recovering those difficult issues and experiences that offset too rose-tinted a view.

Mike Murphy's chapter on the Hope Collective continues to draw upon ideas which surrounded protest and resistance through underground political gestures and concerns of geographical constraints. Based in Northern Ireland, the Collective promoted a sense of community and collectivity. These included alcohol free and all ages entertainment, a place where artists were hosted in homes rather than in paid accommodation, where no contracts were issued and deals were made on the basis of trust, and where bands were invited to participate in gigs to raise money for charitable causes. Murphy outlines how the squat, collective, and co-operative became central in providing a space for the burgeoning punk scene (and, in particular anarcho-punk) and examines the issues which surround the political and ideological everyday and how an ethos of trust and community were apparent.

If the volume has looked at modes of resistance through political demonstrations, zine production, and the aesthetic, then the chapters which were written by Alastair Gordon, Mike Dines, and Pete Dale provide theoretical overviews of anarcho-punk through contributions on ethics, mythology, and music as a means of protest. Firstly, Gordon maps the precarious terrain of what constitutes a relativist ethical practice in its culture. Through this discussion he suggests that the existing 'core' or overarching narratives of what participants consider their personal/group punk ethic is a varied and contested landscape that is constituted by factional division and argument. In short punk ethics are often largely constituted in practice through a series of claims and counterclaims which revolve around a perceived view of a so-called 'punk ethic.'

By drawing upon the 1-in-12 anarchist club and the anarcho-punk scene in Bradford, Gordon illuminates divisions and points of convergence which detail past differences between crust and 'new age traveller' punks, traditional anarchists and anarcho-punks, the rise of US hardcore/straight edge culture, and the challenges of such new forms of resistance in the late 1980s. He draws upon insider accounts to exemplify the difficulties which these ethical 'shifts' posed for the existing 'punk moral compasses' for club members and the way in which these signaled a wider ethical shift in the UK anarcho and DIY punk scenes of the 1980s and '90s. Gordon's conclusions offer a competing, reflexive model of anarcho-punk ethics which t suggests that these views and subsequent practices have profound consequences for punk members of the club, often resulting in a competing factionalism of small sub groups within the wider punk movement.

Using an interview with lyricist and vocalist Dick Lucas, Dines raises questions surrounding the relationship between the individual and a politically charged subculture such as anarcho-punk. In particular, Dines looks at the way in which ideas such as 'freedom', 'identity', and 'anarchism' are unpacked within a musical and subcultural context. As an overview, however, he also challenges the definitional ambiguities around 'anarcho-punk,' pulling in the work of the French philosopher Roland Barthes to explore notions of mythology. As an initial starting point, much of the analysis is provided from the repertoire of Lucas's band, Culture Shock for, through lyrical insight, individual reflection, and musical enquiry, Lucas himself deals with many of the quandaries in definition and delineation.

Pete Dale's chapter, 'More Than Music?: Confusions of Musical Style and Political Attitude in Anarcho-Punk from Crass Onwards' goes back to the roots of anarcho-punk by exploring the musical content of some of the earliest bands, including Zounds, the Mob and, in particular, Crass. Dale explores the ideas of existing critical examinations of 'avant-gardist' practice, examining the limits to the value of attempting to create a radically 'political music': an argument made for anarcho-punk in terms of such attempts. After all, he notes, anarcho-punk has identifiably encouraged radical activity amongst a mass of people over several decades. A question remains, nevertheless, as to how revolutionary a subculture can be, if and when it prioritizes musical taste/style over and above more obviously 'political' issues.

Matt Worley's interview with Steve Ignorant follows. In this context, Ignorant reflects upon his role – and the role of Crass – in providing a new platform of musical and political expression. Here, Ignorant begins by discussing the move from first-wave punk to the emerging of anarcho-punk and the fusing together of theoretical anarchism and punk rock in the late-1970s/early-1980s. Tensions are discussed, including the unraveling of the theoretical in the everyday existence of the band at Dial House, between Crass and the wider punk scene, and the retrospective labeling of 'anarcho.' The chapter provides a metaphorical afterword that grounds the academic and highlights the personal in the scene. Ignorant's own take on anarcho-punk – and his discussion of his own sense of identity in an ever-growing movement – provides a succinct reflection on the volume as a whole.

The volume ends with Free Association's 'The Kids Was Just Crass.' An experiment in collective writing, Free Association provides a reflective contextualisation of punk and, in particular, the emergence of Crass and the anarcho-punk scene. Here, the authors look at anarcho-punk as a way of 'exceed[ing] the pre-existing sense of social, political and cultural possibility,' placing punk within a 'modernist subcultural cycle [which] represents...new possibilities revealed by a moment of excess.' The key to this chapter, however, is the writers' contextualisation of anarcho-punk within an underground continuum that rejuvenates generation after generation. 'Despite the claims of each pop-cultural revolution, there is no wiping out of the past,' they write, 'instead, moments of excess open up the future precisely by reconfiguring the past, unclogging history and opening up new lines of continuity.' This chapter therefore looks to both legacy and the future. It is up to those who live on the peripheral, they remind us, to teach a new generation of agitators and rabble-rousers.

Although the editors have done their utmost to include the diversity of music, politics, and culture that are often defined alongside anarcho-punk, the breadth of the movement makes it difficult to cover in full. An initial volume, for instance, finds it difficult to steer away from the constraints of canon and, in this case, having Crass central to its thesis. What still needs to be unpacked are those bands/individuals who lived on the peripheral; who sprung up on the fringes of the scene. Although beyond the remit of this particular work, the globalization of anarcho-punk is a subject that also needs further investigation, especially in relation to protest movements of the present day.

That said this current volume encompasses the salient features of the initial wave of anarcho-punk. Debates which surround the political, cultural, and aesthetic are explored, from the political contextualization of the 1980s and the rise of Thatcherism, to the significance surrounding the DIY ethos of zine design and record distribution. This comes at a time when there has been renewed interest in the movement. The recent *Tales From the Punkside* (2014) has seen the beginning of a number of books that have collated the tales, art, and photographs from those involved in the scene. *Not Just Bits of Paper* (2015) and '*Some of Us Scream, Some of Us Shout*': *Myths, Folklore and Epic Tales of the Anarcho* (2016)[13] followed close behind. The editors hope, therefore, that *The Aesthetic of Our Anger* is a valuable addition to the consideration and archiving of anarcho-punk.

---

13    The three books in question are Greg Bull and Mike Dines, ed., *Tales From the Punkside* (Portsmouth: Itchy Monkey Press, 2014), Michael Baxter and Greg Bull, ed., *Not Just Bits of Paper* (London: Perdam Babylonis Nomen, 2015) and Greg Bull and Mike Dines, ed., "*Some of Us Scream, Some of Us Shout*": *Myths, Folklore and Epic Tales of the Anarcho* (Portsmouth: Itchy Monkey Press, 2016).

DAVID SOLOMONS

# A BLUE TOMATO
# AND A PACKET OF
# GAULOISES[1]

*Musik ist eine Waffe. (Music is a Weapon)*[2]

## UNDER THE OLD OAK TREE

OF *TEN NOTES On A Summer's Day* (1984), the melancholic and somewhat divisive valedictory release of Crass as a recording unit, Penny
Rimbaud, co-founder and mainstay of the band, once explained: 'It
describes where we'd ended up after all those years of frenzy and madness. You've put everything you've got into something, you've shouted and screamed; and then you suddenly find yourself on your own,

1    This chapter is dedicated to my brother Geoff for his stoicism and courage.
     Special thanks go to Penny Rimbaud (for his generosity of time and inspiration-
     al example), Henning Wellman (for getting the whole thing started), Ms Fiona
     McAlister (for her ongoing love and support) and Mr Richard Fontenoy (for a
     chance given).
2    Berlin street graffiti.

sitting under an oak tree, and you think, "Fucking hell, what was that about?"[3]

Six years after the band released *Ten Notes...* their sworn enemy, Prime Minister Margaret Thatcher, left Downing Street for the last time. Although seated next to her husband in a gleaming black Jaguar Sovereign 4.0 rather than alone beneath an ancient English oak, the same sentiment was clearly etched into her face. Her farewell address had been typically note perfect, the burgundy suit immaculate, the hair flawlessly coiffured, but the hot tears she was visibly stifling back as she climbed into the car beside the dutiful Dennis clearly showed that she was going through her own bleak version of Rimbaud's dark epiphany.

Crass's years of frenzy and madness had begun in the dour and desperate days of the late 1970s, when the so-called 'post-war consensus' of the UK's political and economic establishment had been left cruelly exposed by a worsening crisis. This crisis precipitated a remarkable dual evolution: the gradual ascendency of a powerful new political right and, concurrently, the abrasive new musical form of punk, bred of discontent and suckled on the sour milk of economic stagnation. This new right and punk (specifically the strain that was to become known as 'anarcho-punk') would confront each other with varying degrees of success over the following years. Each represented a very different way of seeing human beings, and fundamentally different visions of what life should be like for them.

## A RIOT OF MY OWN

Dial House, established in the late-1960s by Penny Rimbaud, had always attempted to provide creative space for the seeker, imparting an alternative education as it did so to the refuseniks, refugees, and renegades who washed up on its shores. In creating the community at Dial House, Rimbaud had been seeking '...somewhere I could live outside of the hubbub that I was told was reality. Somewhere I could create my own life by my own values. Basically somewhere I could learn to exist in my own way as the person I wanted to be, without intrusion.'[4] Rimbaud's search for his own personal Eden, a place

---

3  Berger, George, *The Story of Crass* (London: Omnibus Press, 2008), 267.

4  Penny Rimbaud, interview with author, July 17, 2012. All subsequent references are to this interview unless otherwise indicated.

of mental, social, artistic and philosophical discovery, was part of a long and colourful lineage of British experiments in alternative living. Bohemian artistic colonies had developed in Cornwall from the 1880s onwards; flamboyant artist and sexual maniac Eric Gill (designer of the 'Stations of the Cross' at Westminster Abbey) had established his artists' community at Ditchling in Sussex in 1907; the Whiteways Colony in Gloucestershire had been set up in 1898 along Tolstoyan principles, featuring a plethora of anarchists, conscientious objectors and, refugees from the Spanish Civil War. Whiteways was even the base for the publication of the anarchist periodical *Freedom* during the 1920s when its editor Thomas Keell was a resident.

Penny Rimbaud, though, had drawn inspiration from a different source. During the 1960s he had seen the film *The Inn of the Sixth Happiness* (1958), adapted from Alan Burgess's book *The Small Woman*; both of which related the story of Gladys Aylward, a London woman who had lived as a missionary in China's Shanxi province during the 1920s and 1930s. In reality (as opposed to the slightly fanciful artistic licence taken by the two fictional representations), Aylward had co-founded the 'Inn of Eight Happinesses' based on eight virtues: love, virtue, gentleness, tolerance, loyalty, truth, beauty and devotion. Rimbaud looked further into the ancient tradition of the Sino-Japanese inn, where board for the night could be bartered in return for a song, a story or some work in kind, and had subsequently worked hard to forge a similar environment at Dial House: one which would not only allow him to explore his own personal freedoms, but would also offer a creative space for others to do the same.

Whether those arriving at Dial House wished to express themselves and hone their artistic voice, or simply just find a place of sanctuary where they could exist relatively free of judement and interference, space could be found away from the restrictive straightjacket of 'the real world.' As Rimbaud recalls, 'so basically, I suppose for want of a better word, and it's one that is difficult to use nowadays, it was built around libertarian ideas, it's a libertarian project. In the late 1960s, I hadn't got any model to work on, so I invented a model. The idea was that I would abandon my job as an art lecturer, take the locks off the doors and wait to see what would happen. I'm not going to tell anyone anything, or instruct them. This is a space, let people use it as they want. And generally speaking, over 47 years or whatever it is, it's worked very well.' In testament to Rimbaud's vision, during the

1970s a torrent of artistic creativity poured forth from the community at Dial House: written work, fine art, illustrations, organisational input onto large-scale events such as the International Carnival of Experimental Sound Festival in 1972[5] and the British music festivals at Windsor and Stonehenge. Musically too, Dial House had produced a considerable output in the form of the avant-garde performance outfit Exit ('powerful statements presented in a very beautiful way') and its later successor, Ceres Confusion.

By the time punk was detonating Rimbaud was in emotional turmoil and reeling in the aftermath of a dark turn of events which surrounded his close friend Wally Hope. Hope had been a friend of Rimbaud's for many years. Hope was a chaotic yet undeniably inspirational figure from the UK underground who had been instrumental in the founding and organisation of the landmark music festivals at Windsor and Stonehenge. As Rimbaud recalls, 'the Stonehenge Festival was organised from here, from Dial House. It was primarily by Wally Hope, his real name was Phil Russell, but his "hippie name" was Wally Hope. It was his idea, so I and the people here did everything we could to bring it to fruition by helping out, whether it was by making bread or making posters.' In May of 1975, however, Hope had been arrested by the police and charged with possession of LSD, which resulted in ten weeks incarceration in a mental institution and forcible 'treatment' with strong antipsychotic drugs such as Largactil and Modecate. Discharged suddenly, and chronically debilitated from the 'chemical cosh,' Hope survived only a few months more before dying in September 1975. Despite a coroner's finding of suicide, Rimbaud's view of Hope's demise was somewhat more sinister: 'he was eventually incarcerated in a mental institution, sectioned, supposedly for being schizophrenic, which was a complete 'put on' by the state, and eventually he died as a result of that. I actually think that, ultimately, he was assassinated by the state and I proved that he was – conclusively at one point – so that obviously changed my approach somewhat.'

5    The International Carnival of Experimental Sound took place at The Roundhouse in London in August 1972 and featured a number of leading avant-garde musicians including John Cage, Cornelius Cardew and AMM. Penny Rimbaud also performed and, together with Gee Vaucher, put considerable effort into the event's organisation. Vaucher's promotional poster for this 'Woodstock of the avant-garde' depicted a repeating sequence of cartoon ice cream cones.

Two years after Hope's death, Rimbaud was bereft and mired in a trench of despondency in which 'the future appeared as empty as the past.'[6] Unstable and drinking heavily, over a frenzied two week period Rimbaud poured out the long-gestating and now-uncontainable rage of his bereavement – 'attacking everything inside me' – into a lengthy and confrontational prose poem entitled *Christ's Reality Asylum And Les Pommes De Printemps*[7] and, using an old Gestetner printing machine, produced the work in a pamphlet edition of 100 copies.[8] As Rimbaud recalls, 'the whole thing was how the western world is like a concentration camp or asylum. At one point it was going to be 'Christ's Auschwitz' or something. I saw the concentration camps as a template for how it actually was: you had your slaves working at Ford or down the mines. You were perfectly happy to eliminate them through poverty when they ceased to be functioning pawns in your process, or you sent them off to war to be killed. It didn't seem to me to be any different, except with a little bit more room. Basically the western world in my eyes was one fucking enormous concentration camp and if you didn't play the game you were gonna get it.'[9] Rimbaud asked friend and fellow Dial House resident Dave King to design a logo with which to give 'Christ's Reality Asylum' a visual power concomitant with its caustic textual thematic intensity, something that would represent 'the fascism of the state, the fascism of the church, and the fascism of the family.'

Wishing to find an emblem that would underline the themes of structural and institutional power inherent in Rimbaud's work, King began experimenting with designs that integrated a number of visual archetypes – the Christian Cross, the Union Flag, the Greek Star of

6    Rimbaud, Penny, *Shibboleth: My Revolting Life* (Edinburgh: AK Press, 1998), 209.

7    *Les Pommes de Printemps* was actually intended to be a contiguous series of poems by Eve Libertine included with 'Christ's Reality Asylum' as a 'two in one' publication. When Rimbaud printed the cover, he was still expectant that the poems would be delivered. They remained, however, sadly unwritten.

8    In some interviews, designer Dave King has remembered the edition running to 50 copies rather than 100.

9    Alex Burrows, "Penny Rimbaud On Crass and the Poets of Transcendentalism and Modernism," *The Quietus*, last modified Novermber 10, 2010. http://thequietus.com/articles/05258-penny-rimbaud-crass-interview

Life, the ouroboros – all framed with a circle, a traditional Japanese device symbolising clan power which King had noted in a book of Japanese family crests that resided at Dial House. King also incorporated a key memory from his childhood environment, one that was still scarred by the bomb damage remaining from the war: '...at the end of our street...bombs had fallen and obliterated several houses, and it made this fantastic adventure playground for kids. As the sort of background there were a lot of Celtic crosses around, there was even one stone one that had sort of...that was pretty ancient... that had ended up in the centre of a roundabout, so that would just be a cross with a circle around it. That was the first sort of graphic thing that I noticed.'[10] After working through several iterations with Rimbaud, King's final version distilled down these different elements into a powerful sigil charged with multiple layers of allusion and meaning: nation, state, church, flag, ideology, infinity.

Another charming influence on the visual imagery used by Crass was a children's book *The Mystery of the Blue Tomatoes*, in which Rimbaud had first experimented with influences from American pop art. 'Well Gee and myself both used to do illustrations for kids' books back in the early 1970s, that's how we earned a living, doing book covers for a company that produced children's book,' he notes. 'I'd done one called *The Blue Tomato* or something, and I'd done a pop art tomato and put a black circle around it with the title and the author's name in exactly the same way as the Crass singles had a circle around the image, which itself was a rip-off of Robert Indiana and Jasper Johns. Both those American pop artists used stencils...that's what gave me the idea to have the circle as the standard formula singles cover.'

Unbeknownst to either Rimbaud or King, the latter's design was about to take on a significance far beyond any that either had originally envisaged. It was at this point – as an emotionally-dislocated Rimbaud was struggling to define new directions through which to express his creative and political feelings – that a young Steve Williams (soon to be Steve Ignorant) turned up at Dial House,[11] to find others with whom to start a punk band. For what became an endeavour of such seriousness, the moment of its inception was one of pure comedy:

10   MOCAtv, "The Art of Punk – Crass – The Art of Dave King and Gee Vaucher," last modified June 18, 2013. http://www.youtube.com/watch?v=ubzKiomuUB0
11   Williams' brother had been a resident at Dial House.

just as Rimbaud was struggling to ward off an attack by the house's recalcitrant goat, Clarence, in walked Steve Williams. 'I walked in and [Penny] said, 'alright Steve, how are you doing? What are you up to?' So I said that I was into punk rock and that I was thinking of starting a band, and he said 'I'll play drums for you.' I was like 'Right, OK'. That was literally how it started."[12] For Rimbaud, disillusioned and in need of reinvigoration both artistically and politically, his meeting with Ignorant, inspired by The Clash and striving for something new and special, produced a special bond. As Rimbaud recalls, 'when you lose a dear friend at the hands of the state, you realise that just growing vegetables and painting pictures and talking the talk aren't the all. It was at that point that I guess I decided to get out onto the street, which was the formation of Crass really.'

## STRENGTH THROUGH JOY

Through 1977, the stumbling punk zombie that Rimbaud and Ignorant had accidentally animated into being at Dial House began its shambolic lurch towards coherence. Initially constituted as a vocal and drum duo christened 'Stormtrooper,' and with elements of chance playing no small part, a genuine creative unit swiftly began to assemble itself. A new name was also (thankfully) acquired. Rimbaud's favoured option 'Les Enfants Terribles' losing out to the Ziggy Stardust-inspired 'Crass' ('The kids were just crass, he was the nazz'), with Ignorant echoing this metamorphosis further through the adoption of the public persona of Steve Ignorant.

The band's line-up, too, evolved quickly. Through Dial House's dendritic social network connections were quickly made, new members acquired and a first gig staged in a children's playground in the courtyard of a central London squat. A sequence of gigs followed through the rest of the year including the White Lion in Putney, Action Space in Covent Garden, Chelsea Art College, and two notably chaotic and booze-saturated gigs at The Roxy, a former vegetable warehouse in Covent Garden which, though only open for less than eighteen-months, was nevertheless one of the key venues of London's punk movement.

Perhaps more significant in the evolution of the band were four gigs that the band played in New York. Gee Vaucher, artist,

---

12   Steve Williams, interview with author, November 10, 2011. All subsequent references are to this interview.

comrade-in-arms of Rimbaud, and former Dial House resident, had been based in the city whilst progressing her career in the upper echelons of the city's publishing industry. Booking gigs for the band, Vaucher eschewed the obvious venues such as CBGBs, but instead exposed them through local clubs in the Puerto Rican and Polish communities. Anthony McCall, artist and film-maker, remembers seeing one of these gigs: 'I was bowled over by the velocity of the music and the no-kidding seriousness of their stage persona. They lined up across the front of the stage, in black uniforms with Crass armbands and the Crass logo banner behind them and you were hit by this angry, sonic *blitzkrieg* which continued for the duration of the performance without a break. I'd seen punk bands in New York at CBGBs, The Mudd Club, and Tier 3, but their visual persona and music was utterly unique.'

Although the band later looked back on the New York gigs with decidedly mixed feelings, they nevertheless marked an important juncture, after which Crass found themselves facing their first truly important decision. With punk now experiencing its *annus mirabilis* there was little shortage of boisterous and inebriated punk good-timers, but Rimbaud, by dint of age possessing a maturity and experience unusual in the punk genre, wanted something more than this, something that would present a more worthwhile and enduring statement, both artistically and politically: 'To my mind, it wasn't that it wasn't going anywhere, it was going where all Rock and Roll goes, straight up its own arse. I thought, "we've got to find something to make this artistically and creatively worthwhile." Then it doesn't matter whether you sell records or not – the satisfaction of it is judged in creative terms, not financial terms.' On the band's return to the UK, Rimbaud, sensing their imminent arrival at this juncture, laid out an ultimatum for Crass: either they were to become a serious proposition or he was no longer interested in carrying on with the band.

Initially, the gauntlet thrown down by Rimbaud was not picked up with much enthusiasm by the other members, with the result that he left the band, albeit for a period of little more than twenty-four hours. Rimbaud has always maintained that his drastic ultimatum was made safe in the knowledge that the others would, once the heat of the moment had passed, acknowledge that Crass was self-evidently worth carrying on with, and that its potential now demanded a more dedicated and coherent approach. In addition to this short pause for deliberation, the attendant side effect was that of a certain reconfiguration of the band, not only in terms of its personnel but also, subsequently, in its approach and aesthetic.

Moving away from the all-male proposition that Crass had been up until this point, Gee Vaucher and fellow Dial House collaborators Eve Libertine and Joy De Vivre now became an integral part of the band, recalibrating it sexually, musically, and thematically. Just at a time when the 'mainstream' punk movement was showing the first signs of its dangerous veer away from the raucous, libertarian fun, and 'anyone can do it' empowerment ethos of its initial period towards the darker waters of the male-dominated Oi! and its association – rightly or wrongly – with far right politics, Crass were instead moving in the other direction, introducing a combative feminism into their already-potent ideological mixture. By mutual band consent, for example, the word 'cunt' was removed permanently from the Crass lyrical lexicon.

Concomitant with the new phase of the band, a subtle seriousness also began to emerge in terms of the members' personal approach to performing as part of Crass; the shambolic alcohol-fuelled amateurism that had characterised the band's shows at The Roxy was gradually replaced by a concordat that no drink or substances were to be ingested prior to performing. Whereas some of the older members of the band found this newly-imposed stricture relatively easy to adhere to, Steve Ignorant found that the straight-edge mentality, together with the increasingly politicised direction of the band, placed a not inconsiderable burden upon him: '...because I was in Crass I couldn't be seen to be drunk because if I was seen falling over in the gutter, then Crass was falling over in the gutter. That put a really big responsibility on me. Plus, I was being questioned about things that I didn't understand the first thing about like 'trade unions' and 'the role of women in today's patriarchal society...and it really put pressure on me. It was all a really good learning curve.'

As the challenge of punk's first wave was gradually neutered both by tabloid over-familiarity and mainstream appropriation, on their 1978 debut album, *Feeding of the 5000*, Crass declared:

> The social elite with safety-pins in their ear,
> I watch and understand that it don't mean a thing,

The scorpions might attack, but the systems stole
the sting.

The irony of the situation was rich: although the track in question
was entitled 'Punk is Dead,' Crass had in fact proved that nothing
could have been further from the truth. In scarcely a year, the band
had turned from the almost laughable Stormtrooper iteration, into a
cogent, motivated, and politically-infused unit which straddled the
boundaries of age and gender, and whose new-found creative seriousness would see its quest for social justice through music and modes of
living transform it into a force to be reckoned with.

## ANY COLOUR AS LONG AS IT'S BLACK

More than almost any other band of the era, Crass appreciated the
importance of fashioning a narrative of its own. Being a band born
of the punk movement, (albeit one that unusually spanned a wider
spectrum of ages, genders, social classes, and political outlooks than
their contemporaries), from the start of their newfound seriousness,
Crass were intent on fashioning a philosophical framework, a lattice
of ideas and beliefs through which they could interact with the world
and, conversely, through which the world could interact with them.

Rather than the faux-Situationism and decreasingly-effective
shock tactics that Malcolm McLaren engineered for The Sex Pistols,
Crass's aesthetic was both considerably more subtle and, at the same
time, more openly confrontational. As with King's logo, Crass's entire
presentational aesthetic fused wildly diverse symbols at the molecular
level – uniting opposites, inviting contradictions, standing by some
inherent meanings whilst simultaneously playing with, and subvert-
ing, others. With the elision of libertarianism, pacifism, feminism,
and civil rights all within their own singularly non-judgmental and
always-ready-for-dialogue openness, Crass's *Weltanschauung* was as
unique as it was difficult to categorise; and it was this difficulty of categorisation which the band strove consciously to reinforce at almost
every turn.

Mark Twain, a man who knew a thing or two about forging his
own *Weltanschauung*, once said 'clothes make the man. Naked people
have little or no influence in society.' Although, on first reading, this
may seem to be merely one of countless similar Twain witticisms, like
many of his aphorisms it hints at much deeper and darker waters

– class, money, social stratification, accepted mores and manners – and the near impossibility of social mobility when modest origins are written on, or more accurately hanging from, the body. Crass, too, subscribed to the view that clothing was profoundly influential on shaping people's impressions and value judgments. With an element of chance which would have pleased John Cage (an important influence on the band, and whose celebrated composition *4' 33"* inspired the silent section of 'They've got a Bomb' on *The Feeding of the 5000*), it was the malfunctioning of their ancient washing machine which acted as Crass's own particular casting of the I Ching. Following a washing day disaster, when every item in a communal wash was accidentally transmuted into a drab grey colour, the band made a unanimous determination henceforth to dye their collective wardrobe black.

This black-out of Crass's clothing was not only an immensely practical decision for a band and household comprising eight people, it was also an important component of their aesthetic, a defiant statement that operated on several symbolic levels. Initially, the band celebrated the unity that black clothing brought to them as a collective, their disparate ages and genders were made into a coherent visual whole by a standardisation of their bodily presentation.[13] This connection was heightened by the band's conscious decision not to emphasise individual personnel, but instead to present a unified, collective identity in which personalities could not be picked out. In the conventional pecking order of rock band configuration, singers typically accrued the most kudos and attention, followed by guitarists, bass players, and finally drummers. For Crass, however, it was the message, and not the medium, that was of paramount importance, and their identical 'flat black' apparel was intended to act as a leveller for the members of the band, placing them all on an equal visual footing and preventing any potential focus on an individual personality from unbalancing and overshadowing the message and ideology of the band. Though some observers chose to see something threatening or paramilitary in the band's clothing, for once *NME* showed a more

---

13   This contrasted with the early days of the band, notably the presence of original guitarist Steve Herman, whose sartorial style was very much *du jour*, and known to encompass a beard and a rainbow t-shirt. Grainy Super 8 footage of the band's debut live performance at the Huntley Street squat in 1977 provides evidence of this.

nuanced understanding of their intensions, a 1979 interview with the band by Graham Lock concluding that, 'it's true, sometimes good guys don't wear white.'

Soon, however, it became apparent that this unity extended not only to those within the band, but also to the people who became their audience. Through black clothing, a connection was forged with those who bought the band's records, and especially to those who attended their live shows. A huge component in the initial appeal of punk had been its democracy and its ease of access, something in sharp contrast to the remote 'rock aristocracy' who had become an unreachable elite characterised by excessive technical virtuosity and wealth, and glimpsed only as dots on the horizon at vast arena spaces. Punk, however, allowed membership based solely on enthusiasm, drive, authenticity, and need for expression. In its early days punk provided a fellowship for those who did not fit elsewhere, allowing them to find community in its individualistic and non-judgmental approach.

By 1978, however, many were beginning to feel that much of this new fraternity had been undermined by creeping corporate exploitation, flagrant bandwagon jumpers, and by the inevitable over-familiarity bred by punk's transition from underground to mainstream. In Crass, however, many found a band whose music and ideology were purposely resistant to corporate manipulation and, importantly, still had no barriers to access. Here was a band whose members did not look or act like the rock stars that the punk movement had once made such a show of disdaining. With their black clothing, collective rather than individual personality and austere presentation, those who became fans of Crass could feel a deep connection and affinity with the band. They, too, could be dressed in black and emblazoned with the Crass symbol. Should the members of the band wander around amongst the audience after the show, the casual observer would be hard pushed to tell who was a performer and who was an attendee. Penny Rimbaud comments, 'we remained anonymous in name and in form. That was partly because we did not see ourselves as representing ourselves, we saw ourselves as representing the ever-growing body of discontent and that was the effective way to work at that time.'

Reinforcing this lack of differentiation – firstly between band members, and then between band members and audience – lighting at Crass live shows was kept deliberately colour-free and at low intensity (shows were frequently illuminated with nothing more than several standard forty-watt household lightbulbs). As Penny Rimbaud comments, 'it was very much a conscious thing. Basically, the collective at the time, during the time, was not us, it was all of us. It was you, the people up in Glasgow, the people in Seattle, or whoever. The collective was a common body, of whom we might have been the representative, but the reason why our stage shows were not lit was so that we couldn't be picked out as sort of objects or entities upon which to heap the hopes and prayers of all those years.' To this end, right from their early period, the band collaborated with film maker (and one-time Dial House resident) Mick Duffield to incorporate his work into their performances.

Although connected with Dial House and Exit, Duffield had never actively displayed his work with them. However, making the natural linkage between visuals and live sound, and in tandem with a slowly-increasingly political content in his work, Duffield began projecting his film *Autopsy* at the band's live shows. Given the shared undercurrent of anger, defiance, and black humour which are inherent in both Duffield's film work and Crass's music, it was an (un)comfortable marriage, one which served to add an exhilarating visual element to the band's live presentation whilst being totally in keeping with their *détournement* aesthetic. As Duffield later explained, 'It developed as time went on. It started out as a single screen with one film and quickly developed into several screens and specialised loop-projectors, back-projecting and front-projecting.'

As a reflection of the multi-faceted nature of the music – and its serious thematic concerns – Vaucher produced a sequence of striking sleeves combining visual 'photomontage' and dense layers of text, often opening out into a large poster format. With Crass's oppositional stance to the increasingly unrestrained and repressive Thatcher administration, the characteristic Crass record sleeve style was intended, even before the first note of music had been heard, to present an excoriating critique of the political and social status quo of the time. In this, the band's record sleeves bore traces of two artists working decades before in defiance of another, very different regime.

German artist John Heartfield (born Helmut Herzfield) was a pioneer of the modern use of art as a political and satirical weapon, most celebrated for his distinctive photomontages attacking the National Socialism of Germany in the 1930s. Despite struggles with the Stasi in East Germany (where he settled after a period of exile in England during the Second World War), Heartfield's vicious and clever talent was profoundly influential on underground art in the period following his death in 1968. Much of punk's 'cut and paste' defiance bore an unmistakable Heartfield imprint. Siouxsie and the Banshees, for example, took thematic inspiration from the title of Heartfield's 1935 work 'Hurrah, die Butter ist Alle!' ('Hurray, the Butter is Finished!') for their 1979 single 'Mittageisen', featuring his original image on the cover (a family meal at which the members are eating a variety of metallic objects, inspired by Hermann Göring's Hamburg speech where he noted that, 'iron always made a nation strong, butter and lard only made the people fat'). British punk band Discharge would also feature a Heartfield composition, 'Peace and Fascism' (a dove of peace impaled on a Fascist bayonet against a background of the headquarters of the League of Nations, its white cross flag subtly metamorphosed into a Swastika) as the cover of the album *Never Again* (1984).

Hannah Höch too, the sole female member of the Berlin Dadaist group, and one of the original creators of the photomontage form, was also influential in Vaucher's images. Although seemingly less overtly political than Heartfield, Höch's work nevertheless evinced her deep underlying interest in the place of women in media, and its subsequent depiction of them. As early as the Weimar era, Höch had been acutely aware of the distorting lens through which the media projected images of women, driven by the social, commercial, and consumer pressures of marriage, fashion, and female beauty. Whilst marriage was often depicted as turning brides into mannequins, works such as 'Das schöne Madchen' (1920) ('The Beautiful Girl') examine the effect of advancing technology on the female form, depicting bodily parts replaced by machinery, and saturated by male-dominated *Technik*.

As Rimbaud notes, 'both Gee and myself were art school students in the Sixties so we were pretty graced in [Heartfield and Höch], that was very much in our lineage.' Given that Crass shared so many of the thematic concerns of both artists, and were in need of visual imagery to match the sheer visceral power of their music, the influence of Heartfield and Höch on Crass's visual aesthetic was natural and seamless. Echoes of the savage edge which characterised Heartfield's best work can be seen in album artwork such as the cover of *The Feeding...* (even the burnt-out Mini would have been familiar to Heartfield following his 1967 return visit to Britain). The cover of *Penis Envy* (1981) too, could easily bare comparison as a cleverly updated modern latex counterpart to Höch's ambitious 1929 collection of work, *From An Ethnographic Museum* (a complex exploration of racial, gender, and cultural equality examined through depictions of women's bodies as contrasted with images from a museum catalogue). Whereas much of punk's 'shock of the new' visual aesthetic now seems very much of its time, even at times 'quaint', Crass's imagery retains much of its power, benefiting in its photomontage and photorealist approach from the advantage identified by John Berger in the essay 'The Political Uses of Photomontage': 'everything which has been cut out keeps its familiar photographic appearance. We are still looking first at things and only afterwards at symbols.'[14]

Perhaps the most *gloria in excelsis* example of Crass's unique take on the 'fauxtomontage' style, was the cover for the band's 1981 *Persons Unknown/Bloody Revolutions* single (in the company of the estimable Poison Girls), in which The Sex Pistols were portrayed with the heads of the Queen, the Pope, the statue of Justice at the Old Bailey, and Mrs Thatcher. Even Lydon's beer can was replaced with a pseudo-sophisticate glass of white wine. The parody was considered controversial on all sides, ironically the most vociferous coming from the punk fraternity, wounded and outraged that punk's original and most sacred icons could be lampooned in such a way. Few noted that the Thatcher-Rotten hybrid was actually wearing Poison Girls badges on its jacket lapels.

The use of these influences, and their combination with other ideas, was a largely collaborative effort amongst the members of the band; and one undertaken in tandem with the evolution of the band's music, rather than being merely a post hoc attempt to illustrate it. As Rimbaud recalls, '[Gee] would come along to the recording sessions, whatever album it was, whatever we were doing, and from that she would get her own picture and – generally speaking – just get on with it. A lot of the design work for the albums was done by other people; I did an awful lot of design work, in other words putting it altogether, and she produced the imagery...Occasionally I might suggest "Why don't you do such and such..." if I had a particular picture in mind. So

---

14    John Berger, "The Political Uses of Photomontage," in *The Political Uses of Photo-Montage, Selected Essays of John Berger*, ed. Geoff Dyer (New York: Pantheon Books, 2001), 221.

it was the case that Gee and I used to discuss stuff at length, to expand on ideas...That was very much a joint effort in terms of concept. Then it became her job to put it all together.' Vaucher, to whom appearing on stage was unappealing, was in her element designing the covers, artwork and presentation of the band: 'It was...the involvement with the whole aesthetic of presentation, because I think it's really, really important, it's another language, and we were all very interested in not only the words, not only the sound, but the presentation and how we could try something very new and try to cut through and find a new language...'[15]

## THE FACE THAT STARES BACK FROM THE MIRROR

Their timelines having been so closely intertwined, when it arrived in 1984, the end for Crass was, ironically, no less bitter than that for Mrs Thatcher. Though opinions differ as to whether the band was always meant to end in that highly symbolic year, what is not in doubt is the enormous weariness that the years of devotion to the band had engendered in its members. Ignorant recalls the van journey back from the band's final gig, a benefit concert for the miners played in Aberdare in Wales: 'We were driving home and Andy Palmer just said "I want to pack the band in." He'd just had enough of it. He just wanted to have the relationship with his partner that he couldn't have whilst he was doing Crass. The funny thing was that about ten minutes after he'd said this, it was probably me, I said "do you know what? I want to jack it in and all." I was tired of it, and if it hadn't been him, it would have been someone else I reckon. We were all just so tired from it. It had been non-stop for all those years.

The constant expectation that Crass's material would comment on contemporary events, almost like a modern 24-hour rolling news channel, was demanding enough, but added to this, the logistical commitment needed to organise and progress the band, its recordings and its live shows only exacerbated the sense of physical and mental exhaustion further. Crass's aesthetic style compounded this yet further. Just as Thatcher had become imprisoned by the symbols which she had so skilfully evoked[16], so too did those of Crass come to exert

15    Interview in *There is No Authority But Yourself.* DVD. Directed by Alexander
      Oey. Netherlands: SubmarineChannel, 2006.
16    Thatcher harnessed the magnificent pageantry used to celebrate victory in the

an increasingly deleterious influence over those who were involved. Ignorant explains that: 'we had this little portable TV, and the only reason we watched it was to get the worst, most horrific images from it so that we could use it at gigs. At the end there was no enjoyment it in.' Rimbaud, too, reinforces this interpretation, noting that 'for seven years we'd worked on this programme, absolutely resolutely, no question. Every minute of the day and night was taken up with organising, operating, whatever it was, coming up with new ideas, dealing with old ideas, just the usual pattern, and it never fucking stopped... And living in this house, the constant visitors, the constant mail-ins, all the rest of it. It's not an easy place to live in that respect.'

For Crass, since the collective identity of the band went deeper than the mere adoption of pseudonyms that could be cast off as soon as was expedient, so too was the separation of that collective identity back out into its constituent parts much more of a painful process. "It really was a matter of coming down to breakfast, sitting opposite someone you had worked with intimately for seven years and not knowing who the Hell they were – what their thoughts were, what their ideas and aspirations were, what their loves and hates were, because we'd become this sort of common body.' Furthermore, both Ignorant and Rimbaud agree that the years of unrestrained input created an inner bleakness which the members were now struggling to escape from. Rimbaud explains that, 'the grimness was more in realising that we hadn't looked to ourselves for seven years and we couldn't cope with it,' whilst Steve Ignorant says simply, 'we all turned a bit bloody miserable, and I think it was a good thing that it stopped.'

Yet, ironically, if Crass could be said to have had a failing, it was that their symbol system, and the content which it conveyed, started to become negative over the duration of the band's lifetime. During the early years of the 1980s, for those mounting their resistance, mounting *any* resistance, was a huge undertaking. The forces of the establishment were exerted so strongly against them that the energy required to resist them left ever-smaller room for the exploration of

---

Falklands conflict to her own ends. It was she, not the Queen, who took the salute at the victory parade through the City of London in October 1982, declaring during a speech at the Guildhall the same day, 'we, the British people, are proud of what has been done, proud of these heroic pages in our island story, proud to be here today to salute the task force. Proud to be British.'

more positive alternatives. Ignorant articulates the corner into which the band was forced, or into which they painted themselves: 'we were always trying to find different ways to say the same thing. How many times can you say that you don't want nuclear war?' Penny Rimbaud, too, is open in acknowledging that Crass, in directing the entirety of their energy toward combating the Thatcherite machine and its symbol system, did not leave enough for themselves to then be able to paint a clear enough picture of an alternative world, of what such a world could be like: 'no, and that was Crass's failing. We didn't really have a clear enough picture of an operational mode. I mean, one example is the Best Party in Iceland, who I am in touch with, who got voted in in Iceland after the bank collapse, and they are looking for radical ways of actually creating new institutions... they are someone who are working within the system without the system, and certainly I think one of the reasons why... one has to have a clear vision of possibility. I think in some respects the permaculture movement or the transition movement etc have got some of those elements in them – how do we survive? How do we live? What do we do?'

Learning from this mistake, the work that Rimbaud and Vaucher have continued subsequent to the demise of Crass has been predicated on reversing this situation, and focussing much more on the presentation of a definite 'operational mode': 'the only way is through example. One has to offer something better if all we can offer is criticism and disgruntlement. If we can offer joy and love, that touches people. There's nothing nicer than a smiling face in the underground train, because it confirms something, even if we don't know what the smiling face is about, we get some sense of possibility from it. If everyone is looking miserable as shit, all we get is a sense of impossibility.'

Yet it remains true that, whilst the former members of Crass struggled to make their own personal escape from under its rubble, the aesthetics and symbols that had underpinned the band nevertheless proved a jumping off point for many others, galvanising that which later came to be seen as the 'anarcho-punk' movement. Crass were, at best, an unwilling spearhead of the anarcho-punk current, but that does not diminish the importance of their influence, and the fact that they were seen by others as the Ur-source of that movement is testament to the significance of their work. Although bands in the 'first wave' of British punk made great play of 'anarchy' in their lyrics and promotional literature, none went so far as to explore it as a political or social credo. One of the huge – and largely unspoken – questions hanging over punk at the end of the 1970s was whether it could transcend its increasingly caricatured public notoriety and harness its inherent energy and iconoclasm to fashion something more positive.

It was here that Crass made a unique contribution, forming a bridgehead, exploring and developing their own particular brand of anarchy without adjectives; one that drew in and bound together associated – and sometimes even contradictory – schools of thought, such as feminism and pacifism. Once established, through this bridgehead, stormed a phalanx of bands such as Flux of Pink Indians, the Subhumans, Hagar the Womb, Zounds, and Icons of Filth. Although the movement encompassed a diversity of musical, political, and aesthetic styles, it was Crass that provided the tinder with which to start the fire, whether pioneering the feminist politics that initially provided Hagar the Womb with their direction (giving women their voice in the often male dominated realms of anarcho-punk) or by association giving a fillip to the career of Zounds after they sought refuge at Dial House following an automotive disaster which left them stranded on the road in Essex. As with the wider political bridgehead, so too did the influence of Crass permeate the movement's thematic preoccupations, taking the exciting, yet most often hollow, opposition of punk's first wave, and using its energy to explore more serious themes around the failure of capital, gender politics, Northern Ireland, the treatment of animals, war, and racial equality.

Crass were also seen to be fighting to overcome creeping discord amongst subcultures, trying through positive action to unite the dangerous and divisive fractures which are now inherent in youth culture (they understood that the magnitude of the battle ahead would require unity, not division), for example in their singular approach to skinheads, the demons of the age. 'We were the only band in the '77-79 period who weren't aggressive towards Skinheads' notes Rimbaud. 'I mean someone like Sham 69 had a skin[head] following, but certainly at that point, in those early days, people were banning skinheads from gigs and that sort of shit. Well how do you ever get through to people if you never go out to them? Even though we suffered, quite badly on occasions, at the hands of organised idiot gangs, nonetheless we still didn't adopt the policy of segregation. Because how the hell do you ever get through to people if you're not prepared to go out to them? Otherwise you're just compounding the prejudices, rather than undermining them.'

Such a resolute and determined approach to opening up dialogue with their 'adversaries' demonstrated amply that, with Crass, neither the medium nor the message was pose and sway and borrowed threat, but instead an authentic commitment to using their music to win over antagonists; ones which could, moreover, present genuine physical danger.

Whatever failings Crass may have had as a collective; however often they might have fallen short of the astoundingly high standards which they had set for themselves, they were a band that, almost uniquely, managed to reconcile some of the tensions between 'punk authenticity' and high volume sales, between the sticky, creeping seduction of the music industry and 'meaning it, maaaan', creating – through their way of life and through Crass Records – a remarkable Shangri-la of honesty and generosity amidst the endemic deceit and vanity of the music business. It was through this blueprint formulated by Crass that, Rimbaud's reservations aside, the anarcho-punk movement took its inspiration. 'If we're being honest about it,' notes Mark Wallis, member of the mid-1980s Kent band Liberty, 'we learned [everything] from Crass. Because without Crass there wouldn't really be Conflict, or there wouldn't be any bands that we know today, you know. Sometimes people find it hard to admit that, or they don't want to admit that but that's the truth.'[17]

Given Crass's lineage in art, the musical avant-garde, political protest, and alternative lifestyle, it is not overstating the case to say that they introduced a whole new slew of ideas into punk, giving it a seriousness of mind and sense of purpose that the first wave, however musicall inspiring, patently did not possess. It was through Crass's aesthetic that a whole wave of young musicians was introduced to new ideas, ones that inspired them and which they thereafter explored with relish. Crass introduced into Punk riffs derived from Benjamin Britten, political photomontage and avant-garde poetry (to say nothing of an enormous input of 'anti-business' nous, integrity, and generosity).

David Beckham may occasionally be snapped wearing a diamante-studded Crass T-shirt by Jean Paul Gautier (as Penny Rimbaud

---

17    Interview in *There is No Authority But Yourself.* DVD. Directed by Alexander Oey. Netherlands: SubmarineChannel, 2006.

comments, 'Maybe he was wearing it for the right reasons?'), but Crass's legacy has, in the main, proved remarkably impervious to corporate co-option. 'On the one hand I'm glad about [Crasss' resilience to co-option],' notes Rimbaud. 'But there is an arena that I'm not glad about it, in the sense that Crass did nothing more than represent a commonly-held discontent, and that was mirrored in the huge following that we had. It's the following for whom I'm disappointed. We created what was probably one of the most powerful cultural movements of the 20th-Century, certainly on a par with, or more powerful than something like Dada, more powerful even than say the existential group of post-war Paris in terms of popular following...' He concludes, 'I hardly meet anyone who doesn't claim to respect Crass within the world of media...yet they don't write about us or support in any way at all. Crass is a bit like Gauloise – if you've got a packet of Gauloise everybody smokes them, but no one fucking buys them. I think we were the Gauloise of music.'

RUSS BESTLEY

# BIG A LITTLE A

## THE GRAPHIC LANGUAGE OF ANARCHY

MALCOLM MCLAREN, BERNIE Rhodes, Vivienne Westwood, Jamie Reid, and The Sex Pistols may have set the scene, introducing the word 'anarchy' into punk's verbal and visual discourse, but even they could not have predicted the ways in which the circle 'A' and other symbols of anarchist ideology were to become punk visual tropes in the ensuing years. The development of the UK anarcho-punk subgenre was to become key to this trend between 1978 and 1984, but parallel punk subgenres were to take on the circle 'A' and other graphic conventions for political, rhetorical, or simply fashionable reasons.

The use and migration of anarchist symbols across a range of punk graphic material is explored here, with a particular emphasis on the 'official' visual representations of punk groups and labels through record covers, posters, and other graphic ephemera. A range of graphic codes and conventions can be observed, evolving from the relatively sophisticated graphic identity and output of a number of UK anarcho-punk scene-leaders (including Crass, Conflict, Poison Girls, and Flux of Pink Indians) to the often less technically or graphically proficient visual material produced by lesser-known bands and fellow travellers with a desire to contribute or buy into the scene. Anarcho-punk trends and styles should also be seen in parallel to (and, to an extent, in direct competition with) other developing punk subgenres and the wider evolution of anarcho-punk and/or hardcore scenes.

This chapter focuses on the repetition and use of anarchist symbols across a wide range of graphic material associated with historical punk developments, primarily during the 1980s. The often confused or conflicting relationship between punk subcultures and anarchist ideologies is examined through their visual codes and conventions.

## ANARCHY IN THE UK?

*I am an antichrist, I am an anarchist[1]*

*Anarchist, anarchist, an' I kissed a couple of local girls[2]*

Punk's public relationship with anarchism was, at least in part, kick started by The Sex Pistols' performance of their upcoming debut single, 'Anarchy In The UK,' on Tony Wilson's Granada Television late night magazine programme *So It Goes* on 4th September 1976 – the television debut for the group and for a new youth subculture that had already begun to make headlines in the national papers. That programme was limited to the North West of England, with further mainstream exposure for The Sex Pistols offered by London Weekend Television in a programme dedicated to the punk phenomenon which was broadcast on 28th November, and the notorious Bill Grundy interview on the *Today* show on 1st December.

By that time, punk had already developed something of a high profile in the music press, and its rhetorical positioning had taken centre-stage in a publicity campaign based around the notions of change, shock, and the 'new wave'. Sex Pistols manager Malcolm McLaren, alongside colleagues Vivienne Westwood and Bernie Rhodes, had played a central role in providing the new 'movement' with an appropriate vocabulary, drawn from a curious mixture of late '60s underground manifestos, early 20th Century political art movements and more recent cultural commentators from media, film, and literature.

---

1    Sex Pistols, "Anarchy In The UK," EMI, 1976.
2    Water Pistols, "Gimme That Punk Junk," State Records, 1976.

Clothes designed by the trio and sold in Westwood and McLaren's shop in the Kings Road, London, bore slogans drawn from Marxist theory and more recent countercultural manifestos: Westwood and McLaren's 'Only Anarchists Are Pretty' printed shirts bore the slogans such as 'Be Reasonable, Demand the Impossible' (from 'Soyez réalistes, demandez l'impossible!' – anonymous graffiti, Paris 1968), 'Try Subversion, it's Fun,' 'Believe in the Ruins' and 'Anarchy For the UK Means Freedom From Rubber Bullets,' while the 'Anarchist Punk Gang' muslin shirt featured anarchy 'A' symbols alongside a skull and crossbones and the legend 'As You Were I Was, As I Am You Will Be' (from Hunter S. Thompson's *Hell's Angels*). The use of the term 'rubber bullets' was a direct commentary on contemporary political issues in the UK – notably the use of rubber bullets by British troops to suppress protests in Northern Ireland – while the sense of celebration of individual autonomy offered a direct counterpoint to mainstream press warnings of social breakdown as a dangerous consequence of the economic problems dogging the country.

It could be argued that the use of the anarchy symbol by Westwood and McLaren bore no more importance or relevance than other graphic elements such as the skull and crossbones, swastika, the union flag or images of the Queen, Karl Marx, Marilyn Monroe or Mickey Mouse (who in turn featured an anarchy 'A' on his right ear). McLaren also updated his classic 'Vive Le Rock' t-shirt design in 1977, screen printing it onto a muslin shirt and adding images taken from William Powell's *The Anarchist Cookbook* – a notorious countercultural text first published in the USA in 1971 and widely circulated within the late hippie underground. This montage-like approach, mixing symbols of insurrection and revolution with images of authority, religion and popular culture, was largely aesthetic – or at least lacking in a clear focus or specificity of political intent. 'Anarchy' was a threatening term, but its value within the early UK punk scene was usually rhetorical – a device to vaguely suggest freedom from restrictions or convention, rather than a disciplined call to social and political reorganisation.

In this sense, the texts drew upon quotes from art and political radicals such as Marx, Durutti, Debord and the heritage of Atelier Populaire and the Paris 1968 protests, along with popular literature drawn from the late hippie counterculture. Certainly there was a contemporary currency for various interpretations of the anarchist position, as evidenced in the use of the circled 'A' by groups such as Here & Now at their free performances at Meanwhile Gardens, Notting Hill, in the early 1970s. It was also a common trope within the radical circles surrounding the Deviants, Gong, Hawkwind, and the Pink Fairies, and at major events such as the Windsor and Stonehenge festivals – a crossover that would link personally to Penny Rimbaud and Crass in the subsequent development of what would become known as anarcho-punk.[3] Meanwhile, the older schools of anarchist thought centred around Freedom Press in Whitechapel and the squatting and activist communities were continuing a political critique that was largely distinct from the more music and lifestyle-centred hippie movement. A similar pattern would be reflected within later generations with the implied separation between the more 'traditional' political anarchists and the anarcho-punk groups and their followers, drawn to the politics through subcultural engagement.

McLaren, Westwood and Rhodes's obsession with both historical and contemporary radicalism, drawing on images and quotes from both right and left wing intellectuals, was largely centred on an attempt to provoke and shock rather than a clear form of ideological positioning or political allegiance, and others amongst UK punk's early pioneers soon evolved a similar distaste for organised politics and the doctrines of the past. A loose interpretation of the anarchist position – rebellious but unfixed, sceptical, antagonistic, critical of political organisation and centred on the ideology of the individual (at least in terms of its punk definition) – was a relatively easy one to take, particularly for a young and less than studious subcultural group. Interviewed by Nick Kent for the *New Musical Express* in November 1976, Malcolm McLaren stated that the use of the term 'anarchy in the UK' provided a perfect slogan for his new prodigies; 'I just see it as a reaction against the last five years of stagnation.' In McLaren's terms, anarchy was '…a statement of intent, a statement of self-rule, of ultimate independence, of do-it-yourself.' Punk's version of anarchism was, then, partly based on a loosely-informed historical concept but more broadly adopted as a rhetorical position invoking a sense of liberty, personal freedom, individualism and anti-authoritarianism,

3   Penny Rimbaud, (aka J.J. Ratter), *Shibboleth: My Revolting Life*, (London: AK Press, 1999). See also Crass, *A Series of Shock Slogans and Mindless Token Tantrums* (London: Exitstencil Press, 1982).

not totally dissimilar to the sentiments of earlier generations of rock 'n' roll rebels, from Woody Guthrie to Bob Dylan, or from Jerry Lee Lewis to the Who.

## THE FILTH AND THE FURY

Janet Street-Porter interviewed The Sex Pistols for the *London Weekend Show*, broadcast on 28th November 1976. Interspersed with live footage of the group performing Anarchy In The UK at the Notre Dame Hall, Leicester Square two weeks earlier, Street-Porter asked a question directly related to the lyrics of the first verse concerning destroying the passer-by:

> **JSP**: *What do you mean? Do you mean you actually want to destroy them, or...?*
>
> **ROTTEN**: Complacent, apathetic old fucks who walk up and down and do nothing and complain about everything, and watch *Top of the Pops* and send their boring little letters into *Melody Maker*, week after week. That's what I wanna get rid of.
>
> **JSP**: *How do you want to get rid of it though?*
>
> **ROTTEN**: Push them out. Destroy them one way or another. But not violence. Get rid of them.

The group's concerns at this point appear centred on the lack of relevance or excitement within the then-contemporary British music scene (the Rolling Stones and Rod Stewart are cited as part of the 'boring' rock establishment), and on a self-proclaimed sense of 'authenticity' and connection between themselves and their audience – ironically, a keystone within the myth-making and marketing of various forms of 'serious' rock music since the 1960s, with particular artists described as 'keeping it real' or more in touch with their 'roots' than their contemporaries.[4] Anarchism, as either a political ideology or doctrine, is not touched upon in the interview, and the

---

4    Barker, Hugh, and Yuval Taylor. *Faking It: The Quest for Authenticity in Popular Music* (London: Faber & Faber, 2007).

term seems interchangeable with a vague sense of anti-establishmentarianism or general disaffection with the status quo, particularly within the field of popular music. Interviewed by Polly Toynbee on 15th October 2014, John Lydon offered a highly critical interpretation of the politics of early punk: 'What happened to anarchy in the UK then? When did he get serious? "The older you get the more you learn, all right?" Anyway, he says, "I never preached anarchy. It was just a novelty in a song. I always thought anarchy was just a mind game for the middle class."'

Similar anti-authoritarian themes arose across the burgeoning punk movement, with punk 'actors' keen, and willing, to cite their grievances with the world around them, more often than not without the accompanying wit of the likes of Rotten, TV Smith, or Howard Devoto (for whom 'boredom' could be highly ironic – 'You know me / I'm acting dumb / You know the scene / Very humdrum / Boredom / Boredom / B'dum b'dum'). Like Lewis Carroll's famous quote, the term 'anarchy' could mean whatever the orator wished it to mean, and any attempts at a specificity of 'meaning' could be sidestepped in favour of a mutually shared, unfocussed expression of boredom, negativity and dissatisfaction with, basically, anything and everything. 'Anarchy' may have become something of a punk watchword following the rise of the Pistols, but its use-value as a specific term was far from defined, and many imitators chose to adopt the phrasing and rhetoric of 'anarchy, chaos, and destruction' or nihilism and boredom without trying to fix its meaning. Some received criticism from within the subculture itself – the Adverts' 'Safety In Numbers' and Alternative TV's 'How Much Longer?' were disdainful of the direction that the new wave was taking and the narrowing of ambition to a uniform pose, while others took a more directly humorous approach (notably arch punk parodists Alberto Y Lost Trios Paranoias), employing punk clichés as a means to ridicule the naive posturing of some participants. Once a subject can be mocked through a range of widely recognised and stereotypical conventions, as in the Alberto's 'Kill' and 'Fuck You,' then those conventions have lost their authority (in the same way that early punk visual tropes such as the swastika, safety pin, and razor blade were soon to fall out of favour within the punk subculture as their symbolic power was drained by repetitive association and overuse).

How much longer will people wear
Nazi armbands and dye their hair?
Safety pins and spray their clothes
Talk about anarchy, fascism and boredom[5]

According to Dave Laing's analysis of punk lyrical content in the context of wider popular music forms, a greater proportion of early punk songs were concerned with 'social and political comment' and

---

5    Alternative TV, 'How Much Longer?' Deptford Fun City, 1977.

voiced as 'first person feelings' than was usually the case in chart singles.[6] Such 'social and political comment' was, however, broadly limited to anti-establishment sloganeering and the rejection of authority, though again within the context of a loosely individualistic lyrical framework ('I Don't Wanna, I Don't Care,' 'Complete Control,' 'No More Heroes,' 'Don't Dictate,' 'Oh Bondage Up Yours!'). More often than not, early UK punk songs were concerned with self- and group-reflection or commentary on the scene itself ('Bored Teenagers,' 'One Chord Wonders,' 'Your Generation,' 'Problem Child,' 'Clash City Rockers') rather than addressing 'bigger' issues of national or global importance.

> Youth club group used to want to be free, now they want anarchy![7]

While the media attention afforded the Pistols may have inadvertently led to a mass outbreak of bandwagon-jumpers who were keen to exploit the opening offered to anything 'punk,' the group's fiercely intelligent lyrics and Jamie Reid's powerful graphic styles perhaps pushed others to avoid being seen as too closely attempting to copy the scene-leader's 'brand.' Certainly, very few contemporaneous songs reference the term 'anarchy' in their titles, while The Clash's 'White Riot' did at least spawn a wider range of 'riot' themed songs, and other common lyrical tropes included boredom (of course), escape and vague notions of individualism more closely reflecting the B-side of 'Anarchy In The UK,' the more self-referential, and it could be argued traditional in terms of rock 'n' roll themes, 'I Wanna Be Me.' Suitable examples include the Buzzcocks' 'Autonomy,' the Rings' 'I Wanna Be Free,' the Drones' 'Just Wanna Be Myself,' the Rods' 'Do Anything You Wanna Do' and Sham 69's 'I Don't Wanna.' Equally, 'Anarchy In The UK' was unique within The Sex Pistols own repertoire in referring to the concept of anarchy – more widely, lyrics centred on caustic put-downs of often nameless targets ('Liar,' 'Problems,' 'New York'), personal feelings and sentiments ('Seventeen,' 'No Feelings,' 'Pretty Vacant') and diatribes against the establishment and the music industry ('God Save The Queen,' 'EMI'). Meanwhile, interviews and

6   Dave Laing. *One Chord Wonders: Power and Meaning in Punk Rock* (Milton Keynes: Open University, 1985).

7   The Members, 'Sound Of The Suburbs,' Virgin, 1979.

statements from the band referenced 'chaos', and it could be said that a sense of the 'anarchic' held sway over the group and the wider movement, though this was embodied more in terms of a lack of control rather than an ideological position – in part evidenced by the 'get pissed, destroy' coda to 'Anarchy In The UK.' Essentially, the pairing of 'Anarchy In The UK' with 'I Wanna Be Me' on the same seven inch single – whether deliberately or inadvertently intended by the group themselves – indicated two rhetorical positions on the same concept; independence, autonomy, youthful rebellion, and the assertion of individuality. These 'standard' rock themes could be seen to date back historically through the likes of the Who, the Small Faces, and a host of garage bands and rock 'n' roll rebels from the 1950s onwards.

## GRAPHIC ANARCHY

The visual communication of punk's original anarchic message was equally vague. Many designers followed music industry tradition by featuring a photograph of the group on the sleeve of their record, though often the setting was adjusted to a suitably rough and ready urban backdrop. Roberta Bayley's group photograph on the front of the first Ramones album – itself a knowing adaptation of traditional styles of photographic portraiture – had set the precedent for many, including The Clash, Sham 69, and the Cortinas, along with a long lineage of lesser-known groups such as Headache, Blitzkrieg Bop, and the Suburban Studs. The visual trope of the group photographed (usually in grainy monochrome) against a distressed and decaying urban landscape was later re-visited by Chron Gen, the Partisans, the Enemy, Attak, Anti Social, and many others during the second wave of UK punk in the early 80s, a 'punk' convention and visual shorthand that multiplied and grew without much critique or interrogation.

Jamie Reid deliberately chose not to feature images of the group on the record sleeves of The Sex Pistols, a convention also adopted by Malcolm Garrett for single releases by Buzzcocks and Magazine (though Buzzcocks album covers reversed the principle). Reid's initial sleeve design for 'Anarchy In The UK' featured a drawing of a monster attacking a building – a legacy of his earlier work at Suburban Press – but this was rejected and replaced by a red and black anarchist flag (also rejected) and subsequently for the first production run with a plain black sleeve. The single was then issued with a standard EMI company logo paper bag – the symbiotic relationship between punk singles and picture sleeves being yet to fully evolve. In a similar fashion to the group's songwriting, Reid's graphics were provocative and abrasive, but in general bore little or no formal relationship to anarchist theory or political ideology. Iconic elements were limited to the use of colour, appropriated images, and ransom-note typographic styles or rough-and-ready handwriting.

Formal symbols were rarely used on artwork for The Sex Pistols – the swastika made a brief appearance on early posters for second single 'God Save The Queen,' along with a more frequent use of the union flag and, obviously, the Cecil Beaton official photograph of the Queen – but again, the political critique was implied rather than overt, and symbols associated directly with radical or oppositional politics were largely avoided. The same was true across a wide range of early UK punk output – other UK punk sleeve designers (Malcolm Garrett, George Snow, Bill Smith, Jill Furmanovsky, Michael Beal, Phil Smee, David Jeffery, and many others) chose to focus on either the image of the group themselves (a more 'traditional' design approach within the music industry) or on the generally awkward, unusual, innovative, 'new wave' themes of the evolving subculture, utilising a similarly discordant visual style to reflect the zeitgeist. Politics wasn't downplayed as such, but it was more implied through the challenging conjunctions of images and text, the use of provocative reportage photographs, or the distressed and often less-than-harmonious graphic treatment of the visual composition rather than through a reliance on formal or established 'political' codes and symbols.

## ANARCHY AND ANARCHO-PUNK

Punk's until-then rather laissez-faire adoption of anarchism was set to change with the emergence of Crass and the subsequent growth of what would be retrospectively termed the anarcho-punk movement. Initially, as has been well documented,[8] Rimbaud and Ignorant formed Crass in order to engage with and participate in the growing punk subculture, not as a catalyst to some sort of breakaway movement that set itself in opposition to the punk scene, for all its evident faults. That is not to say that Crass didn't start out with a

---

8   George Berger, *The Story of Crass* (London: Omnibus Press, 2007), Ian Glasper, *The Day The Country Died: A History of Anarcho-Punk 1980-1984* (London: Cherry Red, 2006).

critical position in relation to punk, or without a 'political' message to communicate – Ignorant's well-known lyrical pronouncement 'fuck the politically minded' aside. The first record release by the band, *The Feeding of the 5000* (1978), featured eighteen songs, with lyrics attacking the media, the government, the church and state, and the punk scene itself – the track 'Punk is Dead' featured the lyric 'punk narcissism was social napalm / Steve Jones started doing real harm / Preaching revolution, anarchy and change / As he sucked from the system that had given him his name,' though quite why guitarist Steve Jones comes in for such personal abuse, rather than the other Pistols, is unclear. It is clear, however, that part of the Crass 'philosophy' was to critically reflect on punk's failure to bring about genuine change, and to use its misappropriation of the concept of 'anarchy' as a means to engage with punk audiences. On *Sucks*, a direct reference to The Sex Pistols indicates a double-edged sword, alluding to one of the well-known phrases of the subculture while at the same time offering the 'true' meaning as something different; 'Do you really believe in the system? / Well ok / I BELIEVE IN ANARCHY IN THE UK.' Given their broader critique of the 'failure' of punk to live up to its rhetoric, the adoption of such a specific term appears to be both a challenge and an attempt to engage punk audiences with the critique itself.

Crass certainly managed to provide a catalyst for a new form of punk subculture, as young Scottish fan Chris Low – soon to become drummer with Political Asylum and the Apostles – recalls; '...but suddenly, *Feeding* was there, providing, by proxy, an alternative reality that in essence made you think that as the things it was 'against' were things that you couldn't relate to, it was a whole all-encompassing ethos and ideology that you could derive an identity and sovereignty from. It was shortly after that – around the time that Honey Bane single came out – that Crass played the Stirling Albert Hall with a band called Spiked Copy, whose singer I knew. Pretty much everyone I hung about with went along to that and I remember it being fucking brilliant. And so different from the other punk bands I'd gone to see, Clash, SLF, Damned etc., who you saw at big, seated venues where the bouncers would hassle you if you started jumping around, not to mention the fact we wouldn't be able to get in most of the time as most venues were over-18s. But this Crass gig was in a local hall, cost about 50p to get in, and was fucking brilliant. The fact they came

across so intensely on stage just compounding what to us was an un-
believably strong, powerful image.'[9]

Punk was already becoming politicised in the UK, through an
overt engagement by some high profile groups in campaigns such as
Rock Against Racism and a hardening political climate – the Winter
of Discontent of 1978/79 was looming, as was the May 1979 General
Election where Margaret Thatcher would sweep to power and provide
Crass and many other punk groups (from both within and outside
the 'anarcho-punk' camp) with a highly visible bête noire on which
to focus their assault. For Rimbaud, working within the context of
a punk group was a new experience, but also part of a continuum
in terms of his personal ideology, as he indicated to Alex Ogg, when
interviewed for the book *No More Heroes* (2006); '... it was just an
extension of what I'd always done – finding the best way of saying
things. The political thing was the new element. And that was almost
forced on us. Steve and myself were just mucking about. But as rock
'n' roll started exposing its lies, we felt we had to expose our truths.
The anarchist thing wasn't because we wanted to be seen as anarchists,
it was because we were trying to say to both right and left, fuck off, we
don't want to be identified with you. We're not part of any Trotyskyite
scheme or some capitalist heist. We're individuals doing what we want
to do.'[10] Such sentiments echo closely the earlier position within The
Sex Pistols' camp as the group began to attract media attention during
1976, as Jamie Reid had noted retrospectively: '... The Sex Pistols were
at their strongest when nobody knew where they were coming from
– when people would call you anarchist and fascist in the same week
– but that didn't last for very long.'[11]

Rimbaud's position needs to be understood in relation to a number of wider contexts – the birth and subsequent development of what
might be called the UK punk movement (and the co-option by the
music industry of its major figures), the changing political climate of
the country during an economic depression, the rise of the far right
and a counter-offensive by the far left that took 'popular culture' as
one area of potential engagement, and the broadening-out of punk

9    Chris Low, email interview with author, August 2014.
10   Penny Rimbaud, interview by Alex Ogg, 2006.
11   Jamie Reid and Jon Savage, *Up They Rise – The Incomplete Works of Jamie Reid* (London: Faber & Faber, 1987), 57.

and post punk musical and aesthetic styles, together with a willing and engaged audience for 'new' sounds, styles and messages. In short, while the national political climate provided a clear set of ideological positions to attack, critique or question, the punk subculture provided a context, and importantly an audience, for a group such as Crass to find a space to create. The growth of an independent music market, born in part from punk's 'anyone can do it' ideology, gave 'alternative' punk voices a platform, as well as critical, and economic, support.

## MIXING PUNK AND POLITICS

Fellow 'political punk' travellers – the Gang of Four, Delta 5, the Raincoats, the Pop Group, the Au Pairs, the Mekons – may have drawn inspiration from left wing, libertarian or feminist politics, but Crass were soon seen to be firmly allied to an anarchist message, notwithstanding criticisms of their early performances from both left and right-wing commentators that they were on 'the other side.' Anarchism, as something more than a sense of free-thinking, libertarian, personal self-reflection drawn largely from the philosophies of the late hippie underground, was then something that the group were forced to engage with more formally, as Rimbaud noted retrospectively

to Alex Ogg; '...actually, we then had to learn classical anarchism very quickly. We'd always lived as anarchist individuals, but we didn't have any history – it was a crash course. We hoisted ourselves on our own petard in that sense. However artistic we attempted to be, it was always within the political framework, or against the political framework. We got increasingly embroiled in oppositional politics, which is so far from my own thinking. If my own life has been opposed to anything, it's been opposed to the concept of oppositional politics, which is what we came to represent but never actually believed in.'[12]

However, such serious interpretations of the group and their actions could also be opened up to question; '...we became seen as po-faced, hardened anarchists, but there was deep humour. The irony to us was never far from the surface, the fact that we could laugh absurdly at it, while people were taking it so seriously.'[13] Interestingly, this view contrasts with others from those who engaged with Crass as up-and-coming groups who were facilitated by the Crass label to release their own recordings, as Steve Lake of Zounds recalls; 'They made it quite clear they were not even interested in their own music. To them, music was just a vehicle to get their message across. They were an ideological, propaganda machine who used music and art as a medium to propagate their ideas, whereas Zounds were fully fledged, immature, rock n roll children who lived to play gigs, worshipped Elvis and Hank Williams, and just happened to write songs about their lives as disaffected squatters with no ambition.'[14]

> Pogo on a Nazi, spit upon a Jew,
> Vicious mindless violence that offers nothing new.
> Left-wing violence, right-wing violence, all seems much the same,
> Bully boys out fighting, it's just the same old game.
> Boring fucking politics that'll get us all shot,
> Left-wing, right-wing, you can stuff the lot.
> Keep your petty prejudice, I don't see the point,
> ANARCHY AND FREEDOM IS WHAT I WANT.[15]

---

12  Penny Rimbaud.
13  Penny Rimbaud.
14  Steve Lake, *Zounds Demystified* (London: Active Distribution, 2013), 33.
15  Crass, 'White Punks On Hope,' *Stations of the Cross*, Crass Records, 1979.

Crass found themselves at the centre of a debate on the future of the UK punk movement, and a schism ensued between what would come to be described as the politicised anarcho-punk subgenre and developments across the wider subculture, including commercial new wave, post punk, more 'traditional' forms of punk and, especially, the Oi! movement, which in many ways presented itself as an alternative, 'authentic', class-based location for punk's continued evolution. Either way, the punk anarchist 'message' was gaining momentum, and new groups across the wider regions of the UK formed in the wake of scene-leaders Crass and Poison Girls, in part due to the willingness of those groups to travel away from the traditional rock music circuit and to play in more remote and low-key venues. Such a strike for punk authenticity, while not exactly new, found a degree of resonance within the subculture, and many bands and fans were drawn into its wake.

More traditional and formal notions of anarchism, meanwhile, were regaining wider cultural currency. George Woodcock's selected compendium of essays *The Anarchist Reader* was published in paperback form by Fontana in 1977, and its relatively easy introduction to the concept of anarchism from a variety of historical viewpoints made it an accessible volume for a young readership drawn to the concept through punk but wary of complex or unintelligible political theory. Anarcho-punk certainly provided a stimulus for some followers to attempt to engage with anarchist history and politics, in much the same way as Rimbaud's earlier 'crash course' had indicated for the scene-leaders themselves. Debates raged in anarcho-punk` zines, with writers, editors, and readers keen to explore the multiple definitions of anarchism, various 'anarchies', and activist – or pacifist – politics.

A clear divide could be observed between the anarcho-syndicalist ideals of the 'Anarchy and Peace' punk collectives centred around Crass and the more confrontational politics of Ian Bone's Class War and fellow anarcho-punk travellers such as Conflict and the Apostles. Such debates long predated anarcho-punk, of course, with Bakunin, Stirner, Godwin, Sorel, Woodcock, and others positioning anarchist politics in relation to themes of violence, revolution, pacifism, protest, trades unions, and self-governing soviets – anarcho-punk's more seriously engaged participants had a lot to read and discuss. Perhaps because of their perceived position as scene-leaders (and their impact on the mainstream following significant success in the Independent

Charts[16]), the pacifist approach expounded by Crass held sway with the majority of the subculture, at least until the mid-1980s when more militant positions became popular, as Chris Low explains; '... when Class War first emerged it was regarded as an absolute pariah. Anarcho-punk was still to all intents and purposes "pacifist" and Class War's violent rhetoric was anathema to that. It was only when Chumbawamba and Crass arrived at a more "revolutionary" (as opposed to "personal revolution") political position that anarcho-punk moved towards the militancy that now characterises it worldwide.'[17]

Some anarcho-punk groups followed Crass's example and included extended reading material within their record packaging and sleeve notes, with followers encouraged to learn more about the core philosophy of anarchism from a variety of ideological positions, and it is clear that the movement itself spurred on some individuals to construct a more rigorous and intelligent political framework and discourse. Whether this was useful or valuable in the longer term is a moot point – the adoption of increasingly dogmatic and doctrinaire positions by subsequent generations of punk and hardcore groups, labels, distributors, and zine writers (a.k.a. the 'punk police') certainly exacerbated earlier fault lines within the punk movement and alienated a lot of participants within the wider subculture. More contemporaneously, the fracturing of punk and hardcore, with extended public debates on the authenticity and ideological soundness of individuals and groups based on their diets, language, behaviour or associations, can perhaps be seen to have had more of a negative impact than the progressive or positive development such approaches may have originally sought to validate. As Chris Low reflects, '...anarcho-punk did encourage people to "question authority" and reject many aspects of social conditioning – from militarism to religion to the very idea of the idolisation of "rock stars." However, I would argue that much of this was still based on a "received wisdom" of many of the social issues anarcho-punk addressed, and often in a fairly unreasoned manner, i.e. the often espoused claim that slaughterhouses were "no different" to the gas chambers of Nazi Germany. A position that IS, arguably, consistent with an extreme animal liberationist perspective but I would

---

16   Barry Lazel, *Indie Hits: The Complete UK Independent Charts 1980-1989* (London: Cherry Red Books, 1997).

17   Chris Low.

imagine was more a case of anarcho-punk's parroting a simplistic understanding of the Poison Girls' "Offending Article" (a uniquely complex polemic which should probably be read as a wilfully provocative corollary to Valerie Solanas' *Scum Manifesto* in its etymological approach to speciesism rather than taken on face value) and slogans most popularly espoused by Conflict rather than having a familiarisation with Peter Singer's writings. Such a position became part of the language and currency of anarcho-punk and woe-befall anyone who refuted it.'[18]

Some new groups who became wrapped up in what music critics began to describe as the anarcho-punk movement found the politics became foregrounded more than the music, as Steve Lake of Zounds later recalled, 'I never set out to make political statements, promote a point of view or publicise an ideology. In the days I started doing it I didn't even know what an ideology was.'[19] Such attitudes were not unfamiliar, among bands, fans, and active participants under the anarcho-punk' umbrella. For some, a concern with such things as animal rights, feminism, anti-capitalism or a perceived growing threat of nuclear conflict (heightened by the very public animosity between the USA and USSR, the move by NATO to position US nuclear weapons on British soil and a media fixation with the increased tensions of the Cold War),[20] or with more localised issues, drew them to anarcho-punk's (at that time) loosely-defined model of libertarian politics. Equally, the visual communication strategies supporting activist and campaign groups in these areas, largely drawing on the samizdat tradition of low tech print reproduction, closely reflected the punk aesthetic, and graphic design elements could to an extent be simply interchangeable on record sleeves, backdrops, banners, badges and clothing. In turn, some of those concerns (notably animal rights, feminism, anti-war voices and support for CND) became default ideologies for the movement as a whole, as a more clearly defined set of codes and conventions matured and took hold. Steve Lake's lyrical concerns within his song writing for Zounds featured a range of personal, reflective and political themes, some of which were to become

18    Chris Low.
19    Lake, *Zounds Demystified*, 5.
20    Matthew Worley, "One Nation Under the Bomb: The Cold War and British Punk to 1984," *Journal for the Study of Radicalism* 5/2 (2011): 65-83.

more formally embedded in the core philosophy of the burgeoning 'movement' – though Lake himself expressed some frustrations with the resulting narrow categorisation of the group as a 'political' band; Zounds's lyrics contain a lot of politics. They also include satire, absurdism, surrealism, gut feeling, comedy, emotion, contradiction, confession, love, hate, celebration, comment, disgust and a million other things. Zounds is not a political rock band, it's a cry for help.'[21]

Similarly, such embedded and defined tropes became something of a straightjacket for other musicians and groups placed, willingly or otherwise, within the anarcho-punk scene. Some lyrical and musical themes could become overplayed to the point of saturation, leading to frustration for the artists concerned and for some sections of the audience – though it should also be noted that such sets of expectations were also a 'way in' for many others, and while a theme may have become overly familiar, the sentiments expressed need not be seen as worthless as a result. Even the 'scene leaders' expressed concerns with the way the 'movement' was becoming described and stereotyped. Opinions differ as to the root cause – from the machinations of the music press and industry to 'contain' new cultural modes through naming and categorising, to the restricting influence of set ideologies that become static rules and regulations in themselves. As Penny Rimbaud later reflected; '... the anarcho-punk movement was an anathema to me. I wasn't interested in it. I didn't like it. I think it was very divisive in any case. It was a very convenient way for the business to put us outside the business – us and everything we were related to. I don't think we isolated ourselves, we were isolated by the industry, who couldn't contain us.'[22]

For others, anarcho-punk 'politics' may have chimed with personal beliefs, but a critical reflection allows a distinction to be made between cause and effect, as Chris Low recalls; '...I think the main way "punk changed my life" was the vast array of people that one way or another I encountered through it. You truly wouldn't believe some of the social

---

21  Lake, *Zounds Demystified*, 6. It is interesting to note that the debut E.P. release by Zounds on the Crass label included a fold-out poster featuring a quote by Pierre-Joseph Proudhon, a rare case of an anarcho-punk group citing 'traditional' anarchist political theory. The fact that Proudhon's surname is spelled incorrectly perhaps demonstrates a less than rigorous approach.

22  Penny Rimbaud.

circumstances or people I have met who, once the topic of punk came up, there's immediately been a bond with. But that said, I wouldn't want to give punk too much credit for how I turned out. Most of the values I have I'm sure I would have inherited through my parents and those are the same values and beliefs I find most people I socialise with share, many of whom may not even have heard of Crass or anarcho-punk.'[23]

And therein lies the rub – many, if not all, ideological associations apparently embedded within an anarchist punk lifestyle are not too distinct from more widely held 'liberal' values in the late twentieth and early twenty-first centuries. Certainly the notions of 'political correctness' so beloved of the liberal left and cursed by the political right seem to fit quite neatly alongside widely promoted punk anarchist values of tolerance, anti-racism, anti-sexism and anti-homophobia. Perhaps the 'anarchist' tag could be dropped altogether, and the politics of punk could simply be seen as progressive, liberal, and 'modern'. Whether such ideas can be seen as positive is certainly debatable, and may for some even be regrettable, as Amebix singer Rob outlined to Alex Ogg; '...some of the values that were originally propagated by the anarcho scene are directly linked to what has come to be associated with political correctness and Nanny State politics. I am not a fan of censorship and feel that some things have led to an impasse.'[24]

## I STILL BELIEVE IN ANARCHY

The model of punk anarchism embodied by the increasingly dogmatic anarcho-punk groups, particularly from 1980 onwards, was not to completely overwrite the more casual association between punk and 'rebellion' that had been cemented in previous years. The Exploited's 'I Believe in Anarchy,' released in 1980 on the b-side of debut single 'Exploited Barmy Army' and re-recorded in 1981 for their debut album *Punks Not Dead*, references the term 'anarchy' much as it had been embodied within The Sex Pistols and the early UK punk movement, rather than the political vision of the new pretenders to punk's vision and values. The album title was itself a direct riposte to the Crass song 'Punk Is Dead' from two years earlier and the subsequent rise of Crass and the anarcho-punk movement. Anarchy, in

---

23    Chris Low.

24    Alex Ogg, "Children of a lesser guild: An Anarcho A-Z," *Punk & Post Punk* 3:1 (2014): 41-47.

these terms, is contextualised *within* punk, a kind of individualist non-conformism fighting back against the subculture's critics (both internal and external), rather than positioned within a socio-historical context or related to an ideological position in the wider world; 'I'm not ashamed of being a punk / And I don't care, I don't give a damn / And I don't care what you say / Cause I believe in anarchy.' This form of punk anarchism, a theme that would later be wrapped up within critiques of lifestyle anarchism, harked back to the origins of the term as incorporated within the punk subculture, and while this marked something of a distinction between anarcho-punk followers and the wider punk community, particularly in the early 1980s, in practice these contrasts were often far less rigid than might be assumed

– Honey Bane's debut single on Crass Records, with its chorus 'You can be free / The real you / You can be you' appears far closer to the individualist punk youth revolt model than the ideologically-driven political anarchism supposedly defining the anarcho-punk' groups as a distinct, self-identifying movement.

On the other side of the 'divide', hardcore punk groups embraced the anarchist message, particularly its anti-war themes that held a high degree of cultural currency during a heightened period of Cold War nervousness.[25] Discharge, Chaos U.K. and Dead Mans Shadow produced records that focussed on anti-war messages, and were, at least initially, unafraid to adorn their record covers and group logos with the anarchist symbol. Interestingly, typographic composition also comes into play here – the visual balance offered by a circled 'A' in the original Chaos U.K. logo helps to anchor the composition and offers a central axis around which to build the rest of the graphic form. While slightly less compositionally successful, the 'A' in the middle of the group name Reality offers a similar approach to the logo designer. In fact, adopting a group name with the letter 'A' strategically placed – particularly for those attracted to the anarcho-punk scene – was something of a priority if the group was to create a successful visual identity. This presented something of a problem for the Disrupters; having successfully managed to get a track onto the first *Bullshit Detector* (1980) compilation album issued by the Crass label to showcase a selection from the assortment of demo tapes which were sent for consideration by hopeful groups around the country, a change of group name would be unhelpful, but the original moniker lacked the strategic letter 'A'. The group got around this problem by simply turning the circled 'A' through 90 degrees to form the capital letter 'D' of their name – not altogether successfully. Meanwhile, Leeds band Icon A.D. signed to Radical Change, the label run by the Disrupters, but declined the obvious graphic trick of circling the 'A' in their name, though the incorporation of the symbol on the sleeve illustration for their second EP *Let The Vultures Fly* (1983) is rather awkward, to say the least.

### POST ANARCHO-PUNK REFLECTIONS

From the outset, Crass had set out to wage their punk campaign through to 1984 – the year being significant for a number of reasons, obviously

---

25   Worley, *One Nation Under the Bomb*.

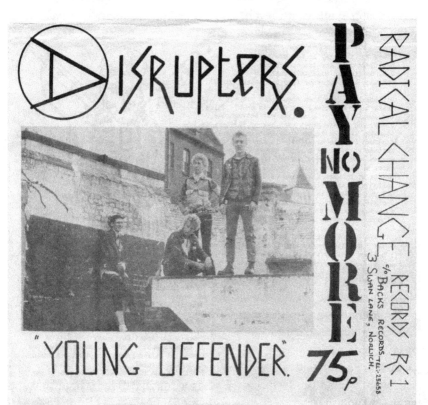

DISRUPTERS.

"YOUNG OFFENDER".

PAY NO MORE 75p

RADICAL CHANGE RECORDS RC1
c/o BACKS RECORDS TEL:-25655
3 SWAN LANE, NORWICH.

PHOTOS BY I.M.D.

ARTWORK BY THE DISRUPTERS

PRODUCED BY JON WARD
AND THE DISRUPTERS

ENGINEERED AND MIXED
BY DAVE KNOWLES

JULY 1981
RECORDED AT WHITEHOUSE STUDIO

NO PLACE FOR YOU
U.K. SOLDIER
Side two

YOUNG OFFENDER
Side one

GIBBON - Guitar
KEV - Drums
TIM - Bass
DISRUPTERS ARE :- STEVE - Vocals

THANKS TO:- CRASS, ANDY CHAPMAN,
JULIE, JANE, JOANNE, COCKNEY,
BILL (FOR THE BASS), SCRUFF THE
BUDGIE, TIM AND BEVERLEY, &
PAULEEN (FOR REHEARSALS)

A BIG FUCK OFF TO:-
OI! AND G. BULLSHIT.

linked to Orwell's book but equally significant within the punk scene for its reference to the lyrics of The Clash's '1977' and its use as a metaphor for a sense of foreboding doom ('no future' indeed). Combined with other familiar hardcore and anarcho-punk tropes – riots, inner city decay, the Cold War, nuclear destruction, war, police oppression – the casual political doctrine of 'anarchy and peace' formed a central theme in the lexicon of early 1980s punk output and discourse. Obviously, such clichés were open to critique and ridicule from those inside and outside of the subculture, in the same way that earlier generations had been satirised for their overuse of certain words and symbols. Comic hardcore punk satirists Chaotic Dischord's perhaps best-known song, 'Anarchy in Woolworths,' released in 1984, turns the cliché of punk anarchy into simplistic, stupid, and very funny comedy; 'Went into Woolworths to buy some dye / A bloke came up and punched me in the eye / What did he do? He punched me in the eye / How many times? Two-three-four.' Of course, the joke wouldn't work if the symbiotic relationship between punk and the politics of anarchism hadn't by then become so well-known and stereotypical to the point of saturation.

Cross disbanded in 1984 as planned (a few minor offshoot experiments notwithstanding), and the impetus for the anarcho-punk scene seemed to dissipate with them. Obviously, some groups continued the campaign and the notion of punk 'anarchism' wasn't lost on subsequent generations of hardcore and punk followers, but the clearly-announced political 'badge' indicated by the anarcho prefix was softened, or forgotten, depending on the reader's critical position and association. Meanwhile, the *rhetorical* form of punk anarchism, that notion of free-spirited individualism and youthful rejection of authority, continued unabated, only marginally losing impact as the 'punk generation' began to age, becoming more concerned with jobs, families, and everyday life than with the difficult task of maintaining ideological credibility under the critical gaze of their peers. In many ways, the anarchist punk 'experiment' had come full circle – earlier, less fixed or politically engaged notions of punk 'anarchy' continued unabated, while the more considered, or serious, anarcho-punk movement came and went. The circled 'A' stereotype prevails, on t-shirts, badges, jackets and record sleeves, but ultimately its 'meaning' has been reduced once again to a stereotypical symbol of rebellion, no more dangerous or ideologically considered than the skull and crossbones, clenched fist, studded jacket, or mohican hairstyle.

ANA RAPOSO

# RIVAL TRIBAL REBEL REVEL[1]

## THE ANARCHO PUNK MOVEMENT AND SUBCULTURAL INTERNECINE RIVALRIES

**AS A RATIONALE** for starting Crass, Penny Rimbaud claims that when 'the Pistols released "Anarchy in the UK", maybe they didn't really mean it ma'am, but to us it was a battle cry.'[2] Implicitly this classifies The Sex Pistols as poseurs – a horrific crime in subcultures – and Crass as the real punks. When a member of one punk faction

---

1    This chapter is part of a doctoral research which concluded in 2012. As such I would like to thank my supervisory team at the University of Arts London: Roger Sabin, Russell Bestley and Andrew McGettigan for their constant support, encouragement and endless enthusiasm throughout the research. I am in particular debt to Russell Bestley for all the support and help in this chapter. I would also like to thank Matthew Worley for the valuable feedback.

2    Penny Rimbaud, "The Last of the Hippies: A Hysterical Romance", in *A Series of Shock Slogans and Mindless Token Tantrums*, ed. Crass (London: Exitstencil Press, 1982), 12.

criticises other elements within the same subculture – for selling out, promoting violence, or defending different political views – they demarcate themselves as the authentic punks. Other punk movements retaliated against the anarcho-punks' righteous attitude. The discourse of authenticity is rife in these relationships.[3]

A contemporaneous punk offshoot – street punk or Oi! – was singled out for particular criticism by participants within the anarcho-punk movement. While both scenes arose through the sense of disappointment which was felt by participants that the radical vows of early punks had been left unfulfilled, the relationship between them was often convoluted. Although some bands, particularly Oi Polloi, called for unity between factions, the discourse was often one of division. An additional punk offshoot both targeted by and targeting the anarcho-punk movement was the hardcore scene. While crossovers occur, such as the controversial Admit You're Shit; other bands, such as The Exploited and Discharge, who also integrated anarchist rhetoric in their lyrics, overtly engaged in a dispute over authenticity and what they saw as a more 'real' interpretation of a true punk ideology.

This analysis is made with an emphasis on the ways in which the music graphics produced by the bands reflected this discourse of authenticity. Visual media offer a way of expressing a strong, direct, intelligible message, and it is no surprise that bands use music packaging as a medium for contention. In this context, graphics have the function of exposing poseurs and iconic visual allegories become a representation of authenticity.

## PUNK IS DEAD

One of the first attempts to ally punk and organised politics was Rock Against Racism (RAR). The foundation of the movement was

---

3   According to Hugh Barker and Yuval Taylor "Punk, in its confused regard for authenticity and its rejections of fakery, created a series of traps. For all its confusion it was an exciting, revitalising music. But it was also a simulation that came to be seen as authentic, a failure cult that wanted to reinvent music, and a progressive genre in which incompetence and emotional immaturity were badges of honour." (Barker and Taylor, 2007: 291). This left a space for diverse interpretations of authenticity. After punk's official 'death', a number of punk offshoots claimed different interpretations of punk as authentic. For more on authenticity see Barker and Taylor (2007) and Thornton (1995).

triggered in part by Eric Clapton's support for Enoch Powell's *Rivers of Blood* speech in the summer of 1976 and what was seen as a growing empathy between major rock acts and right wing political agendas. RAR was explicitly socialist and the organisers "were all veterans of the 1960s libertarian politics and agit-prop work (now ensconced in the Socialist Workers Party)."[4] According to Dave Laing, "if punk rock's concerns with political and social topics took its cue from general ideological trends, its achievement was nevertheless to introduce such themes into songs, something which the mainstream of popular music had successfully resisted for a decade."[5] RAR acknowledged this aptitude and formed an alliance with punk.

But if RAR's organisation was clear about their political standing, the audience lacked the same involvement; "...to the untrained eye there was little difference between the racist and the anti-racist punk, especially given the familiar sight of youths with an RAR button on one lapel, an NF button on the other."[6] The commitment of some of the participating musicians was also mixed, as can be observed in the response of Knox from the Vibrators to a zine writer: "Q: 'Why did you do the RAR gig? Because you believed in it?' Knox: 'No, actually what most people don't realise is that bands do get paid for it. We just did it because it was a gig to do...'"[7] The inter-relationship between politics and punk in RAR was never fully achieved, as according to David Widgery "the Left thought us too punky and the punks feared they would be eaten alive by communist cannibals."[8] According to Crass "We even played a Rock Against Racism gig, the only gig that we'd ever been paid for. When we told the man to keep the money for the cause, he informed us that 'this was the cause'. We never played for RAR again."[9]

---

4    Simon Frith and John Street, "Rock Against Racism and Red Wedge: From Music to Politics, From Politics to Music", in *Rockin' the Boat: Mass Music and Mass Movements*, ed. Reebee Garofalo (Boston: South End Press, 1992), 68.

5    Dave Laing, *One Chord Wonders: Power and Meaning in Punk Rock* (Milton Keynes: Open University Press, 1985), 31.

6    Frith and Street, op. cit, 70.

7    Roger Sabin, *Punk Rock, So What?: The Cultural Legacy of Punk* (London: Routledge, 1999), 6.

8    David Widgery, *Beating Time* (London: Chatto & Windus, 1986), 59.

9    Crass, *Best before* (Crass Records, 1986).

Rock Against Racism 'used' punk, but was not an outlet arising from punk. RAR acted as a recruiting and propaganda tool for the parties who were involved and its politics were imposed on musicians and subcultures. According to Ian Goodyer:

> If cultural exclusivity within RAR draws the fire of some critics, then the organisation's determination to tap the energy of punk rock draws fire from another direction. Some commentators contend that RAR's intervention in punk represented a conservative influence. Which inhibited punks from freely exploring the radical potential inherent in their repertoire of shocking and spectacular modes of behaviour and display.[10]

By 1978 a group who was disillusioned with the commodification of punk and alienated by political organisations which were scavenging on its body, set out to spawn the anarcho-punk movement. To do so Crass 'officially' announced the death of punk in their first release, *The Feeding of the Five Thousand*, through the track 'Punk is Dead':[11]

> Punk is dead
> Yes that's right, punk is dead
> It's just another cheap product for the consumers head
> Bubblegum rock on plastic transistors
> Schoolboy sedition backed by big time promoters
> CBS promote The Clash
> Ain't for revolution, it's just for cash[12]

---

10 Ian Goodyer, *Crisis Music: The Cultural Politics of Rock Against Racism* (Manchester: Manchester University Press, 2009), 4.

11 Although Crass were the first to publish the announcement in an 'official' punk medium, the feeling that punk's spirit had died had been present within a year of its emergence. By the time the first punk record was released by a major label, critiques of the commodification of the 'rebellious' subculture had already arisen.

12 Crass, *The Feeding of the Five Thousand* (Small Wonder Records, 1978).

In 1979, the track 'White Punks on Hope', from the album *Stations of the Crass*, took the argument one step further, stating "They said that we were trash, well the name is Crass, not Clash."[13]

The date of the 'death of punk' is a disputed issue, ranging from early 1978 to 1979 (symbolically marked by the death of Sid Vicious). The reason for punk's official demise is not in dispute: its incorporation into the mainstream. It had been 'made safe' and a generation that had adopted the revolutionary proto-political concept of punk felt betrayed. By announcing the death of punk, Crass declared themselves as the authentic punks following the original proto-politics proclaimed by punk's early pioneers. Anarcho-punk aimed to free punk – and punks – from corporate industries and organised politics. Placing a strong emphasis on individuality and DIY (do-it-yourself) politics, it produced a current that diverged from what punk was becoming. Because if punk died in the late 1970s, it was reborn, as a more self-conscious movement where political stances were more overtly exposed.[14]

In 1980, one of the most blunt critiques was made through the visuals of the split single 'Bloody Revolutions' by Crass and Poison Girls. The suggestion of betrayal and the notion that the 'Pistols didn't really mean it' was achieved through an iconic image of The Sex Pistols (taken for the promotion of the single 'God Save the Queen'), where the faces of these punk forerunners are morphed to those of Queen Elizabeth II, the Pope John Paul II, Lady Justice and Margaret Thatcher; standing for the entire establishment: the monarchy, church, law and state. The single presented a polemic against both the music industry and punk subculture. According to Penny Rimbaud not only was it banned by HMV due to the "inflammatory nature of the cover",[15] but "more disturbing by far was a phone call we received from a

---

13 Crass, *Stations of the Crass* (Crass Records, 1979).

14 For more on punk's death and rebirth see Sabin (1999) and Clark (2003).

15 J.J. Ratter, *Shibboleth: My Revolting Life* (Edinburgh: AK Press, 1998), 123. This point is rather contentious – HMV did indeed operate a banned list, which included most record releases on the Crass label among others, but the rationale for selection was often more arbitrary and not record-specific, other than through association with similarly 'offensive' material by the same group or label. The fact that *The Feeding of the Five Thousand* had caused such controversy within the record industry, and subsequently Crass had released the offending

very angry and rather drunk Glaswegian punk. 'You fucking bastards,' he slurred, 'how dare you defile The Sex Pistols like that. Don't you know they're fucking sacred?'"[16] Arguably, the 'inflammatory nature' of the cover was different for the subculture and the record retailer. It is clear that for some members of the former, it is the desecration of high-ranking figures – The Sex Pistols, however for HMV, the reason for the ban is not clear and is arguably the debasement of figures of power. Notwithstanding the ban was possibly not directed towards *Bloody Revolutions* itself but was rather due to a reluctance of HMV to stock potentially polemic records that was later officialised when "HMV had compiled an Obscene Products list, which was dated 16 February 1987 and included all records on the Crass label, all Dead Kennedys records, Conflict's *Increase the Pressure*, Microdisney's *We Hate You White South African Bastards*, Ian Dury's 'Four Thousand Week Holiday' and various punk and satanic metal records."[17]

Crass were not the only ones to criticise the rotten apple in the barrel of punk subculture. The centre label of the EP *Capitalism is Cannibalism* by Anthrax, features a punk as a puppeteer manipulating a punk. The label presents a critique of 'unauthentic' punk exploiters and punks blindingly following 'instructions' from other punks as put by Anthrax "Exploiting the exploited in their sly clever way, cheating on their own crowds because its them that have to pay, and the people that are conning us, used to be part of us, and with their money-making solution they think they've got it sussed!"[18] The illustration was upgraded from the centre label to the front sleeve of their next release the seven-inch EP *They've Got It All Wrong* released on Small Wonder Records the following year.

The exposure of punks following the puppeteers is also present in the lyrics of the track 'Take Heed', on the album *Strive to Survive Causing Least Suffering Possible* by Flux of Pink Indians from 1982. The lyrics read:

---

track, *Reality Asylum*, as a single on their own label, meant that it was highly likely that *all* subsequent releases by the group would be banned by the store, irrespective of their specific content.

16   Ratter, *Shibboleth*, 123.

17   Martin Cloonan, *Banned!: Censorship of Popular Music in Britain, 1967-92* (Aldershot: Arena, 1996), 69.

18   Anthrax, *They've Got It All Wrong*, Small Wonder Records, 1983.

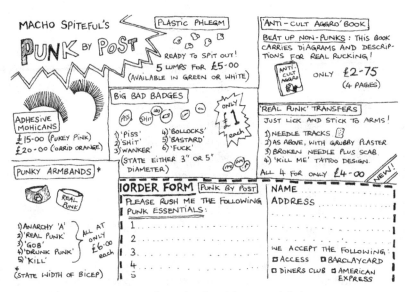

The gutter press said punks should spit and fight
And the puppet punks were fooled alright
They began to sniff aerosol and tubes of glue
Because the paper said that's what real punks do[19]

The twelve page booklet inserted in the gatefold sleeve of the album addresses a myriad of orthodox anarcho-punk issues from fake punks to animal testing, nuclear weapons, war and religion. One section contains a mock advertisement, "Macho Spiteful's Punk by Post", of a mail order service for punk 'essential' accessories, from coloured adhesive mohicans, to plastic phlegm – "Ready to spit out!", to transfers of needle tracks to stick on the arms, to the essential 'Anti-cult Aggro' book – *Beat Up Non-Punks*: This book carries diagrams and descriptions for real rucking!"[20] The critique targeted the flamboyant fashion of punk and ready-made punks, drug abuse and the violence in the subculture.

## SKIN DISEASE

Amidst the turmoil within punk in the late 1970s, a new offshoot of punk emerged – Oi!, or street punk, was a punk variation trying to reconnect to working class culture. Presenting faster and more

---

19   Flux of Pink Indians, *Strive to Survive Causing Least Suffering Possible* (Spiderleg Records, 1982).

20   Flux of Pink Indians, *Strive to Survive*.

aggressive sounds, it reflected its roots in pub rock, reviving the sing-a-long with songs about drinking, football, aggro, sex and class. Oi!, which was at its core apolitical, united punks and skinheads. The term was coined in 1980 by Garry Bushell, a writer for the music paper *Sounds*, who was the main promoter of the genre.

In a similar fashion to the anarcho-punk movement, Oi! emerged out of disappointment with what punk was becoming – if at its emergence punk had claimed to be the angry voice of kids of the streets it was being taken over (arguably from the very start) by middle-class art school people. Oi! claimed to be the 'real punk', reviving the working class background of the original subculture (although not all of its participants were indeed working class). Even though both Oi! and the anarcho-punk movement emerged with similar purposes – reviving the authentic punk promise – their relationship was far from cordial.

Crass released a track criticising the violent faction of the subculture, on the flexi disc 'Rival Tribal Rebel Revel', inserted in the *Toxic Grafity* zine in 1980. Although it was a reaction to a spike in violence, such as when punks were assaulted by bikers at the Stonehenge festival or by British Movement skinheads at Conway Hall, the use of cockney on both the track and the graphics accompanying the limited edition on hard vinyl, focuses its target as a critique of all violence through reference to an Oi! stereotype.

In 1982 they released the track 'The Greatest Working Class Rip-Off'[21] on *Christ: The Album* where the accusation of violence is made clear: "Punk's got nothing to do with what you're trying to create/ Anarchy, violence, chaos?/ You mindless fucking jerks".[22]

Despite the contemporary political debate surrounding Oi! or the genre's aptitude for violence,[23] the core of the critique was not targeted

---

21 The tile is a clear reference to the single *The Greatest Cockney Rip Off* released in 1980 by the Cockney Rejects – one of the major Oi! bands.

22 Crass, *Christ: The Album* (Crass Records, 1982).

23 According to Matthew Worley "A masculinity based on strength and pride could all too easily give way to 'bullying and bigotry', as in the lumpen 'yob' of media caricature. Political disillusionment too could bleed into extremist views that rejected conventional politics, or to an impulsive nihilism that found solace in violence, the glue bag or drugs such as tuinal. Indeed, the tendency for some young skinheads in the late 1970s to align themselves with the politics and signifiers of the far right seemingly fused both possibilities." (Worley 2014: 9). For

at these but mainly at what was seen as a subversion of punk precepts. According to Rimbaud:

> To say that punk is, or should be, 'working class' is to falsely remove it from the classless roots of 'real rock revolution' from which it grew. (…) Oi! and, more recently, Skunk, have been promoted in the pages of *Sounds* as the 'real punk', real sucker maybe, but not real punks. Whereas punk aims to destroy class barriers, Oi! and Skunks are blind enough to be conned into reinforcing them.[24]

The blame was attributed to Bushell as despite acknowledging that some of the bands could have good intentions Rimbaud states that "by accepting the label of Oi! they must also accept responsibility for what Oi! is – one man's dangerous, ill-considered power game that backfired on them all."[25]

From the other end Bushell accused Crass of a hippie, middle class and disengaged from 'reality' attitude. When comparing Crass and Conflict Bushell stated that:

> Whereas Crass seem trapped by their (ho ho) 'classless' communal lifestyle, Sixties hippy drop out / cop out ineffectualism dressed in nihilistic puritan black rather than narcissistic promiscuous technicolour, Conflict have the potential to mean much more because they follow the Pistols ultimatum of being the poison *in* the machine, keeping their dissent on the streets, arguing with people instead of bellowing at them from any safe Epping Forest bunker.[26]

Bushell's band, The Gonads, released the *Peace Artists* EP in 1982, mocking pacifist anarcho-punks, and particularly Crass, using the Campaign for Nuclear Disarmament (CND) symbol created on the

---

more on Oi! and politics see Raposo (2012) and Worley (2014).

24  Rimbaud, "The Last of the Hippies", 5.

25  Rimbaud, "The Last of the Hippies", 5.

26  George Berger, *The Story of Crass*, (London: Omnibus Press, 2008), 168.

sleeve by having a drunken skinhead smashing into a lamp post.[27]

Chumbawamba successfully engaged in the task of mocking Oi! from within. Under the alias of Skin Disease they released the track 'I'm Thick' in Garry Bushell's compilation EP *Back On the Streets* in 1982. When called to record after sending Bushell a proposal posing as an Oi! band from Burnley, Chumbawamba recalled the story "And there we were thinking, 'What's the most we can get away with here? How about shouting 'I'm thick!' sixty-four times?' It was really funny because the producer couldn't quite tell whether we were serious or not..."[28] Nick Toczek also had a track released on one Oi! compilation on which he comments "I also had a track on one of the Oi! albums, *The Oi! of Sex*, on which I was the token anarchist among predominantly far-right-leaning skinhead bands. That was cool though; at least I wasn't preaching to the converted on that track."[29] Despite being willing to engage with Oi!, it is noteworthy to reveal the misinformation regarding the Oi! scene. Although, atypically, *The Oi of Sex* was indeed the only one of the six Oi! albums compiled by Garry Bushell to include a far-right leaning band (A.B.H.), it was countered by the inclusion of Burial (with connections to Red Action) and avowedly socialist ranters Swift Nick and Little Dave. Additionally, one of the points of the manifesto included on the record states "Oi! is... proud to be British, but not xenophobic"[30] distancing Oi! from far-right politics.[31]

One of the few bands to actively pursue uniting punks and skinheads under the umbrella of anarchist politics was Oi Polloi. In an interview given to *Axe of Freedom* zine, Deek Allen assesses the split between the two movements.

27  From its initial gigs, Crass placed the CND movement at the centre of a new punk subcultural capital. If the symbol had been omnipresent in the hippie subculture, although often disjointed from its origin, Crass imported it to punk with remarkable success. The symbol can be observed on a myriad of sleeves of the anarcho-punk movement, from bands which integrate the symbol as the main component of their logo to its placement in various spaces of the inserts.

28  Ian Glasper, *The Day the Country Died: A History of Anarcho Punk 1980 to 1984* (London: Cherry Red Books, 2006), 379.

29  Glasper, *The Day the Country Died*, 397.

30  *The Oi! of Sex* (Syndicate, 1984).

31  For more on the Oi! compilations check Worley (2014).

*Don't you think the 'Oi!' label has split the punk move-
ment in half (the old ploy of divide and conquer) and it
never really came from the street but from a shitty journal-
ists [sic] (Bushell) weak minded attempt to make money?"*

**DEEK:** 'Oi!' could have been a great forum for unity
bringing skins and punks together, but it was twist-
ed by Bushell who used it as a vehicle for personal gain and influenced it to such a degree that on
the whole it became "anti-Crass-bands" (whatever
a "Crass-band" is supposed to be) and when Crass
in turn responded then the split was complete. I
wouldn't overestimate the damage done though and
I certainly wouldn't say it split the punk movement
in half, since 'Oi!' became mainly for skins and so it
was mainly them who became distanced from anarcho-punk, it didn't so much split the punks. Its pretty much over now though I'd say, and the only big
'Oi!' bands left I'd say are The Oppressed (a good
anti-racist, anti-fascist band) and Nabat from Italy
who are really into unity between punks 'n' skins
and even admit to liking Crass.[32]

Oi Polloi dedicated two albums to unity amongst the factions. The
first was *Unite and Win!* released on anti-fascist Roddy Moreno's label
Oi! Records in 1987. And the second was the seven-inch EP *Punks
'n' Skins*, released on Fight 45 Records in 1996, re-issuing a track first
included on *Unite and Win!*. Additionally, one of the main Oi! bands,
The Business, did a cover of 'Do They Owe Us a Living' from Crass.
But the willingness to make punk offshoots to 'unite and win' was
frequently scarce.

## AND I DON'T CARE WHAT YOU
## SAY 'CAUSE I BELIEVE IN ANARCHY

An additional punk offshoot both targeted by and targeting the anarcho-punk movement was the hardcore scene. While crossovers occur,
such as the controversial Admit You're Shit whose records were released

---

32   Craig, "Interview with Oi Polloi", *Axe of Freedom*, Issue 3, 1985, 6.

by Mortarhate:[33] other bands, such as The Exploited and Discharge, who also integrated anarchist rhetoric in their lyrics, overtly engaged in a dispute over authenticity in their outputs.

The Exploited released their debut album *Punk's Not Dead*, in 1981, as a direct response to the track 'Punk is Dead'. Crass engaged in a quarrel with the Exploited: in 1981, the EP *Merry Crassmas*, released by a reverse acronym of C.R.A.S.S., Creative Recording and Sound Services, announced a competition with the following prizes: First prize – Bath salts; Second prize – One Exploited single; Third prize – Two Exploited singles. The proclamation of anarchy of the Exploited was seen as void by those who were involved in the anarcho-punk movement. According to Deek Allan from Oi Polloi "Yeah, to those of us for whom punk means a little bit more than having a mohican on your head, getting pissed and causing chaos, The Exploited really epitomise a kind of sad cartoon of punk, devoid of any real politics or positivity."[34]

Discharge occupy an atypical place in the anarcho-punk milieu. Some academics consider Discharge as part of the anarcho-punk movement, due to sharing a similar ideological targets despite different musical approaches, as according to Michael Dines "If Crass had appropriated the form and musical style of first wave punk, so

---

33 Admit You're Shit's vocalist, John 'Weeny' Cato, had racist beliefs and was a member of the British Movement. Admit You're Shit, or AYS, brought out their first record through Mortarhate Records in 1985, the seven-inch EP *Expect No Mercy If You Cross Your Real Friends*. In true anarcho-punk fashion, the record relied heavily on an informational insert. The back of the sleeve stated that "within this EP there will be at least one insert. If you do not get one, write us and you will receive one. Note: This E.P. is fukkin worthless without it. [sic]" However, the EP forged links not only with the anarcho-punk movement but also displayed iconic references to the neo-fascist movement. The back sleeve displays the slogan 'Integrity and Intelligence' in which the capital 'I's are used to form a Celtic cross. Additionally, two dragons, frequently used to represent England, surround the track list revealing a nationalist posture uncharacteristic of the anarcho-punk movement. Atypically, the sleeve also references the American hardcore movement, from the symbol for UK Hardcore (UKHC) to thanks to Ian MacKaye of Minor Threat amongst others.

34 Ian Glasper, *Burning Britain: The History of UK Punk 1980-1984* (London: Cherry Red Books, 2004), 360.

as to convey a more intellectualised form of dissent, then Discharge used the punk aesthetic to retreat into writing music that involved a new level of musical simplicity and 'in your face' forthrightness."[35] However they moved in a different milieu than most in the anar-cho-punk movement. George Berger suggests the reason as "any suggestions of a genuine alliance [with Crass], however was shattered when members of Discharge ridiculed Crass in interviews ('I'm going to boot the bald bastard up the arse')."[36] With Crass being the unwilling 'leaders' of the anarcho-punk movements this segregated Discharge from its core.[37]

Oi Polloi criticised the ascent of Discharge-like bands in the booklet that accompanied the seven-inch EP *Let the Boots Do the Talking* from 1999. The booklet presented the 'Free patent Oi Polloi Dis-band "song" generator ™' fully explaining a tool to help lyrical creation. (See next pages.)

## PROPA-GIT

The anarcho-punk subculture was not exempt from critiques from within, particularly from the 'hideous crime' of selling out. Chumbawamba made their debut on the Crass Records compilation *Bullshit Detector 2* in 1982. Following the authentic anarcho-punk ethos they created their own label Agit-Prop in 1985. The label's first release, *Revolution*, presented a call for action on the front sleeve: "If our music makes you happy, but content, it has failed. If our music entertains, but doesn't inspire, it has failed. The music's not a threat: Action that music inspires can be a threat." The eight-page booklet that housed the seven-inch single contained several attacks on the music industry, such as: "HMV, in their moral righteousness, refuse to sell records which contain four-letter words as they're regarded as obscene and in bad taste. Yet, Thorn-EMI, their parent company, manufactures and export weapons of war and instruments of torture world wide. Does that cause a public outcry? Does it fuck." or "Stop

---

35  Michael Dines, "An Investigation Into the Emergence of the Anarcho–Punk Scene of the 1980s" (PhD diss., University of Salford, 2004), 98.

36  Berger, *The Story of Crass*, 172.

37  Although none of the punk offshoot covered on this essay were closed in its essence with a centralised organisation but composed of several bands with different affiliations, the gig tours and labels defined to some extent a common milieu.

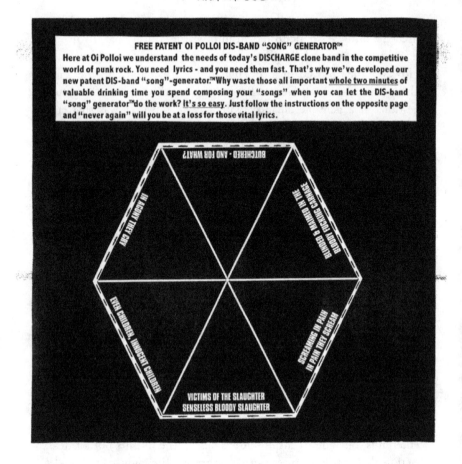

**FREE PATENT OI POLLOI DIS-BAND "SONG" GENERATOR™**

Here at Oi Polloi we understand the needs of today's DISCHARGE clone band in the competitive world of punk rock. You need lyrics - and you need them fast. That's why we've developed our new patent DIS-band "song"-generator.™Why waste those all important <u>whole two minutes</u> of valuable drinking time you spend composing your "songs" when you can let the DIS-band "song" generator™do the work? <u>It's so easy</u>. Just follow the instructions on the opposite page and "never again" will you be at a loss for those vital lyrics.

taking orders from His Master's Voice!" A further attack on the music industry was made in 1989, with their participation in the *Fuck EMI* compilation released on Rugger Bugger Records. However, despite their previous attacks on the music industry and particularly EMI, in 1994 they would sign to this label who were particularly loathed within the anarcho-punk movement. They were excommunicated by many within the anarcho-punk movement.

A derogatory statement towards the band was made on a compilation EP released on Ruptured Ambitions Records, with the participation of Riot/Clone, Anxiety Society, Oi Polloi and the Bus Station Loonies. *The Anti-Chumbawamba EP – Bare Faced Hypocrisy Sells Records*, with the ironic catalogue number Propa Git 5, mocked Chumbawamba's album

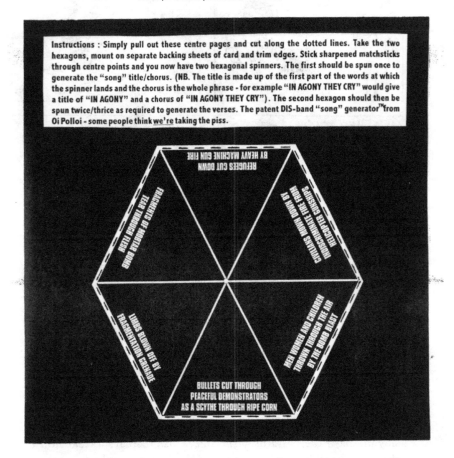

Instructions : Simply pull out these centre pages and cut along the dotted lines. Take the two hexagons, mount on separate backing sheets of card and trim edges. Stick sharpened matchsticks through centre points and you now have two hexagonal spinners. The first should be spun once to generate the "song" title/chorus. (NB. The title is made up of the first part of the words at which the spinner lands and the chorus is the whole phrase - for example "IN AGONY THEY CRY" would give a title of "IN AGONY" and a chorus of "IN AGONY THEY CRY"). The second hexagon should then be spun twice/thrice as required to generate the verses. The patent DIS-band "song" generator from Oi Polloi - some people think we're taking the piss.

*Pictures of Starving Children Sell Records;*[38] the graphics presented an act of *détournement* of Chumbawamba's album *Never Mind the Ballots... Here's the Rest of Your Life*, itself adapted from a 1968 Atelier Populaire poster – *Le Vote Ne Change Rien, La Lutte Continue.*[39] The insert and back sleeve present numerous attacks on the band 'selling out'.

---

38   *Pictures of Starving Children Sell Records* was a direct attack on the Live Aid events. It portrayed the events as a superficial and unauthentic approach to famine and third world exploitation and as a way to soothe consciences rather than addressing the roots of the problem.

39   By using references to previous countercultural movements, an attempt was made to establish its position within this lineage of protest and dissent, drawing legitimacy and authenticity from the radical family tree.

Although The Apostles's milieu was the anarcho-punk movement, they consistently derided the punk scene (and often anarcho-punk). Their first EP, *Blow It Up, Burn It Down, Kick It Till
It Breaks*, released on their own label Scum Records in 1982 presented an attack on the pacifist approach taken by Crass. While
using the black and white fold-out sleeve, by then iconic of the
anarcho-punk movement, the cover displayed a militaristic insignia of an eagle carrying a sword and a rifle with the title of the
EP *Blow It Up, Burn It Down, Kick It Till It Breaks* written on
a banner surrounding it. The back cover bluntly brandished the
slogan "Bash the bastards". The sleeve also displays a clear nod to
the Ramones logo. On the centre of the insignia in the front sleeve
the date 1985 is displayed so as to dismiss the Orwellian prophet-
ic countdown of Crass Records arguing there will be a future of
struggle post-1984. On the sleeve of their second EP, released the
following year, they state:

> For everyone who's asked "What the fuck does
> '1985' stand for?" – Right! 1985 is our way of giving
> a big V-sign to all the pessimistic George Orwell tot-
> ing 1984 crap-rap and doomsday-drivel brigade. For
> us, survival beyond 1984 is a foregone conclusion and
> The Apostles will still be together, and going strong, in
> that year and in years to come. It is also a snipe at the
> copyright laws since all bands copyright their material

either present or past. 1985 is a state identification, a symbol of hope and determination to survive as well as being a way to recognise anything to do with The Apostles.[40]

While clearly establishing a visual link to the anarcho-punk movement – the first five EPs took the form of a black and white fold-out sleeve with a strong presence of a circle on the front sleeve – The Apostles' stance was clearly opposed to the contemporary pacifist approach. A cartoon in the interior of their first EP reveals the contrasting destinies of pacifist and non-pacifist sheep. However the most controversial release by the group mixed anti-fascist songs and neo-fascist songs, including 'Kill or Cure', directly addressed at homosexuality (though the band included homosexuals in its line-up), and 'Rock Against Communism' apparently offering support to that far-right organisation. The sleeve integrated the *RAC News* symbol].[41] The same year the symbol was used by Skrewdriver for the sleeve of the single *Invasion*. Despite being undoubtedly a satirical statement with the intent of jostling the anarcho-punk audiences, the irony was not perceived as such by all including even some members of the band. Their fifth EP – *Smash the Spectacle*, released on Mortarhate Records, in 1985 – included a note regarding disagreements amongst band members as a result of the previous release. The sleeve of *Smash the Spectacle* urged for armed class war, referencing renowned socialist symbols – particularly one inspired in the hammer and sickle, a wrench, representing the working class, crossed with an AK-47 assault rifle.

All the artwork of The Apostles' releases was created collectively by members of the band. The fact that the printed products produced were central to its members is revealed in a statement in the album *The Lives and Times of the Apostles* (released in 1986 in Children of the Revolution Records). It is a call for action – "Punk groups everywhere: expand your work to art and literature now – you can't play records when they cut off all the power!" However

---

40   The Apostles, *Rising From the Ashes* (Scum Records, 1983).

41   RAC News was a section of Bulldog: Paper of the Young National Front launched in 1979 to promote the new Rock Against Communism movement and chronicle the scene's evolution.

despite the call for punks the front sleeve of the same album featured the plans of action of two punks criticising the drug use and even the intelligence of punks:

Panel 1: Punk 1 – ...well, okay we're both agreed then: the world is gradually being ruined by humanity, or at least parts of it. so let's wage a peaceful protest and lay in front of a few police cars, nuclear trains and that... you can sing the songs and I'll make the fires, yeah? Seriously, we ought to do something about the state of things instead of simply moaning and complaining all the time... you reckon?

Panel 3: Punk 2 – Yes but dat's no good cuz dey'd get de army an' beat seven shades o'shit outa the lot of us. Aw dat peace flowers love an Joni Mitchell means getting' covered in mud an' walkin' home wit tractor tyre marks over our arses, doan it?

Panel 4: Punk 1 – You could be right, I suppose. Well, we'll make a few petrol bombs and carry out night raids, design home made guns and teach those bastards in authority a lesson! We could pick on targets outside our town so nobody suspects we are behind it, and concentrate on hit and run tactics, dressing really straight so we don't invite suspicion. What about hitting all those army recruitment offices in the town and the abattoir in the village...

Panel 6: Punk 2 – Yes but we'd jus get nicked wootn't we? Dat's no good. I'd miss World Of Sport, The Sweeney, Minder an' James Burkes' commentary on sections of de M4 mot away... an' I don't fink all dat frow in' bomz an' brix does any good. Ow'd we make bomz? We'd avta visit dat anarchist geezer on the east side a' town an' ee jus goes on an' on about prolitaryan autowhat sit an' we only wanna borrah some boox on makin' letter bomz outa fag lighters.

Panel 7: Punk 1 – Well, we've gotta do something. Ah! Got it: propaganda. We'll put out a large magazine giving addresses of vivisection laboratories, army training centres, fur warehouses, trade union official and information on squatting, rioting, survival, how to understand The Apostles music...

Panel 9: Punk 2 – Yes but we'd need money to print it anyway, I can't draw an' I can't write anyfing, y' know, good, an 'oo reads 'zines deez days? Fuckin' no-one mate. It's no werf de effort if you ask me.

Panel 10: Punk 1 – Well what... I mean, you... I... (sigh) oh for Crass sake, we could... I mean we could at least live our lives fully, setting an example by being truthful, honest, caring, sharing and spreading trust and respect.

Panel 12: Punk 2 – Yes but I wanna enjoy meself, doan I? 'oo cares what uvver people fink? I wanna get pissed so I doan affta fink abaht nuffin at all an', y' know, get out avit an' dat... (burp) anyway me giro arrives on fursday, doan it?

Panel 13: Punk 1 – Really? Tell me, what's it like being out of what is left of your brain for 99% of the time?

Panel 15: Punk 2 – ...well... it's orlright, innit? (Buurrrpp!) 'cept for 'angovers an' 'oles in me gluebags...

Panel 16: Punk 1 – Look, as you evidently hate life so much why don't you kill yourself now and get it over with? Punk 2: (cough, burp, wheeze.) ...what, an waste the uvver two pots of Evo I got left?

Arguably the sleeve could be addressed to the general punk subculture. However, the targets and modus operandi of Punk 1 are idiosyncratic of the anarcho-punk movement.

## BULLSHIT CRASS

The anarcho-punk movement was itself also subjected to direct critique. Special Duties released the single 'Bullshit Crass' in 1982, accusing the band of being too elitist. The Crass-like sleeve, using the iconic white stencil lettering ring, contained the single whose lyrics tweaked some of Crass's slogans:

Fight Crass Not Punk
Anarchy and peace promote the Crass

It ain't for freedom it's just for cash
They don't mean what they say
What they preach there is no way
Bullshit Crass you've been detected
Duties have your shit rejected
Bullshit Crass you've been detected
We'll free the punks that you've injected
Bullshit Crass you've been detected
Crass were first to say punk is dead
Now they're rightly labelled as red
Commune hippies that's what they are
They've got no money Ha! Ha! Ha![42]

According to the vocalist Steve 'Arrogant' Green,[43] "It was the fact that they said that 'Punk was dead', and they played this really tuneless music. Also, none of the punk bands I was into ever preached at their audience. I mean, The Clash were political, and had some very intelligent lyrics about the state of society, but they never really preached. Crass were just so extreme, I saw them almost as a religious cult."[44] Regarding the Crass-like sleeve he also mentions that "it sold quite well, but that may have been because it looked a bit like a Crass record and their fans were so stupid they thought it was one."[45]

The critique didn't stop in the subculture. As the title of the twenty-eight page booklet inserted in the boxset *Christ: The Album*, released in 1982, Crass quoted a highly unflattering article by Steve Sutherland from the *Melody Maker:*

> Crass by name, even worse by nature, like it or not, they just won't go away. Crass are the distempered dog end of rock 'n roll's once bright and vibrant rebellion. That they're so unattractive, unoriginal and badly unbalanced in an uncompromising and humourless sort of way, simply adds to the diseased attraction of their naively black and white world where words are *a series*

---

42   Special Duties, *Bullshit Crass* (Rondelet Music & Records, 1982).

43   A clear play with Crass's vocalist pseudonym Steve Ignorant.

44   Glasper, *Burning Britain*, 226.

45   Glasper, *Burning Britain*, 226.

*of shock slogans and mindless token tantrums* to tout around your tribe and toss at passers by.

Good old Crass, our make believe secret society, our let's pretend passport to perversity. They're nothing but a caricature and a joke.[46]

Furthermore it didn't stop in the 1980s. In the few appearances in contemporary publications regarding punk and post-punk the position of the authors is often derogatory and one of dismissal. Clinton Heylin's *Babylon's Burning: From Punk To Grunge* expresses derision towards the anarcho-punk movement, which according to the author accounts for its absence from the book. While discussing the Gang of Four and the emergence of new 'regional' punk bands he argues that:

> These bands were filling a vacuum created by *reac-*
> *tionary racketeers* like Crass, UK Subs, Sham 69 and
> Skrewdriver, then *inflicting themselves on London audi-*
> *ences in the name of 'punk'*. Perhaps the future direction
> of rock's new wave could yet be wrestled from these
> self-righteous oiks. [emphasis mine][47]

Despite the more politically correct approach of Simon Reynolds in *Rip It Up and Start Again* the argument is similar, although in this instance he speaks in the guise of 'they' – the 'authentic' post-punks:

> When it came to politics in the conventionally un-
> derstood sense – the world of demonstrations, grassroots
> activism, organised struggle – post-punk was more am-
> bivalent. Art students and autodidacts alike tended to
> prize individuality. As bohemian nonconformists, they
> were usually made uncomfortable by calls to solidarity
> or toeing the party line. They saw the plain-speaking
> demagoguery of overtly politicised groups like The Tom
> Robinson Band and Crass as far too literal and non-aes-
> thetic, and regarded their soapbox sermonising as either

---

46  Berger, *The Story of Crass*, 210.

47  Clinton Heylin, *Babylon's Burning: From Punk to Grunge* (London: Viking, 2007), 351.

condescending to the listener or a pointless exercise in preaching to the converted.[48]

## CONCLUSIONS

Authenticity is highly valued within the subcultural context. Anarcho-punk, particularly through Crass, announced the death of punk so that punk could be reborn. By criticising what punk was becoming they laid the path for what they believed punk could be. This argument created controversy within the punk subculture. Other factions within the subculture criticised the anarcho-punk movement, particularly Crass, for their self-righteous attitude. Value was placed on individuality, commitment, and authenticity. On the back sleeve of the seven-inch EP *Rising From the Ashes*, The Apostles present their view of what punk was becoming:

> I've seen punk born and die. I've seen R.A.R. become C.R.A.P. I've seen punk reborn. I've seen the mod revival and mod death. I've seen Sun, Sea and Piracy walk the plank. I've seen positive punk turn into negative junk. I've seen Oi The Hero become Oi The Zero. I've seen electronic wizardry born from the metal womb of the computer age... but WE are still here and Crass are still here. So what now? How long will it be before the electronic 'wild planet' dream is woken up rudely by a power cut. How much longer/will people wear/safety pins/and dye their hair?[49]

Additionally they add, "I have more respect for Skrewdriver than I have for the Redskins, regardless of how sincere both bands undoubtedly are."[50] Although The Apostles unarguably shared more ideological concepts with the Redskins than with Skrewdriver, the emphasis here is placed on commitment rather than principles.[51]

---

48   Simon Reynolds, *Rip It Up and Start Again: Post-Punk 1978-84* (London: Faber & Faber, 2006), xxiii.

49   The Apostles, *Rising From the Ashes*.

50   The Apostles, *Rising From the Ashes*.

51   In fact, in the name of free speech Andy Martin from the Apostles inserted an ad

The treasons most condemned by the anarcho-punk movement included 'selling out', by signing to major labels or becoming mainstream, and becoming 'poseurs', pretending to be something they were not. The poseur is notorious in the context of both punk and skinhead subcultures, and the theme became increasingly important within a variety of punk and post-punk offshoots including anarcho-punk, Oi!, hardcore and street punk. The claim for authenticity was ubiquitous, and the internecine rivalry between different groups, factions, and political allegiances was played out through lyrics, statements and artwork. The importance of this ideological battle for the legacy of punk should not be underestimated.

"Punk is dead. Long live punk."[52]

---

for the White Power EP from Skrewdriver in his zine *Scum*. The add disclosed the way to buy the record adding "This record has been *banned* by Garry Bushell of *Sounds* and by all the other music papers. This record has been banned by all the major record labels. This record has been *banned* from nearly every record shop. BEAT THE BAN!" (Martin 1983, 10)

52  Graffiti in use since the 1970s.

HELEN REDDINGTON

# THE POLITICAL PIONEERS OF PUNK
## (JUST DON'T MENTION THE F-WORD!)

WRITING ABOUT PUNK has always been a risky business, especially when one is approaching it from an academic perspective. Punk is anti-academic, and supposedly anti-formal; it prioritises the lived experience over both scholarly theory and mediated opinion and later in this chapter I will underline the importance of being real as opposed to following theoretical directions, both in the living of a subcultural life itself and also in the approach to writing history.

It is a complicated path one must follow in order to negotiate potential accusations of hypocrisy in one's writing. Indeed, Furness notes the irritation expressed by Penny Rimbaud, initiator of the Crass collective, at the *No Future* punk conference which was organized by David Muggleton in 2001. Rimbaud declared the concept of a scholarly approach to punk as 'absurd... academics sitting round talking about something so anti-academic.'[1] I was there, having overcome my

---

1    Zak Furness, *Punkademics: The Basement Show in the Ivory Tower* (Wivenhoe/

own misgivings about exactly the same issue, but found the conference to be hilariously affirming. As far as I know, Rimbaud didn't actually attend any of the sessions where academics supposedly sat round 'talking about something so anti-academic', but he did attend to make his own keynote speech, alongside Caroline Coon and Gary Valentine. Both he and Caroline were remarkably helpful to me as I sought to find women to interview for the book which I later published. So this chapter is written with the awareness that (after the writing of McRobbie[2]) firstly, I am a subjective writer, and secondly, that there are those who believe that anarchic music making should be excluded from academic discourse. Furness, of course, robustly defends those of us in particular who were actively engaged with punk as musicians during the 1970s and who now find ourselves as lecturers and researchers from a destination we had never envisaged, Higher Education.

From this position we have been able to insert our empirical experiences into more high-falutin' historical discourses, sometimes interrupting their flow with an insistence on revision based on our own experience of participation in a multi-stranded subculture; in my own case, this meant collecting the experiences of women who played rock instruments in punk bands and beginning to contextualize these within the greater punk, gender, political, and historical discourses.

There are several reasons for writing this chapter. In my earlier research, I was aware that I could only scratch the surface of the areas of punk and women's music-making that I was investigating; I had not documented the actual music,[3] I had not addressed race or LGBT issues, and I had not explored the connection between the women in anarcho-punk bands and feminist practice. Here, I hope to begin to discuss the importance of the women musicians of anarcho-punk and the way their feminism was and is embedded within their musical praxis.

The women in the punk subculture were visible and vocal, making their presence felt on the street, as artists (Vivienne Westwood,

Brooklyn/Port Watson: Minor Compositions, 2012), p15.

2    Angela McRobbie, "Settling Accounts with Subcultures: A Feminist Critique," in *On Record: Rock, Pop and the Written Word*, ed. Simon Frith et al. (London and New York: Routledge 1990).

3    Reddington, forthcoming in *Popular Music History*.

Gee Vaucher, Linder Sterling), and as writers (Julie Burchill, Lucy Toothpaste) as well as musicians. This was of great importance: they were audible for the first time as rock beings, not only following in the footsteps of 'hollerers' like Janis Joplin, Tina Turner, and the other strong female vocal role models who had come before them, but also appearing on stage playing electric guitars, electric basses, drums, and keyboards and making 'boy-noise', redefining it as aesthetically and technically their own. This chapter focuses on a subculture within a subculture: the explicitly pacifist and feminist (amongst many other things) subgenre of anarcho-punk, which stubbornly celebrated its subculture-ness even as the Birmingham School definitions of sub-cultures began to be deconstructed with the onset of Thatcherism and the beginnings of the 20th century *fin-de-siecle* philosophy, postmodernism.

I will be focussing on the period in the UK between roughly 1978 and 1984; this is because during this period the political changes in the British social landscape were tumultuous and made a transition from entropy to proactive monetarism, and the most influential of the anarcho-punk bands, Crass, dissolved in 1984. Using the context of moral authority, anger, anarchy, and uniformity (all issues that beset discourse on punk), I will discuss some of the women-focused bands of anarcho-punk and some of the ways they encouraged more partic-ipation in their activities.

## MORAL AUTHORITY AND PUNK
## SUBCULTURAL AUTHENTICITY: A CONTEXT

At the beginning, punk's rules were set out by men. Johnny Rotten's 'moral authority'[4] was a strong foil for the hypocritical moral stance of the mainstream British media, which had been intent on demonizing the current generation of young people. Hebdige describes the historic friction between the mainstream and perceived threats to established culture, citing Williams's 'aesthetic and moral criteria for distinguish-ing the worthwhile products from the "trash,"'[5] the 'moral conviction' of Barthes' beliefs[6] and Gramsci's critique of the social authority of the

---

4    Peter York, *Style Wars* (London: Sidgwick and Jackson, 1980), p48.

5    Dick Hebdige, *Subculture: The Meaning of Style* (London: Methuen, 1979), p8.

6    Ibid., p10.

mainstream.[7] It is no wonder that punk, with its celebration of its own trash aesthetic, excited academia. The hippy project had apparently failed, its alternative approach quickly appearing to become commercialized and its libertarian politics leading to, for instance, the *Oz* trial that revealed a darker side to the peace and free love message.[8]

Although Johnny Rotten was savvy enough to abandon punk just as it was being consolidated and fought over, he and others who instigated the phenomenon left a powerful legacy of self-empowerment.

It was disappointment at the apparent success of the record industry in commodifying, or co-opting, the music and political stance of The Sex Pistols and The Clash, that splintered the punk subculture. Clark summarises the odd polarity that had happened: '… when the mainstream proved that it needed punk, punk's equation was reversed: its negativity became positively commercial.'[9]

Hebdige enlarges on this recuperation process and quotes Sir John Read, then Chairman of EMI, who was delighted that money appeared to be more important than the message to a selection of traditional 'brilliant nonconformists'[10] who 'became in the fullness of time, wholly acceptable and can (*sic*) contribute greatly to the development of modern music.'[11] Poison Girls' 1984 lyric: 'Made a bomb out of music/ Made a hit with a record' could not have been more apt.[12] However, the 'selling out' and consequent opportunity to communicate challenges to the opinions of a wider audience had a positive effect, according to Laing:

> …the example of The Clash in developing a dia-
> lect of political comment within the rock mainstream

7    Ibid., p16.

8    Despite this Geoff Travis (who set up Rough Trade and The Cartel which distributed punk records all over the UK and Europe), Penny Rimbaud and many more who formed the framework for branches of punk and post-punk activity were firmly rooted in hippy ideals and aesthetics.

9    Dylan Clark, "The Death and Life of Punk, the Last Subculture", in *The Post-Subcultures Reader*, ed. David Muggleton and Rupert Weinzierl (Oxford and New York: Berg, 2003), p233.

10   Hebdige, *Subculture*, p 99.

11   Ibid.

12   The Poison Girls, "Take the Toys," *Their Finest Moments*, Reactive Records, 1998.

should not be underestimated. Without that example (as well as punk's general impact) it is unlikely that the songs of UB40 and of 'Two Tone' groups like The Specials would have found the general popularity they enjoyed from 1979 onwards.'[13]

Even Cogan, who dismisses the politics of The Clash as 'vague political leanings', admits that '… the more commercialized bands could be seen as a gateway to the more ideologically involved bands.'[14] As it became apparent, however, that being in a punk band could set musicians en route to mainstream success, The Clash template (a rock band becomes a punk band becomes a rock band again) began to function for other artists. Moral authority passed on to those punks who embedded moral issues into their music and who eschewed commercialization by taking on board the *idea* of anarchy espoused by The Sex Pistols and the overt political sloganeering of The Clash, but opted out of the drive to become wealthy. The vacuum left by the transition of The Clash and The Sex Pistols into the formal music industry was filled by amongst other subgenres, anarcho-punk, and the 'dialect of political comment within the rock mainstream' described above by Laing encouraged bands to approach not only lyric writing but also rock music in general with a refreshed and refreshing activist vigour.

It is in the nature of innovative creative activities that as they become more widespread, and inspirational beyond their central core, new 'rules' are created, and ironically the group of people who created anarcho-punk (which included Crass and Poison Girls), as an authentic political resistance to the commercialization of the music genre spawned a style template of their own. Allan Whalley from Chumbawumba observed much later on: '… it quickly became obvious that they were setting up a kind of blueprint, and a lot of people just followed that blueprint blindly.'[15] This contributed to a conflict

---

13   Dave Laing, *One Chord Wonders: Power and Meaning in Punk Rock* (Milton Keynes: Open University Press, 1985), p117.

14   Brian Cogan, "'Do They Owe Us a Living? Of Course They Do!' Crass, Throbbing Gristle, and Anarchy and Radicalism in Early English Punk Rock," *Journal for the Study of Radicalism* 1:2 (Summer 2007), p87.

15   Ian Glasper, *The Day the Country Died: A History of Anarcho-Punk 1980-1984*

within the greater punk community itself about exactly what punk was; was it a London-centric fashion phenomenon based on Chelsea's King's Road that finished almost as soon as it started; or was it intended as a blueprint for subcultural activities in hotspots all over the UK? Was it a return to working class roots (the journalist Gary Bushell's 'Oi' vision), was it a corruptible concept that exposed weaknesses in the British Record Industry, or was it the missing link between politics and music making for a dispossessed generation?

In reality, it could be any of these things; as Laing says above, the environment created by even those bands that had 'sold out' enabled those who were more purist or even obscurantist to thrive. Lyrically, punk's discourse could be said to be an expression of the concerns of a generation who felt forgotten; sonically, the intention was still to assault the mainstream aesthetic. To those who are outside the subculture, it probably all sounded the same; to those within it, it was nuanced by a multitude of delineations.

## AUTHENTIC ANGER

Within this forgotten generation was a forgotten gender. The women who experienced the loss of identity stimulated by the readjustment of post-60s society struggled to assert their diverse agendas within the open format of punk[16] We too felt anger, and we too wanted to express this alongside our contemporaries. With regard to women in bands, active engagement in music making alongside male peers, *being punks* through *doing the music*, and visibility were factors that consolidated a realist feminism at the time, far from theoretical discourses that sought to ignore the lived experiences of women by setting their sights on grander and more abstract horizons; it appeared to be natural, which was one of its strengths. To some women punks, 1970s feminism seemed to be yet another set of rules, '…seen as excluding other things', according to The Raincoats's guitarist Ana Da Silva, who remembers that it was only later that she understood that the 'anyone can do it mentality' applied to both feminism *and* punk[17]. Some of those in the anarcho-punk community had made a transition from the hippy subculture and its

---

(London: Cherry Red, 2006), p 379.

16  See Helen Reddington (2012) *The Lost Women of Rock Music: female musicians of the punk era*, Sheffield: Equinox

17  Ana Da Silva, unpublished interview with Gina Birch, 2009

free festival ethos into punk; this development included many of the principles of access and sharing that had been articulated in, for instance, the free festival movement in Britain which gained momentum after the first Glastonbury Fayre in 1971 and which led to free festivals being held at Windsor and Stonehenge in following years. For the older members of the anarcho community, Penny Rimbaud and Vi Subversa, punk probably provided a platform for making a better version of the hippy ideal that could include greater respect for women and a more active and engaged approach to politics in general; lack of consideration for 'Women's Lib' had been a major problem in the countercultural movements in the 1960s.[18]

## ANARCHY

Because punk, unlike previous British subcultures, had the creation of music at its heart from the outset, it had developed 'inescapable links' with the music industry, as Laing noted. It had begun as an

> ...outlawed shadow of the music industry and its fate depended equally on the response to it of the industry. And while punk as a life-style developed a certain distance from the fate of punk rock, it remained dependent on the existence of a musical focus to give its own identity a stability.[19]

Disentangling these links and putting an alternative in place was an act of great ambition; punk bands sought out new venues to play and new ways of performing where accessibility came to the forefront; this benefited potential women punks who wanted to participate in music making because they did not have to negotiate traditional gate-keeping barriers. Zillah Minx, founder member of Rubella Ballet, says that in spite of the idea of anarchy being introduced by The Sex Pistols, the practical political application came later:

> I believed I was part of the whole creating of punk. The music then was what was being created by artistic

---

18  See Sheila Rowbotham, (1973) *Women's Consciousness, Man's World* Harmondsworth: Penguin

19  Laing, *One Chord Wonders*, p xi.

people to do whatever they thought was weird and different. It wasn't until Crass came along that it seemed
[overtly] political. Previous to that The Sex Pistols and
X Ray Spex didn't seem anarchist [in the way they be-
haved]. We looked up the word anarchy, and that started to make us think politically.

Zillah describes the first contact that she had with the Crass collective at a gig with UK Subs at The crypt at North East London
Polytechnic:

That's where I first met them. They were there in
the audience talking to people, which was really different. Not only were they in the audience, they were
sharing. So if you got there earlier and they were having a cup of tea, they would ask you if they wanted a
cup of tea. They weren't being a 'famous band'. They
were being part of the audience and part of the whole
experience.[20]

In London Crass played at political centres such as the Centro
Iberico in West London that hosted Spanish anarchists from the
Basque country; through doing this they underlined the message in
their music in a way that seemed more genuinely anarchic than the
interactions of some of the first wave bands that had been co-opted
by the music industry:

I knew it was political... the police kept turning
up and having fights with everybody, along with the
skinheads, and the skinheads would object to what
they were saying. And also Crass were known for playing strange places like the Anarchy Centres. So that's
where we knew that the anarchy thing was happening.
The difference was that people were actively being political, using anarchy as the framework. We took it as
meaning 'do what you want' as well.[21]

---

20   Zillah Ashworth, interview with author, 2003.
21   Zillah Ashworth, interview with author, 2003. It should not be forgotten that

## UNIFORMITY

The anarcho-punk bands struggled with the way that they presented their ideas; as McKay writes, their '...utopian politics [is] presented through dystopian cultural formations'[22] and in their constant questioning of the status quo struggled against a phenomenon articulated by Plant:

> Questions of where the revolution comes from must
> be joined by those which reveal the means by which
> revolutions are betrayed, an interrogation which might
> suggest that remnants of counter-revolutionary desire
> are invested in even the most radical of gestures.[23]

Artists are often pursued by their own desire for the safety of consolidation, and petrified into stasis by being defined by the pronouncements which they make and the activities which they undertake that were originally intended to be fluid or transient. Radical art is terrifying and dangerous; a world without boundaries is much more difficult to negotiate than one with obvious and distasteful political, commercial and social parameters.

The brand of anarchy which was practiced by Crass encouraged bands that were associated with them (mainly by playing gigs with them but also for some recording on their self-titled label) to define themselves any way they wanted to. Unfortunately, the 'blueprint' identified earlier by Chumbawumba's Whalley became a default setting for some of the bands who were originally inspired by Crass. Indeed, Kay Byatt from Youth in Asia remarks that although she remains committed

---

both Ana Da Silva, guitarist in the Raincoats, had become politicized in her native Portugal, and Palmolive, who drummed for both The Slits and The Raincoats, hailed from Spain, where in 1975 Franco's death led to the gradual introduction of democracy through a difficult transition period. This is not to say that all of the women who played in punk bands were overtly politically active; it is undeniable, however, that amongst some of them there was a level of political consciousness that may have set them apart from their peers. This was not always overtly present in their music.

22  McKay, *Senseless Acts of Beauty*, p89.

23  Sadie Plant, *The Most Radical Gesture: The Situationist International in the Postmodern Age* (London: Routledge, 1992), p123.

right to the present day to the same non-conformist causes that she wrote lyrics about while an active band member, she eventually left the group because 'punk's formality' started to tire her:

> [I had] thought the scene was about breaking rules, not making them. It became a very 'right on' movement, and maybe a little too puritanical for its own good, with Crass looked upon as virtual gods towards the end.[24]

Although the aforementioned viewpoint is very personal in nature, the fact that Kay felt strongly enough about the formalization of some aspects of her former band's behavior indicates that perhaps not every band was flexible enough to embrace differences of opinion. From another perspective Zillah observes that audience safety was behind one of the dress-codes that might have looked to an outsider like a uniform; the bleakness of Crass's garb had practicality at its heart:

> That's what happens, I think – you start off with all the interesting, arty people, and by arty people I mean people who do stuff for themselves, not necessarily art college, just people with imagination, and then as things get popular everyone seems to think they've got to join in with the popular look rather than their individual look. The whole Crass thing: they (the audience) all started dressing in black, they all had to have their hair a certain way, and for the macho bit what happened really was not that the people within the anarchy scene got macho, it was the opposition that came. The skinheads that came to beat you up, the normal people that came to beat you up. I think that got really scary and therefore the men and women in that scene would start to wear their Doctor Martins in case they had to have a fight, their black trousers in case they had to hide. People toned it down a bit more, wanted to hide a bit more.[25]

24   Ibid., p164.
25   Zillah Ashworth.

This was also affirmed by Vi Subversa, who cited the need to wear 'fairly armoured clothes to feel safe';[26] regardless of her comments above, Zillah's band Rubella Ballet dressed in day-glo colours and indeed, Steve Ignorant himself refers to Rubella Ballet's colourful rule-breaking as 'a breath of fresh air', a change from the uniformly dour and black-clad presentation that was favoured by Crass and other bands within the genre.[27] Rubella Ballet's colour was an exception. In general, anarcho-punks rejected the more camp side of punk, for as Sontag says, 'To emphasize style is to slight content.'[28] The first wave of punk had had layers of irony throughout it, and could be read as purely style (hence Hebdige's focus). Those who historicize punk as following on from David Bowie's short-haired glam image rightly saw a camp androgyny embedded within it, and this was simple to read. The 'pervy' clothing sold by Westwood and McClaren, and the slogans were easy to recuperate and commodify. This rapid absorption into the world of fashion threatened the validity of punk and contributed to the many heated authenticity debates of the time; there was a discourse of resistance to this, too, in anarcho-punk.

## THE FEMALE PRESENCE IN ANARCHO PUNK BANDS: CRASS AND FEMINISM

Although creating an all-female rock band was a radical political act in itself[29] some of the male punks found this idea difficult to engage with; being an 'out' feminist could be seen as a risky option.[30] Isolated from each other largely by a 1970s ideology that can be explained by reference to Potter's writing about tokenism[31] many of the female

---

26  Sue Steward and Sheryl Garret, *Signed, Sealed and Delivered: True Life Stories of Women in Pop* (London and Sydney: Pluto Press, 1984), p37.

27  Glasper, *The Day the Country Died*, p58.

28  Susan Sontag, "Notes on Camp," in *The Susan Sontag Reader* (London: Penguin, 1982), p107.

29  This would possibly come as a surprise to all-female German skiffle band 'Lucky Girls' and British 1960s garage band 'Mandy and the Girlfriends.'

30  Helen Reddington, *The Lost Women of Rock Music: Female Musicians of the Punk Era* (London: Equinox, 2012), pp 182-189.

31  Potter, Sally, (1997) 'On Shows', in Parker, Roszika, and Pollock, Griselda (eds) (1997) *Framing Feminism: Art and the Womens' Movement 1970-1985* London: Pandora p 30

punk groups at the time were regarded by the media as being in competition with each other,[32] although in reality their personnel had often collaborated musically in different configurations before their bands consolidated and made recordings. The feeling about the exclusionary nature of feminism articulated by Da Silva and shared by many other female focused bands led to a reluctance to identify with feminism much to journalist Caroline Coon's frustration.[33] In the music that emanated from Britain's Women's Centres during the mid-1970s, however, feminism could be regarded as of equal importance to the music that was created[34]. Within the anarcho-punk movement that consolidated towards 1980, feminism was often integrated into the ethos of the bands, as part of the general force for change that was expressed in the lyrics; these lyrics explored themes of pacifism, vegetarianism, revolution, and acceptance of queerness (the A-heads' 'Isolated') amongst other issues[35].

This willingness to engage directly with feminism set the anarcho bands in general apart from some of the more feted women in punk bands. There were many bands under this umbrella that had female members; these included Dirt, Lost Cherrees, and Hagar the Womb; I have chosen here to focus mainly on Poison Girls (originally formed in Brighton and later, based in Epping) Rubella Ballet (sometimes also labeled 'Positive Punks' because of their colourful visuals) and Crass. Poison Girls were particularly influential on feminist discourse and practice in anarcho-punk bands, partly because they were active from a relatively early date (1977) and toured with Crass from 1979 onwards building an audience alongside them. They introduced feminist ideas to, for instance, Dirt[36] who say they were inspired by them

---

32  Op cit. Reddington., p188.

33  Op cit. Reddington p183.

34  More details about this can be found at http://womensliberationmusicarchive.co.uk/

35  The free speech encouraged by the movement also led to some unfortunate pronouncements such as those made by 'Admit You're Shit's John Cato, who aligned his views with the racist British Movement. Found in Glasper, *The Day the Country Died*, 120. However, most anarcho-punk bands were anti-racist, although in common with other punk bands, predominantly consisting of white people.

36  Glasper, *The Day the Country Died*, p60.

and other female-fronted bands; Youth in Asia, who celebrated their own 50/50 gender split[37] and who also cite Crass as an inspiration; and Flowers in the Dustbin (who also cite Patti Smith as being influential).[38] In anarcho-punk bands there appears to have been little fear from either male or female personnel of identifying with feminist politics. Steve Battershill, a founder member of Lost Cherrees (who started in 1981), recalls:

> The feminist stance (sic) was struck very early on and has never wavered; equality in all walks of life is essential to us. The issue had already been raised by Crass and Poison Girls, so, although it wasn't that widespread, people were starting to seriously address such problems.'[39]

Between them, Poison Girls, Rubella Ballet, and Crass covered a broad area of feminist music making and performed to mixed audiences in a distinctive subcultural area which was carved out by the activities of Crass themselves, although both Rubella Ballet and Poison Girls had originally formed as a direct result of the catalyst effect of earlier punk activity in the UK. A feeling of agency was a vital element in the development of the genre as a whole. The music and atmosphere at live gigs continued to strike a chord long after punk's first burst of activity in west London had died away. Eve Libertine describes visiting the Dial House in Epping after being so 'moved by the raw energy' of their performances that she would sometimes be the only audience member left at the gig, as the band emptied venues with their uncompromising sound. She describes her feeling that '... there was a rather one-dimensional quality to what was then an all-male outfit. The onstage politics lacked a feminist angle, a problem that was easily solved by Joy and myself joining the band.'[40] Crass then embedded feminism into their ethos, according to Joy De Vivre,

---

37  Ibid., p160.

38  Ibid., p171. See also Sheila Whiteley, *Women and Popular Music: Sexuality, Identity and Subjectivity* (London: Routledge, 2000).

39  Ibid., p149.

40  Maria Raha, *Cinderella's Big Score: Women of the Punk Rock and Indie Underground* (Emeryville: Seal Press, 2005), p94.

who was able to state that: 'It is not easy to isolate feminist activities of the band, they're so tied in with the wider philosophy about compassion, respect, pacifism.'[41] The 1981 Crass album *Penis Envy* brought to a head the willingness of the collective to invest time and energy into a specifically feminist approach to the art of making music. The decision by Crass to release this album, which was voiced entirely by Joy De Vivre and Eve Libertine, was a deliberate response to the perception of the band (and in particular their community of followers) as being unconcerned with the importance of gender politics. As Rimbaud explains,

> An exclusively feminist album would be a challenge both to us and to our predominantly male audience… with the notable exception of the Poison Girls' stunning *Hex* (1979) album, no one had ever before set out to create an album dedicated solely to feminist issues[42]

Prior to this, Raha describes De Vivre's song-poem 'Women' as being related from a 'nonacademic perspective' and thus appealing to everywoman (and man).[43] This simplicity of expression was also embedded into the language of male members of the anarcho-punk music community. Hence Crass member Steve Ignorant's name: he was, he says 'ignorant of politics'[44] when he first came to the collective. Delivering a direct anti-sexist message alongside the other concerns associated with anarcho-punk meant that the message was validated and communicated in a simple and uncompromising way, at a great distance from theoretical feminism that many of the protagonists in the subculture might have found indigestible or possibly even hostile. The affirmative impact of the male figurehead of what (according to Rimbaud) was becoming an increasingly male-dominated movement, in stepping aside and making way for women's creative voices should not be underestimated. The importance of his active pro-feminist decision can be contextualised by referring to the way Bayton underlines

---

41    Ibid.

42    Penny Rimbaud, sleeve notes to *Crass: Penis Envy The Crassical Collection*, Crass Records, 2010

43    Op Cit. Raha., p95.

44    Op Cit. Raha., p24.

the importance of men's understanding of the support that women may need in music, saying that some '… may think the whole issue is irrelevant to themselves, but they are (unwitting) beneficiaries of a set-up that is skewed in their favour, in terms of a whole range of material and cultural resources'[45].

One of Crass's more high profile pranks involved the duping of 'teeny romance' magazine *Loving* into releasing a white vinyl version of their track *Our Wedding*, which had been created in a spirit of sarcasm. Once the hoax had been discovered, the *News of the World* presented it as 'Band of Hate's Loving Message', quoting the obviously distressed editor of *Loving*, Pam Lyons's response to the 'sick joke.'[46] Whether this was a feminist act or an act of internalized sexism[47] is debatable; feminism involves choices and freedoms that are surely espoused by anarchists. It is possible that a teenage girl (especially during the dour 1970s) should be entitled to dream about whatever she wants to,[48] even if an anarchist collective that represents an older generation deeply disapproves.[49] This type of cross-generational moral friction continues to happen to the present day, with every party feeling that the other is simultaneously manipulated and manipulative, and at the time of writing is being played out predominantly in a relationship between the mainstream pop music industry, pornography and shock tactic.[50]

Crass were creating a politically active framework-by-example for the punks around them who were disappointed by what they saw as

---

45  Bayton, Mavis (1998) *Frock Rock: Women Performing Popular Music* Oxford and New York: Oxford University Press .p 205

46  Crass, *Penis Envy*, (sleeve notes) Crass Records, 2010.

47  See Duguid, Michelle M. and Thomas-Hunt, Meilissa C (2015) *Condoning Stereotyping? How Awareness of Stereotyping Prevalence Impacts Expression of Stereotypes* Journal of Applied Psychology, 2015, Vol. 100, No. 2 343-359

48  See Valerie Walkerdine, *Daddy's Girl: Young Girls and Popular Culture* (London: Macmillan, 1997).

49  At the time, I remember a discussion with my peers who felt that although the idea behind this action was exemplary, the eventual target was a soft one that would probably be horrified at the thought of living in an anarchist collective

50  Oddly enough, this looks to the deviation popularized by the original London punks as an inspiration, as Linder Sterling could attest after seeing Lady Gaga's Meat Dress.

the petering out of the energy associated with the first burst of energy that The Sex Pistols had instigated; they were creating a different way of being. As Zillah remarks: 'We were all really gutted when The Sex Pistols split up. We wanted everyone to think our way.'[51] Zillah cites Crass as showing her contemporaries 'how to *live* as anarchy', even if she and the other members of Rubella Ballet rejected the polemic and harsh visual style of their friends. The open-mindedness of the collective allowed them to examine gender roles to a point as we have seen.[52] But anarcho-punk was not always a site of equality; in London, the predominantly female band Hagar the Womb were founded after: '...finding it hard to get ourselves heard or involved in any sense. Anarchy in Wapping or no, the battle of the sexes continues...'[53] As Ruth Elias, founder member of the band, says, "Pre Crass-invasion" the Wapping Anarchy Centre had been male-dominated, and out of anger, [our] "band of defiance" was set up to give women from the Centre a chance to participate actively in the scene.'[54]

Women in marginal political groupings had often found themselves in the position of handmaidens to the folk heroes, without agency and operating as a mirror image of those in the world outside their political sphere. This phenomenon was clearly articulated by Rowbotham in 1973[55] and had not been effectively addressed in previous political movements in the UK. Anarcho punk embedded into practice the mentoring of up and coming punk bands, importantly with integrated female personnel, and the facilitation of gigs and events for those bands to perform at. From Mark Perry's original instruction 'This is a chord, This is another, This is a third, Now form a band' to the sleeve notes on the Desperate Bicycles 1977 single The Medium was Tedium' b/w 'Don't Back the Front', 'It was easy, it was cheap, go and do it', there was a clearly-defined articulation of do-it-yourself empowerment that was as easy for young women to follow as young men. In punk, acquisition of instrumental expertise was not restricted to man-to-man peer

---

51  Zillah Ashworth.
52  Although within the nucleus of the collective itself, it was still the women who sang and the men who (mostly) played the loud instruments
53  Ibid.
54  Glasper, *The Day the Country Died*, pp154-155.
55  This has still not really been successfully counteracted in the present day, which is why the Pussy Riot Collective has had such a strong impact.

learning, and in this respect anarcho-punk took general punk musical practice a stage further by active mentoring of female musicians.

## THE MENTORING ROLE OF
## WOMEN IN ANARCHO PUNK: VI SUBVERSA

Fronting the band Poison Girls at the age of 40, Vi was an older woman and a mother in a scene that was predominantly (although not exclusively) youth-based. If Vi felt that she could stand in front of an audience with a guitar and sing punk songs with her band, so should anyone else; the enabling factors of her example at the time should not be underestimated. All of the punk women who took to the stage were pioneers of their time[56] but in respect of being an older woman, Vi's pioneering activity was doubly inspiring. She challenged not only gender assumptions, but also assumptions about what a middle-aged parent ought to be doing, and thus caused many young male punks to question many more of their attitudes than simply those associated with the 'fun' aspect of punk. Unlike the Mom-rockers of Middle America[57] Vi was overtly political and fully understood the implications of living what was essentially a rock'n'roll lifestyle with her family both in tow and actively engaged in live events. As Bayton notes, Vi, with her daughter playing beside her, could inspire a three year old girl to want to play guitar in a band, and was one of the many '... women that I interviewed [who] were highly aware that they... were serving as role models for other women'. In response, Vi remarked: 'I feel really privileged to be part of that.'[58]

During her years in Poison Girls, Vi was the embodiment of difference, the proof that subversion was happening and that the world that the young punks lived in was challengeable and could look very different. This type of discursive production put issues of performativity at the heart of the main stream of anarcho-punk, during the time that Poison Girls toured with Crass; she had developed this practice originally in Brighton at the very beginning of the punk moment.

---

56  Explored further in Reddington, *The Lost Women of Rock Music: Female Musicians of the Punk Era*. (London: Equinox, 2012).

57  Norma Coates, "Mom Rock? Media Representations of 'Women Who Rock,'" in '*Rock On': Women Ageing and Popular Music*, ed. Ros Jennings and Abigail Gardner. (Farnham: Ashgate, 2012), pp87-101.

58  Bayton, *Frock* Rock, p62.

Vi put into place informal musical mentoring of both male and female musicians; this was common practice in the feminist music making circles that she was also part of.[59] Vi practised the blend of hippy
and punk ideals that later contributed to anarcho-punk's feminist musical agenda when she relocated to Essex and contributed to the Crass
collective In Brighton's local music scene she encouraged many of the
up-and-coming bands, in particular urging them to infuse their music
with political consciousness. Her earlier involvement with the music
for the 1975 theatrical production *The Body Show* led to a nucleus
of musicians that included female bass-player Bella Donna, a friend
of The Buzzcocks. Vi had been proactive in setting up a ramshackle
rehearsal complex in the cellars of a Presbyterian Church in North
Road in Brighton. This necessitated joining the management committee of a community group that included Church Elders, '...and
because I was middle-aged, they trusted me.'[60] Poison Girls went on
to lend equipment and even band members to start-up bands in the
Brighton punk scene that subsequently developed, giving support and
encouragement to scores of bands.[61] This facilitation of music making
by lending equipment, putting on gigs, and other forms of support
was inherent to punk and was a major catalyst for encouraging people
to perform who could not have done so otherwise; this practice was
also common with feminist music circles of the time[62]. Even within the much more popular stream of pop punk music Siouxsie and
the Banshees, for instance, had borrowed equipment from Johnny
Thunders and the Heartbreakers when they first started.

## ZILLAH ASHWORTH: APPRENTICESHIPS

Zillah's approach to Rubella Ballet, supported by her partner Sid, was
also to embed mentorship into the ethos of her band by encouraging novice female instrumentalists to join the band and learn their

59  Mavis Bayton, *Frock Rock: Women Performing Popular Music* (Oxford: Oxford
    University Press), p72.
60  Vi Subversa, letter to author, 2000
61  The extent of the activity centred around The Vault as a rehearsal and gigging
    space, and its significance to the Brighton punk scene can be seen at www.
    punkbrighton.co.uk, the website set up by ex-punk Phil Byford to archive the
    Brighton bands.
62  Bayton, *Frock Rock*, p72.

playing skills onstage. Starting with female bass-player Gemma (Vi's daughter), who started with the band, she later employed her sister and other female players. 'I thought it made a statement', said Zillah,

> I wanted as many girls as possible and sometimes that didn't really help when the girls weren't very good as musicians because they hadn't had the experience that the men had had. It was different for them as well, being that forward on bass at gigs with blokes jumping on you or spitting at you or whatever.[63]

Later on, the band employed a very skilled young musician:

> …Leda Baker, who was Ginger Baker's daughter, she'd been to one of our gigs and someone mentioned to her that we were looking for a guitarist; when she rang up and said that she was interested in coming over, I was thrilled, I thought, 'A girl guitarist, brilliant!' and when she came over, I couldn't believe it – she played like Jimi Hendrix. We didn't know who she was; and it was some time before she told us who her dad was. We couldn't believe it but it sort of went with what she was playing. And she was only 18.[64]

Fluidity of line-up was part of the ethos of Rubella Ballet, who had no expectations of formal relationships with their personnel; because Zillah had been very taken by the fact that at an early Crass gig, the band had mingled with the audience and made them cups of tea:

> With Rubella Ballet there was this whole thing of 'singers in and out, bass players in and out', so it was very fluid, who was playing what and who was singing what so for the first half dozen gigs there was different people in the band. Like the band being in the audience![65]

---

63   Zillah Ashworth.
64   Ibid.
65   Ibid.

# RE-BRANDING HISTORY:
## FEMINISM VERSUS POSTMODERNISM

The feminist writer MacKinnon had in the 1970s 'imagined that feminists would retheorise life in the concrete rather than spend the next three decades on metatheory, talking *about* theory, rehashing over and over in this disconnected way how theory should be done, leaving women's lives twisting in the wind.'[66] The revision of the meaning of the punk subculture seen through decades polluted by the concept of postmodernism downplays the importance of the active role of women during the punk moment. After punk, as anarcho-punk has widened its scope to a global perspective and slipped deeper underground only to materialize at Stop the City and other anti-capitalist events, the movement retains the gender awareness, that was developed at the outset, as Nicholas confirms:

> Anarcho-punks concerned with deconstructing gender engage in specifically *feminist* poststructuralist tactics, which work from the assumption of a historicised, reified gender order and evade a simplistic, voluntaristic solution.... These deconstructive readings are ensured either through the tactics of exaggeration or literalization or through the fostering of a critical framework of perception for scene participants (via the wider cultural creations of punk) to be able to read gendered acts ironically and anti-foundational. This fostering of modes of perception stay true to the DIY anarchist ethos of autonomy and remains non-coercive and non-authoritarian by making these tactics 'scrupulously visible', relying on participants' ethico-political choice that the post-gender ethos is indeed preferable.[67]

In this, contemporary anarcho-punk arguably evades the fate of more (ironically) 'mainstream' subcultures; Clark writes that,

---

66  Catharine A. McKinnon, "Points Against Postmodernism," *Chicago-Kent Law Review* 75:3 (2000): 25.

67  Lucy Nicholas, "Approaches to Gender, Power and Authority in Contemporary Anarcho-Punk: Poststructuralist Anarchism?" *eSharp* 9 (2007): p18.

...commodification and trivialization of subcultural style is becoming ever more rapid and, at the turn of the millennium, subcultures are losing certain powers of speech. Part of what has become the hegemonic discourse of subcultures is a misrepresentative depoliticization of subcultures; the notion that subcultures were and are little more than hairstyles, quaint slang, and pop songs. In the prism of nostalgia, the politics and ideologies of subcultures are often stripped from them.[68]

The rebranding of subcultures as *only* variations of style, recuperated in selective nostalgia and inauthenticated by default, has culminated in a sneering dismissal of youth culture by writers such as Heath and Potter, who in their 2005 book *The Rebel Sell* distil a rationale for capitalism as a logocentric ideal, and to some extent fulfill MacKinnon's fears about the legacy of postmodern philosophy. MacKinnon derides the way that postmodern theorists swerve around reality, dealing in 'factish things;'[69] their dismissal of social frameworks has retrospectively affected attitudes to the histories of young people, women and all of those not in the hegemonic layers of society. If we refer to Plant's observation, it is possible that such writers often simply do not possess the radar that enables them to register subversive activity; she talks of the '...networks of subversion which continue to arise even in the most postmodern pockets of the postmodern world...'[70] Plant continues: 'That a great deal of cultural agitation is hidden from the public gaze is sometimes indicative of its tactics rather than its absence.'[71] This was apparent in the way that Riot Grrrl functioned in the 1990s. It is also entirely likely that in the 21st century, the public is simply gazing in the wrong direction, as Huq asserts, and as much as 1970s and 1980s punk is most often remembered as a male subculture, with its politics part of a left-anarchic historical discourse, it provided a practical and affirmative platform for the development of feminist practice on the street, that complemented its discussion within academia.

---

68    Clark, "The Death and Life of Punk," p231.
69    McKinnon, "Points Against Postmodernism," p67.
70    Plant, *The Most Radical Gesture*, p176.
71    Ibid.

Looking back on punk, historians often struggle to define its meaning; Sabin discussed this problem as he tried to delineate the scope of his anthology on the cultural legacy of punk. As hard as it was to delineate at the time, it has been even harder to delineate in retrospect; it could seem destructive, but creativity was at its heart. Politically it was fluid and could/can appear to affirm whatever the writer or researcher looks for within it. In Young's utopian book, *Electric Eden*, he remarks that:

> It's interesting to speculate what might have resulted had punk's musical cleansing spared some notion of folk – which was, after all, the culture of citizens, not aristocrats; a music for the leveled society... In Germany, France, Italy and elsewhere, punk was a way of life more associated with the peace movement, animal rights, squatting and environmentalism. In Britain, popular opinion was swift to cast such righteous communitarianism as the enemy within.[72]

We need to add feminism to Young's list; as citizens with no space for their voices to be heard except within the narrow parameters of mainstream stereotypes that so rapidly re-established themselves as punk's opportunities were replaced by Thatcher's enterprise culture. Women with power are acknowledged as such only when they fit the template created by men with power, and are measured against it. As Nicholas writes:

> Particularly relevant to feminist ideas has been the notion that discourses constitute us and thus both enable and limit us through the subject positions they make available to us. Thus the limits of discourses

---

72   Rob Young, *Electric Eden: Unearthing Britain's Visionary* Music (London: Faber & Faber, 2010), 535. According to Young, Crass were the only punk band to succeed in fusing the ethos of both, and he describes them as 'folk-punk-anarchist,' 535. But the Raincoats were also labeled as punk folk music, largely due to their willingness to experiment with non-amplified instruments associated with non-Western cultures.

within which subjects can 'be' represent the limits to subjects' agency.[73]

Feminism still operates in a limited environment. In parallel with the subculture of punk itself and matched against the affirmation of power of the mainstream that punk created by its very existence, feminism is and was necessary because misogyny and sexism exist; but just imagine what women could do with their energy if they were not expending time and energy being feminists. Resistance to male domination takes up space that could be used for better purposes; and because feminism has had as many definitions as punk, the whole idea of 'fourth generation feminism' at the time of writing seems risible; a comment on the anarchist collective CrimethInc's blog, quoted by Nicholas, sums this up perfectly: 'Thus we find the ironic but coherent corollary in anarcho-punk gender politics that 'feminists fight to put an end to gender.'[74] One of the struggles of feminism has been the impossibility of creating a shape that fits all women. Radstone talks of 'the void' as she attends a feminist conference in Glasgow in 1991 and becomes aware of the differences in articulation and experience between not only a very direct Women's Studies Network Conference the weekend before and the Feminist Theory Conference at which she was presenting a paper, but also the 'tough journey from the Gorbals' described in the speech of welcome by the female Lord Provost of Glasgow. Gender discourse does not belong exclusively to anyone, but it appears that it can best be articulated and tested in the margins of politics and the academy. In writing about feminism, gender, and punk there is always an underlying issue of whether the women that I write about are punks first, women first, or musicians first. Lest this seem simplistic, this was an issue that often came to the forefront *at* the time and it sometimes seemed, *all* the time (See Reddington, 2012, pp. 182-190)

In conclusion, it can be affirmed that anarcho-punk appears to have made a formal clearing within its practice for the discussion and articulation of feminism that was probably encouraged by the inter-generational nature of its protagonists. With Vi Subversa very much part of the subcultural group, Poison Girl's explicit lyrical issues

---

73   Nicolas, "Approaches to Gender," pp4-5.

74   Ibid., 8.

nailed feminist colours to the mast, as it were. It would have been difficult to avoid the frank and focused subjects that they sang about and the expectation that these subjects were important regardless of one's social background. Within anarcho-punk, feminism was out into practice by mentoring of female musicians, the assertive inclusion of feminist issues into song lyrics and an acceptance of age and gender deviations from the 'rock band' norm. Zillah describes very young anarcho-punks ('ten, eleven') and also 'the son and daughter of one of the mothers in another band' (Vi Subversa's son and daughter, Dan and Gemma, both in Rubella Ballet). The family aspect of anarcho-punk, I feel, was very much rooted in its hippy approach to living, and members of this extended family were encouraged to participate in every aspect of its activities. It was never the intention of anarcho-punk to become part of the mainstream of the music industry (although paradoxically it was defined in part by its very opposition to the industry as part of the capitalist structures that the movement critiqued and fought against); this made its relationship with feminism less risky. Bands such as The Slits and The Raincoats, while still at the margins of pop, seemed to be closer to the epicentre of punk music making and did not have the ideological context and support that the Crass provided; engaging with feminism became one of their biggest challenges. The anarcho-punks relished antagonizing mainstream women's magazines and were also prepared to risk alienating their male fans by focusing their music on women's experiences and voices. This was an efficient way of counteracting the controlling 'macho' element of the movement which was described by Zillah when she talked about the uniformity of the black-clad audiences at some of the Crass gigs. Belief in the political importance of anarchy authenticated their music and their art. Their position on the bridge between oppositional and alternative activity allowed them to incorporate feminism as a positive part of that action.

It is my belief that one of the most powerful things that we can do for our gender is to reinsert women into historical discourses and to understand the reasons for our omission. Nicholas (above) writes from the perspective of relatively contemporary anarcho-punk feminism, still alive and well, but hidden. Documentation of the moment still emerges, gradually: Zlllah's film *She's a Punk Rocker* (2010) presents a series of very different women talking personally about the meaning of punk. Documentaries such as hers facilitate a feeling of authenticity that captures a moment between the camera starting and the end of filming: her subjects (who include Gee Vaucher and Eve Libertine from Crass, Poly Styrene from X-Ray Spex, Gaye Black from The Adverts, Hagar the Womb and others, are talking to a friend who understands them as much as to a camera. The conversation will continue, and perhaps Crass will make the tea.

RICH CROSS

# 'STOP THE CITY SHOWED ANOTHER POSSIBILITY'

## MOBILISATION AND MOVEMENT IN ANARCHO-PUNK

*'All officers should bear in mind that this is not a lawful protest/ march/demonstration. It is a deliberate attempt to paralyse the financial heart of the country by mainly unlawful means… All [protestors] are anti-establishment, uncooperative with the police, and in the case of some extremists, potentially violent…'*[1]

*'Who is going to take any notice of anyone who smashes windows? You go round like that, your hair all done up, you'll frighten a lot of people – as well as the coppers.'*[2]

---

1   City of London Police, *Stop the City Briefing*, March, 1984.
2   Pub worker, the City of London, March 1984, quoted in *Peace News*, April 27, 1984.

*'The banking community struggled to keep money flows moving, despite the unrest. They succeeded – but only just. [...] Bank balances were £11m below target overnight.'[3]*

**ON 29 SEPTEMBER** 1983, the City of London (the powerhouse of British financial services, domestically and globally) played host to an unruly, radical, and uncompromising demonstration, which had drawn thousands of young militant activists onto the crowded streets of the London financial district.

A large proportion of the demonstrators were punks; and amongst them the predominant contingent were anarchist-identified punks. Unlike so many of the standard demonstrations of the early-Thatcher era in the UK, this 'Stop the City' (STC) event was not organised by an officially-sanctioned pressure group or single issue campaigning organisation. The event had no endorsement from any political party, trade union, or charitable agency. The demonstration had no official organising committee, had not met with either City officials of the City of London Police to discuss its requirements or to agree the route and stewarding of the march.

In fact, 'Stop the City' was not to involve a march of any kind, nor conclude with a traditional rally at which the marchers would gather and listen to speakers from political leaders and supporters. Instead, the participants in Stop the City were encouraged to share collective responsibility in the delivery of a day long series of direct action events which cumulatively, it was hoped, would bring the business of the City to a standstill. All of this was in protest at the operation of the financial-military-industrial complex which the demonstrators insisted was responsible for war, poverty, exploitation, and oppression across the globe, and which now threatened to pitch the planet into a final nuclear conflagration.

The politics of those who were drawn to this unusual style of demonstration were diverse to the point of incoherence; but the 'demands' raised by the action were distinguished by their very scope and ambition. There were few requests for the City to reform its business, or to act more equitably or with a greater sense of moral responsibility.

---

3    *The Times*, quoted in *Freedom*, May, 1984.

Few of the leaflets or banners which were carried by protestors called for 'reductions' or 'moratoriums' on global debt or arms race expenditure; or 'reforms' in the operation of the City's business practices. The demands that the demonstrators had raised on the streets of the City were absolute and uncompromising (and completely beyond the ability of the City to concede).

As a 'Carnival against war, oppression and destruction', Stop the City demanded that the City (and the capitalist system that it served) cease its profit-making activities, end its subsidy of systems of human and ecological exploitation, and renounce its role in financing the international arms industry and the proliferation of weapons of death and destruction. In effect, the demonstrators were demanding that the City cease to be, and the state system which it underpinned be simultaneously dissolved. Beyond such 'absolutism', the demonstrators were far less clear about what their response would be if their demands were not met. 'Half riot, half carnival', was Crass founder member Penny Rimbaud's assessment of the Stop the City initiative. The demonstrations 'attracted thousands of people who in their own ways protested against the machinery of war and the oppression that it represented.'[4]

Crass identified with the potential of Stop the City (STC) from the outset. Rimbaud later reflected that Crass took seriously the 'major commitment [...] to promote and to take part in' the demonstrations; approaching STC as an enthusiastic advocate rather than as an initiator.[5] (The fact that the proposal did not originate from Dial House in many ways made it easier for Crass to embrace it so wholeheartedly; precisely because it did not ensnare the band in unwanted organisational baggage.)

STC occupies a unique position in the history of British anarcho-punk and provides an illuminating illustration of the movement's attempts to project its political practice at a collective level: taking the messages of the culture's musical and printed output and mobilising around them (in an autonomous, confrontational way), in territory which the movement considered to be the 'belly of the beast'. In the context of the anti-Thatcher opposition of the early 1980s, STC posed a sharply different model of radical political expression to both

4    Penny Rimbaud, *Shibboleth* (Edinburgh: AK Press, 1998), 245.

5    Ibid

the prescriptions of the Left and of the mass pressure groups such as
the Campaign for Nuclear Disarmament (CND). STC showcased the
political and cultural pre-occupations of anarcho-punk, in a context
of direct confrontation with the forces of law and order and the business logic of the City – at no little cost to its activist base (in terms of
injuries, arrests and court cases). It is plausible to argue that:

> Stop the City represented anarcho-punk's collapse
> of the protest space and the pop space, bringing the
> seriousness of the demonstration to the gig, and the
> revelry of the gig to the demonstration.[6]

The Stop the City events broke new political ground for the activists who they attracted, and redefined the terrain on which anarchist
and libertarian groups would attempt to mobilise (and against which
they would be compared). While Stop the City initially enabled the
demonstrations to seize the initiative and out-manoeuvre the police
and City authorities, (enabling them to secure greater impact than the
numbers mobilised by the demonstration might have warranted), the
Metropolitan and City police forces quickly adapted to the demonstrators' methods and within a year had been able to overwhelm and
neuter the activist breakthrough which STC represented.

During the short life of the Stop the City initiative the event showcased many bold, imaginative actions; some strikingly effective symbolism; and a mischievous sense of playfulness – all of which distinguished the protests from the drab and routine 'march from A-to-B
for a rally' which remained the stock-in-trade of so much of the po-
litical-cultural opposition to Thatcherism. For all of its innovative
qualities, Stop the City also highlighted some of the key blindspots in
anarcho-punk's revolutionary manifestos; revealing tensions and un-
certainties over questions of strategy, agency, alliance-brokering and
the future orientation of the movement. The evolution of STC also
reflected the shifting attitudes within the anarcho-punk milieu over

6    Palmer Foley, "Stop the City: Identity, Protest, and the Punks who Occupied
     London's Financial District in 1983", *gadflyonline.com*, 1 October 2012,
     http://www.gadflyonline.com/home/index.php/stop-the-city-identity-protest-
     and-the-punks-who-occupied-londons-financial-district-in-1983,    accessed
     August 1 2014.

# STOP 'THE CITY'
## OF LONDON
# THURSDAY 27 SEPT

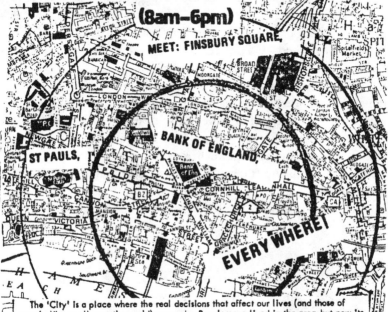

(8am–6pm)

MEET: FINSBURY SQUARE

ST PAULS,

BANK OF ENGLAND,

EVERYWHERE!

The 'City' is a place where the real decisions that affect our lives (and those of people like us all over the world) are made. People once lived in the area, but now its just packed with the Headquarters of Banks, Companies, multinationals and places like the Stock Exchange. Billions of pounds change hands every day making profit for a few, whilst millions of people all over the world are starving. Money is made from weapons dealing, destroying nature, and generally by exploiting and controlling us all.

# PROTEST AND CARNIVAL AGAINST WAR EXPLOITATION AND PROFIT

During the day there'll be constant protests all over the area, including leafletting, talking to 'City' workers, taking over the streets, street theatre and music etc...

– join in or organise your own events..

Flyer advertising the first Stop the City demonstration in September 1983, widely circulated in the months running up to the event, 1983.

the form that direct physical confrontation with the 'forces of the state' should take.

## ORIGINS AND INITIATIVE

Popular histories of 1980s' British counterculture often mistakenly credit Class War as the organising force behind Stop the City.[7] In fact, Class War were entirely peripheral to the initiative. The catalyst for Stop the City was an ad-hoc alliance of radical anti-militarists, peace activists, and punk militants. The class struggle anarchist group later acknowledged: "Individuals in Class War might have taken a small part in organising it but as a group Class War took absolutely no part in organising it and we didn't attend as a group."[8] Even that modest assessment risks over-stating Class War's input.

The impetus behind Stop the City came from two principal directions. On one side, the idea gained support amongst radical currents within the mass anti-nuclear movements that had mushroomed across Europe in response to a new superpower nuclear arms race in the early 1980s. This movement had a vociferous antimilitarist fringe that organised more militant, (though usually avowedly nonviolent) actions against different elements of the 'war machine'. A group of activists within that radical coterie had begun to argue the case for a shift from the (largely rural) focus at the nuclear bases and towards the loci of political and economic power:

> Many felt that if we were, in the short term, to be
> able to stop the arrival of the new missiles, and, in
> the long run, challenge the whole war machine, then
> there needed to develop opposition within the towns

---

7   Marshall makes the less specific (but no more accurate) claim that: 'Class War members (and fellow travellers) were prominent in the 'Stop the City' of London campaign in 1984.' Peter Marshall, *Demanding the Impossible: A History of Anarchism* (London: Harper Perennial, 2008), 495. Franks notes that: 'Class War took part in the Stop the City (STC) demonstrations', but does not discuss STC's organisation. Benjamin Franks, *Rebel Alliances: The Means and Ends of Contemporary British Anarchism* (Edinburgh: AK Press, 2006), 79.

8   Andy Brown [interviewer], "Solidarity and Class War Meet Uptown", *Solidarity*, 13: 3-10; Class War, *This is Class War: An Introduction to the Class War Federation* (Stirling: AK Press, 1989).

as well. For it is in towns that decisions are made and also where people live and work who will all need to be involved if we are to be successful.[9]

On another side, the idea won support amongst a new generation of specifically anarchist activists who had been drawn into revolutionary politics through the anarchist punk movement. The political energies of the activists of anarcho-punk found expression in a wide range of protest and oppositional arenas – including the anti-nuclear lobby, the hunt saboteurs' movement, and anti-Thatcher mobilisations of all kinds. Anarcho-punk's particular reading of the anarchist impulse meant that this activity was, in the main, decentralised, uncoordinated, and pursued independently by those militants. Anarcho-punk attempted to rally its forces in a collective way only rarely: the most significant attempt to do so came with Stop the City itself.

Militants from both sides had been looking for a way to extend and redefine anti-war protests in a way that drew attention to what they identified as the root causes of militarist bloodshed – a global system of capitalist exploitation which generated war and in which periods of 'peace' were only, in the words of Poison Girls: 'an illusion. A short space between the bullets'.[10] The idea that protestors could swarm into the financial centre of the British capitalism and 'wreak havoc' with the smooth running of the economy of war and exploitation, if only for a day, struck a chord with activists from both these oppositional movements.

The London Greenpeace group became an important organisational conduit,[11] but as the campaign's publicity group were soon keen to emphasise: 'no one organisation is in charge of the action; it is a collection of all interested people who want a world without war or the threat of it'.[12]

In the early summer of 1983, the radical activist group circulated a discussion document exploring the idea of 'spreading our opposition into the towns as well'.[13] The paper made the case for generalising the existing oppositional momentum:

---

9    "Together We Can Stop 'the City,'" *Freedom*, 44:19, September 24, 1983, 6.

10   Poison Girls, *Total Exposure* tour flyer, November 1981.

11   George Berger, *The Story of Crass* (Oakland, CA: PM Press, 2009), 246.

12   Stop the City Publicity Group, "Together We Can Stop the City" [leaflet], 1983.

13   London Greenpeace, "Occupy 'the City'? This autumn?" [leaflet], 1983.

Already there's been protests in town – at bunkers, recruiting offices, town halls, courts, police stations, and recently at prisons too. For these to become effective, we need to develop actions similar in strength to those at the bases.

The document drew parallels between the proposal and the history of radical post-war protests, which had:

happened before in many places at different times: the Gdansk workers' council (Poland, 1980), Wall Street anti-nuclear blockade (New York, 1979), Cable Street and Lewisham anti-fascist takeovers of the streets (London, 1936 and 1977), the anti-bomb sit-downs of the early sixties, Derry occupied to stop repression (Ireland, 1970), etc. The situation now needs such actions, in even greater strength (London Greenpeace 1983).[14]

It was a wide ranging (and somewhat surprising) mix of historical comparisons; and, with the exception of the Lewisham and Committee of 100 (anti-nuclear) references, any claim that STC could hope to emulate the political significance of the name-checked events seemed entirely implausible. Although the list included actions which stood far outside the tradition of 'nonviolent civil disobedience', it was notable for omitting any reference to the wave of urban riots which had convulsed (and effectively brought to a halt) several British inner-cities, just two years earlier, in the summer of 1981. Neighbourhood or estate riots were clearly not seen as any kind of relevant model, practically or philosophically.

Absent, too, were any references to that experience of activist-led anti-capitalist actions in urban settings which were arguably far closer to the premise of Stop the City than most of the other entries in the list: the 1970s street confrontations which were initiated by militant autonomist groups in western Europe; the 'carnivalesque' happenings and cultural disruptions that were engineered by the King Mob group in London in the late 1960s; and the militant three-day 'Days

---

14   Ibid

of Rage' ruckus held in October 1969 on the streets of Chicago, in the US, organised by The Weathermen – then a current within the Students for a Democratic Society group.[15]

In effect, there was little or no attempt to theorise what the symbolism or metaphor Stop the City was intended to be, or to codify its exemplar status. The aspiration to fuse a defiant 'carnival' with a militant 'protest' was frequently referenced, as was the aim to break with the norms of the 'ordinary' demonstration format. But it remained unclear if STC's claim was that it was an unparalleled innovation or the extension of an existing radical historical method. This reluctance to engage with theory, and weak sense of radical political history, was not imported directly from anarcho-punk, but it did strongly reflect the impulses of that subculture's body politic.

As Stop the City's frame of reference began to take shape, interested parties were called to a planning meeting at the Tonbridge Club, Judd Street, London on 2 July. Infused with libertarian sentiments, and mindful of the imperative not to be prescriptive, the invite tentatively proposed 'an action in London, this Autumn, which – because of its nature – might appeal to others in our area and beyond'. The prospective target?

> an area with a concentration of people who make decisions about (and profits from) the warfare state – The City – where once people lived. Now it's crowded with banks, company headquarters, and places like the Stock Exchange.[16]

The document raised the possibility of occupying the area, or of holding a celebration of life in the City streets, and suggested that 29 September 1983, 'one of the four annual "days of reckoning"'

---

15    George Katsiaficas, *The Subversion of Politics: European Autonomous Social Movements and the Decolonization of Everyday Life* (Stirling: AK Press, 2006); Hari Kunzru, "The Mob Who Shouldn't Really Be Here," *Tate Etc.*, Issue 13 (Summer, 2008) available online: http://www.tate.org.uk/context-comment/articles/mob-who-shouldnt-really-be-here, accessed August 2 2014; Jeremy Varnon, *Bringing the War Home: The Weather Underground, The Red Army Faction and Revolutionary Violence in the Sixties and Seventies* (Berkeley: University of California Press, 2004).

16    Geoff Price, "Closing down the City," *Peace News*, June 24, 1983, 7.

might provide the ideal opportunity. It was to be, in the words of Conflict: 'an occupation to stop people at theirs'.[17] An announcement in *Freedom* anarchist newspaper declared that the event would be:

> a chance to show that the will of the people is stronger than the institutions of war and destruction. [...] Together we can reclaim the City, for ourselves. There will be a carnival on the streets, and a chance to show our opposition to the death machine.[18]

The timing was just right to excite anarchist punk activists. Enthused by the idea:

> it was through the anarcho-punk scene that a lot of the information circulated about Stop the City, and through which many people came together to organise themselves to get to London from all over the country.[19]

And as the initiative developed, the militants of anarcho-punk became the most populous of Stop the City's principal agents on the ground. Moreover it was 'the DIY communication networks which were established within the anarcho-punk scene that allowed for the demonstration's viral, decentralized organization'.[20] And in this analogue, pre-internet era, promotion and publicity within anarchist punk networks was 'basically a word of mouth thing'.[21]

## AMBITION, PUBLICITY AND PREPARATION

The Stop the City initiative thus became an audacious attempt to close down the financial nerve-centre of the City of London on the

17    Conflict, "Stop the City," *Increase the Pressure,* Mortarhate, 1984.

18    "Stop the City," *Freedom,* 44:17, August 27, 1983, 7.

19    A2, "Stop the City 1984," *History is Made at Night,* October 30, 2011, http://
      history-is-made-at-night.blogspot.co.uk/2011/10/stop-city-1984.html,      ac-
      cessed 2 August 2, 2014.

20    Richard Metzger, "The Original Occupy Wall Street: Stop the City, 1984," *dan-
      gerousminds.net,* October 16, 2011, http://dangerousminds.net/comments/the_
      original_occupy_wall_street_stop_the_city_1984, accessed August 2, 2014.

21    Metzger, "The Original Occupy Wall Street: Stop the City, 1984".

Leaflet produced by Nottingham Anarchist Group to promote Stop the City, parodying the reaction of the 'privileged classes'. 'It says here that thousands of degenerate hooligans [will] lay siege to the City of London despoiling it with their inane idea of justice. Whatever next?', 1983.

day when quarterly revenues were calculated (or as *Vague* more luridly described it, the day when: 'fat corrupt purveyors of this disgusting trade counted up their money and drooled over their profits'[22]) using a combination of a mass presence in the streets, and a whole array of loosely coordinated disruptive activities. This was in the era before the so-called 'big bang' of Information Technology had hit the City. At this time much financial information (held on paper ledgers, print outs and 'computer tape') was still moved around the streets by runners and couriers. Attempting to snarl up the streets, the protestors judged, could therefore tangibly frustrate business dealings.

Publicity and promotion for the first event appeared in the press of the radical peace and anarchist movements in the spring and early summer of 1983, at a time when other large set-piece direct action events (particularly those associated with the nonviolent direct action wing of the disarmament movement) were also in preparation, and when movements against different iniquities of Thatcherism (including the People's March for Jobs) were also mobilising. CND had held a huge march and rally in London the same year, which had attracted hundreds of thousands of supporters (and at which an anarchist 'black bloc' had gathered to rally, chant and disrupt the speeches of speakers from the party political establishment).

Some on the left feared that the pitch of STC was a dereliction of duty and a denial of responsibility on the organisers' part: drawing hyped-up militants to confrontations with the forces of law and order without plan or management methods in place, and then denying any culpability for the events that might follow. Such anxieties echoed the concerns of the City and the Metropolitan police forces who criticised organisers for refusing to negotiate on any aspect of the day's events.

The issue of political violence was a recurring one in discussions which preceded the first Stop the City. The editors of the radical pacifist magazine *Peace News* reported:

> Some people have expressed doubts about the action – it is called on the basis that 'it is intended to be peaceful, not involving violence to people' – but

---

22  Tom Vague, "Stop the City," *Vague*, 15, archived online at *vaguerants*: http://www.vaguerants.org.uk/?page_id=135, accessed March 23, 2014.

they felt that some of those involved were hostile to nonviolence.[23]

*Peace News* continued to urge pacifist involvement in the action (as a counter-weight to the influence of other forces), while the organisers reaffirmed their intention that the action would not involve violence (although damage to property was not foresworn; the involvement of non-pacifist activists welcomed; and no absolute commitment to the *principles of nonviolence* [as distinct from a tactical agreement not to commit violent acts] was forthcoming).[24] Some peace activists, unconvinced by the organisers' reassurances, made clear their public opposition to the action. Writing in *Peace News*, one such critic anticipated disaster, condemning the 'dangerous experiment', and insisting that the planners' preparations for:

> an action in a dense, congested urban area, full of politically sensitive buildings, seemed woefully inadequate. A 'carnival' is planned: as far as I can see only negative and indiscriminate disruption can be guaranteed. Such disruption will terrorise innocents (tourists, shop assistants, residents, for example), interfere with essential services (fire, ambulance) and be unable to demonstrate the truth of London Greenpeace's analysis of the link between capitalism and war.[25]

Of acute concern to many was that 'an action resulting in violence [...] will be a gift for the media less than a month before CND's major demo on October 22'.[26]

The traditional anarchist movement did provide support and encouragement for the action (even though the catalyst for it did not come from within its ranks), with the 121 anarchist bookshop in Railton Road, Brixton providing logistical support with accommodation

---

23  "Stop the City?" *Peace News*, July 22, 1983, 18.

24  See, for example, the defence of the commitment to non-violence by one of the 1983 STC organisers. Dave Pitt, "Stop the City 2," [letter] *Peace News*, August 5, 1983, 20.

25  David Cormack, "Stop the City," [letter] *Peace News*, August 5, 1983, 20.

26  Ibid

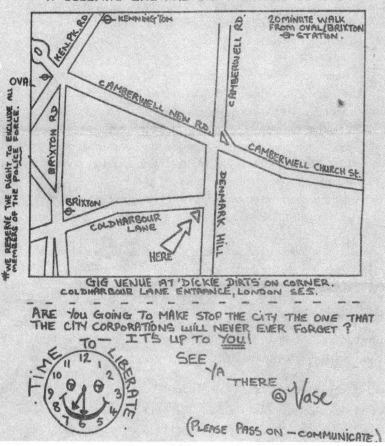

Leaflet promoting the second Stop the City demonstration – called on 29 March 1984.

(with its efforts south of the river Thames mirrored by crash spaces in Tollington Place, Islington to the north).[27] Organisation remained ad-hoc and informal, with logistical responsibilities shared out between working groups at open planning and co-ordination meetings.[28]

## THE FIRST STOP THE CITY

By late August 1983, plans had been finalised: between 6am and 6pm on 29 September, decentralised, autonomous actions protesting against war, militarism and oppression would be linked by a continu-ous 'carnival' which would:

> peacefully reclaim the streets to show that commu-nity and creativity can replace the commercialism and death-dealing of the area.[29]

Assembly points on the steps of St Paul's cathedral, at Finsbury Square and at Tower Hill were to provide contact, logistical support, and jumping off points, but responsibility for the specifics of all pro-tests would be in the hands of those turning up. There would be no central decision-making or co-ordinating body, but consultative 'on-the-spot evaluation meetings' would assess the next steps every three hours throughout the day. Those unable to attend would be encour-aged to join in the telephone blockade, which was intended to over-load company switchboards, and lock-up telephone lines into and out of the City.[30] As they passed responsibility over to the participants, the

27  "Stop the City," *Peace News*, September 16, 1983, 9.

28  See, for example, the report of the July 2 STC planning meeting; "Stop the City!" *Freedom*, 44:14, July 16, 1983, 1. Working groups were established around the themes of 'press; publicity; legal; contacting 'city' workers; research; children's area; carnival; [*and*] co-ordination on the day'; "Stop the City," *Freedom*, 44:18, September 10, 1983, 7.

29  "Stop the City," *Peace News*, September 16, 1983.

30  To facilitate this, lists of the phone numbers of 'some of the institutions involved in "objectionable" practices' were printed off and circulated ahead of the pro-test. This practice grew with each successive event. The 'Great Phone Blockade 1984' leaflet lists the address and telephone details of dozens companies un-der headings including 'Animal Exploiters', 'Meat/Murder', 'Arms Traders', and 'Merchants Banks', but acknowledges that there 'are too many disgusting

organisers affirmed that, if the police attempted to ban the demonstration, 'it will go ahead as planned anyway'.[31] Large scale arrests were considered likely (albeit many of them were expected to be for offences such as obstruction and minor criminal damage), and legal briefings were circulated (backed up by a volunteer legal support telephone service on the day). As well as outlining the rights of arrestees, some documents urged total non-co-operation with the police once in custody; the aim being 'to use up as much police time as possible' and to cost the courts 'time, money and effort, discouraging future mass arrests'.[32]

In the event, the demonstration was not banned outright, although the police carried out a series of early morning raids; including a major fishing-operation at the Islington Peace Centre, where many demonstrators had bedded down.[33] At the centre, there had been a rising sense of anticipation as 'loads of people started arriving from all over the day before.' At a planning meeting prior to the raid 'the mood was [*one of*] excitement as ideas of taking over buildings, burning flags, sit-downs, etc., buzzed about'.[34]

From early the next morning, several thousand demonstrators gathered at the Mansion House and at sites across the financial hubs of the City. Direct action events, spontaneous and prearranged, which were carried out by individuals, crowds, and tight-knit affinity groups, took place right across the densely packed streets of the City. Crowds seethed and surged throughout the area, roaming across streets to blockade traffic (amidst whoops, cries, shouts and songs), before regrouping at the Mansion House and then racing off in a fresh direction. Crass's Penny Rimbaud recalled:

> We soon developed the enjoyable tactic of forming large groups of between one and two hundred people who would suddenly break away from the main gathering and rush into the narrow streets shouting slogans

institutions in the City to list them all here.' "The Great Phone Blockade 1984," [leaflet] March, 1984.

31　"Stop the City," *Peace News*, September 16, 1983.

32　"Non-co-operation with the Police," [leaflet] 1983.

33　"Earwiggings," *Peace News*, October 14, 1983, 24.

34　Skinz, "Stop the City," *Death on a Summer's Day*, 2, 1983.

Protestors link hands around the war memorial in the heart of London's financial centre, during the first Stop the City demonstration in September 1983.

Photo © camera_obscura [busy]

and generally causing as much confusion as possible. [...] Meanwhile city workers peered from behind the smoked-glass windows of their offices, confused, bemused and bewildered.[35]

*Peace News* reported that the actions, 'cramming parts of the City with the sorts of people not usually encountered there', were, 'unstructured and free flowing'.[36] Facing an event 'without leaders', and without an agreed structure, police officers from the Metropolitan and City forces were at a loss as to how to police the demonstration. Of particular concern to the senior officers was the decentralised nature of the demonstration, and the absence of single focus or linear destination (such as a rally point). Occupations, breakouts, 'die-ins', blockades and invasions of financial buildings occurred, without notice or warning, at venues and locations across the City. An article in *Catalyst* fanzine sought to capture the innovative nature of the demonstration:

> Humour was a tactic the police didn't expect either. A dozen of us formed a moving, dancing, musical blockade that ran and skipped down streets, singing 'I'm only doing my job' at the top of our voices. We found a police van waiting at traffic lights. We circled it – dancing, laughing.[37]

---

35  Penny Rimbaud, "Stop the City!" *Punk Lives*, 10, 1983.

36  "News," *Peace News*, October 14, 1983, 3.

37  "Stop the City," *Catalyst*, 6, January, 1984.

Some demonstrators displayed strong Ghandian, hippy sensibilities in relation to the City authorities and their police defenders. 'Chris' (whose leaflet included his home address) addressed the police directly:

> If you joined the police force to serve the community, not the corporations, then help the people to find their stolen lives – and look for yours too. Let us dance and sing in the street. Join us.[38]

If it was clear that these demonstrators were unlike the usual marchers of the left, it was just as clear that they were unlike the usual cooperative peace demonstrators; more militant, less predictable, and distinctively less compliant. If the police response was marked by uncertainty (and very low levels of specific intelligence on the demonstrators' plans) then, at this first gathering, the demonstrators had no clear, agreed sense of what the actions of the event might cumulatively deliver; how the crowd might deal with the police's attempt to contain the demonstration; and what the key messages and symbolism of Stop the City might be. During the course of the event, the temperature of the demonstration rose and the sense of confrontation and resolute defiance on the participants' part intensified.

Much press attention focused on the appearance, behaviour and cultural practices of the punk and activist participants. *Peace News* observed, in some frustration that, 'it was almost laughable, the absurdity of these gents working for god knows what loathsome, harmful enterprise, getting upset about the "so-called ecologically minded people" leaving beer cans around', but remained worried about the movement's apparent lack of concern with the presentation of its self-image.[39] *Death on a Summer's Day* fanzine suggested:

> It seemed that everybody concerned with the anarchist 'movement' had made the effort to get there: groups like Crass, Flux, The Subhumans, The Mob, Faction, Chaos UK (who are not a 'chaos' band), The Alternative and numerous others.[40]

---

38  'Chris,' "Dear Policeperson," [leaflet] n.d., but September 27, 1983.
39  "Stop the City," [editorial] *Peace News*, October 14, 1983, 3.
40  Skinz, "Stop the City."

As the day wore on significant numbers of demonstrators were arrested by the police, often on charges of obstruction (both of the highway and of police officers), in some instances for acts of criminal damage, and in a smaller number of cases for assault. During the latter stages of the demonstration, the focus moved to the magistrates' court where those arrested were being fast-tracked from bail or remand – a 'suicide mission,' Rimbaud suggested, 'but one that we felt was important… [to] let compatriots who were being held inside know that the day had been a success'.[41] A large solidarity gathering assembled outside the courtroom to greet each defendant that was bailed (and to taunt the police lines which were protecting the court).

Rimbaud chose the unexpected outlet of the glossy, commercially-produced *Punk Lives* magazine to celebrate the achievements of the first event and to urge the wider involvement of punks (of all types and hues) in future demonstrations. He reported excitedly:

> Royal Exchange messengers had been prevented from operating; British Telecom workers had refused to work in the City; restaurants and cafes had been stink-bombed; fur-shops had been attacked; people had spent the day jamming telephone lines to banks and offices; there had been lie-ins and sit-downs, street theatre and music and innumerable acts of individual subversion from lock gluing to flying anarchist banners from the various statues that decorate the City.[42]

In the aftermath of the demonstration, participant perspectives on the event were generally extremely positive, and widely reported in the radical, anarchist and libertarian press. A correspondent to *Freedom* declared that 'the day surpassed everyone's expectations', adding:

> We had succeeded in creating a well organised event without any 'leaders' or central organisation. Also an effective public action against war in a very sensitive area, without any contact or negotiation with police,

41   Rimbaud, "Stop the City!"
42   Rimbaud, "Stop the City!"

and where people of many differing views and groups acted in solidarity and with respect.[43]

Key members of the London organising group who were keen to see the demonstration as the opening salvo on a new front declared it, 'a historic, though only partial, success,' which had to be recognised as integral to the advance of a campaign of, 'anti-nuclear, anti-militarist and anti-authoritarian actions'.[44]

Discussion did focus on the question of the number of arrests which were made during the demonstration, and the frustration of experiencing the police thwarting efforts at occupation and other actions (despite the widespread acknowledgement that fluidity and unpredictability all clearly played in the demonstrators' favour). Rimbaud took particular heart from the demonstrators' flexibility: 'Taken aback by the diversity of our tactics, the police were [...] unable to co-ordinate a response'.[45]

Chumbawamba judged that the event had been: 'happy and constructive and peaceful and interesting, for both demonstrators and "public"'.[46] The band Conflict, whose politics were far less shaped by pacifism and the experience of the counterculture than Crass's own, offered a more measured assessment of the day, enthused and frustrated in equal measure. On the *Increase the Pressure* album, the band suggested:

> The carnival was enjoyed, but the City was not stopped
> They worked well under siege; even though many
>     visited the carnival out of curiosity
> Their dull day was brightened, but it left no mark
> The next day most walls had been scrubbed of their
>     graffiti messages
> But the fact remains – power has been tested.[47]

---

43  "Stop the City," *Freedom*, 44:20, October 8, 1983, 3.

44  'Dave, Clare, Steve and Dave,' "A Time to Act," *Freedom*, 44:21, October 22, 1983, 3.

45  Rimbaud, *Shibboleth*, 246.

46  Chumbawamba, "We've Been Asking For Far Too Long," [leaflet] 1984.

47  Conflict, "Stop the City."

What remained less certain was whether the initiative could develop sufficient momentum to pull in greater numbers in future. The dire predictions of calamity, which were raised by some peace movement critics had proved to be without foundation; but there will still concerns about the future direction of the event. That supportive-but-critical perspective was writ large in the editorial position of *Peace News*, which praised the innovative and radical qualities of the actions, whilst sharply criticising STC's hostility to formal organisation, press liaison, and the reluctance to agree tactical ground-rules – all of which, the paper suggested, left atomised and unsupported demonstrators vulnerable to police violence and provocation, and opened the door to uncontrolled escalation.[48]

What appeared to have little negative impact either on future participation or the assessment of the success of the day itself was the large number of people who were arrested. There are a number of related reasons why the impact appeared to be muted. For less serious offences, such as obstruction of the highway, or minor criminal damage, there was no automatic translation from arrest through charge to court-case. Most arrestees could expect to be released without charge later (albeit much later, in many cases) the same day. Many radical activists, with experience of demonstrations at nuclear bases or during hunt-sabbing, were familiar (sometimes extensively so) with the inside of a police van; and for many the potential for arrest was a known and acceptable risk of participation. In anticipation, the STC Legal Group fixed the date for a defendants' meeting prior to the action.[49]

Amongst radical peace activists there was also some support for a strategy of civil disobedience which aimed to 'fill the gaols' with protestors arrested for principled political actions. Influenced by Ghandian thinking the idea, previously advocated by the Committee of 100 in the 1960s, remained contentious; yet the idea of *seeking*

---

48 "Stop the City" [editorial], *Peace News*. *PN*'s criticisms of the apparent lack of legal support offered to demonstrators was misplaced; as both legal back-up on the day and subsequent support and solidarity campaigns were provided. In the next issue, *PN* suggested that the paper had published 'what was perhaps an over-critical report of the action, based on a limited number of eye-witness accounts.' "Stop the City," *Peace News*, October 28, 1983, 5.

49 'Martin,' "Re-appraising Stop the City," [letter] *Peace News*, October 28, 1983, 17.

*arrest* still had some currency.[50] Some activists saw court cases and solidarity campaigns as a political extension of the original action, while many low-level offences only carried the likely cost of a small fine or a suspended sentence. These factors combined to reduce the intimidating effect which was posed by the spectre of arrest. That sense of confidence was reflected in the fact that many police stations which were packed with arrested demonstrators became sites of active protest, with cells being flooded or graffitied and processing being slowed to a crawl by non-co-operation. The danger posed by more serious charges of assault, major criminal damage, or theft (the expropriation of companies' property) were recognised, but overall the sense that the risks were acceptable reduced the deterrent impact. This sober cost-benefit calculation, it should be acknowledged, ran in parallel with a reckless lack of calculation on the part of many young activists who were caught up in the febrile atmosphere of the day, who 'went for it' regardless. For those amongst the 200 arrestees facing charges, most court dates were set for November 1983, with the major trial dates of 4 and 11 November 1983 immediately designated as 'Action Against Banks' days of solidarity actions, with pickets of the Guildhall Court arranged to coincide with the defendants' appearances.

What pulled in greater numbers for the second demonstrations was the percolation, through the fanzine reports, correspondence, word-of-mouth, and active promotion of the initiative by bands, allied to the efforts of the radical and anarchist press. Self-assessments of the effectiveness of the first STC within anarcho-punk remained extremely positive. In the view of Subhumans's lead singer Dick Lucas, that sense of political momentum 'gave people a lot of fresh motivation, I think'.[51]

A follow-up meeting in London of around 50 in London in October 1983, noted that (against the expectations of numerous critics) the demonstration had been a success, and took both *Peace News* and CND to task for their alleged efforts at the 'suppression of the idea' of STC.[52] Such trenchant criticism of national peace organisations view of STC gained traction. Worthing CND Chair Ian Svennevig (an enthusiastic STC participant) claimed that the 'insidious lies that

---

50   'Ali,' "Should we Fill the Gaols?" *Peace News*, March 16, 1984, 16.

51   Quoted in "Subhumans Interview," *Crisispoint*, 1983.

52   "Stop the City," *Peace News*, October 28, 1983, 5.

were being spread throughout the peace movement' ahead of the demonstration led many CND members to 'disgracefully ignore the call for help'.[53] It was an atypically strong reaction from a local CND officer, but it reflected a wider unease; allied to a growing sense that the British disarmament movement remained politically timid and over-cautious in the face of an impending nuclear catastrophe.

## THE SECOND AND THIRD STOP THE CITY

As news of the excitement of the first STC spread, larger numbers were drawn to the idea. A planning meeting in London in early January 1984 drew up to 100 people.[54] It was quickly agreed to plan for a larger, follow-up Stop the City, to be held on the next 'profit calculation' day: March 29 1984. This second Stop the City event would have the largest impact and attract the greatest level of interest in the series. Activists who were enthused by the idea were keen to extend and generalise the experience around the country. On the evening of 21 March 1984, demonstrators in Bristol daubed and super glued bank premises across the city; rallying the following morning outside the local police station (in solidarity with arrested comrades). At the same time, a roving group of demonstrators occupied banks, army recruitment offices, and the offices of the city council in Glasgow.[55]

This second event offered a fuller programme of opt-in events throughout the day, giving the demonstration slightly more structure than previously. Picketing was scheduled to begin at 8am; followed by simultaneous 'women's actions' (including the liberation of tampons from a major branch of Boots), animal rights protests in the fur trade area, and 'alternative energy' actions outside the headquarters of the Central Electricity Generating Board (CEGB) an hour later. At noon, symbolic 'die-ins' were timetabled at different sites which were associated with militarism and war, with rally times set for the Royal Exchange and Bank of England in the afternoon. The day was scheduled to wrap-up at 6pm with pickets at any police stations holding demonstrators.[56]

The organisational framework around Stop the City was continuing to evolve. In addition to the outline timetable of events, the

53   Ian Svennevig, "CND and STC," [letter] *Peace News*, October 28, 1983, 17.

54   "Spring in the City," *Peace News*, February 3, 1984, 5.

55   "Stop the Cities," *Peace News*, April 13, 1984, 3.

56   "Stopping the City," *Peace News*, March 16, 1984, 17.

Leaflet listing the regional contacts (and the key political themes) of the second Stop the City demonstration, 1984.

pre-demonstration briefing included details of legal support services, details of crèche and first-aid support, the post-STC defendants' meeting and pre-arranged benefit gigs to raise defence campaign funds.[57]

Writers for *Vague* reported, with evident pleasure, that the 'pinstripe ranks were once again infiltrated by spiky tops and soon black flags were being raised outside the Royal Exchange'.[58] From the other side of the fence, *The Times* noted the assembly of 'a combination of punks, anarchists, nuclear disarmers, and people demanding the liberation of gays, women or animals'; a gathering of 'people in multi-coloured hairstyles and all sorts of dress' who 'cavorted round the City'.[59] The paper acknowledged that, in terms of scale and reach, the event was 'vastly more impressive' than the first event. Many participants shared that sense of growing self-belief (albeit from a very different perspective to that of *The Times*):

> At first it looked like nobody was going to show up. Then it went from almost no one there, to hundreds and hundreds of people streaming into the area within a matter of just minutes. [...] It was an absolutely magical moment to partake in as people seemed to 'materialize' in the light London rain that morning.[60]

This second Stop the City is the most extensively documented of the series, in large part due to the reportage documentary of the event which was filmed by three members of Crass: Mick Duffield (camera), Joy de Vivre (sound) and Andy Palmer (interviewer). A rough-cut edit of the film, assembled by Duffield, was released for screening within the radical milieu later in 1984, and was widely shown at anarchist and other events in the years that immediately followed. This initial cut, filmmaker Duffield explained, had 'been released early in the hope that it will inspire people for the next Stop the City' that was arranged for the Autumn.[61] The raw edit captures much of the

---

57   "Come in Your Thousands: Stop the City," *Peace News*, September 21, 1984, 21.

58   Vague, "Stop the City."

59   Rupert Morris, "383 held in City protest," *The Times*, March 30, 1984, 1; 28.

60   Metzger, "The Original Occupy Wall Street."

61   Crass, *Stop the City. London. March 29th 1984*, [booklet] (London: Crass, 1984). The booklet accompanying the video indicated that: 'Copies of the final

rough-and-tumble, excitement, volatility, anger, and passion of the demonstration, and also reveals the huge breadth of motivations and expectations of participants (not all of whom are anarchist punks, or indeed punks of any hue).

While images in the press coverage of the first Stop the City focused on the appearance of the 'fancy-dress mob',[62] the defining media image of the second demonstration was Ken Towner's photo of a young policewoman (recklessly and pointlessly) throwing a spewing smoke canister back across a busy street crammed with vehicles, commuters and protestors; an act of unauthorised stupidity variously described in the press as 'brave', 'courageous' and 'determined'.[63] In fact, throughout the day, the police again struggled to contain the protestors' ire and ingenuity.

> Rather than get caught up in ritual set piece confrontations with the police, there was endless movement with groups heading off in all directions and no direction, blocking traffic and forcing the police to spread themselves thinly. There was a tangible sense of power – it was the first time I had seen people de-arrested.[64]

Even so, the arrest toll remained high. With around 550 police officers deployed (including plain clothes officers and undercover *agent provocateurs*), more than 400 demonstrators were arrested.[65] The context this time was also different. This Stop the City took place on the same day that a far larger labour movement protest,

---

film, which will be radically different, will be available towards the end of the year'; but no completed edit was forthcoming.

62    Neil Darbyshire and Peter Dobbie, "Peace, Punks and a Little City Anarchy," *The Standard*, September 29, 1983, 3.

63    The image was used in: Standard Reporter. "The Strong Arm of the Law," *The Standard*, March 29, 1984, 1; "Take that! Police Girl Hurls Back a Demo Smoke Bomb," *The Sun*, March 30, 1984, 7; Ian Black and Don Cooligan. "The Bobby Strikes Back!" *Daily Express*, March 30, 1984, 2-3; Robert Norris. "383 held in City Protest," *The Times*, March 30, 1984, 1; 28, and [untitled photo story], *The Guardian*, March 30, 1984, 1.

64    A2, "Stop the City 1984."

65    "Stop the Cities," *Peace News*, April 13, 1984, 3.

called by a number of trade unions in protest at the Thatcher government's attacks on local government, marched through central London (its route took it from Malet Street, WC1 to Jubilee Gardens, Southbank). As industrial conflicts with the Conservative administration intensified, the start of the national Miners' Strike of 1984-85 was only weeks away. Yet despite the geographical and temporal proximities, the extent of cross-over and connection between the militants of Stop the City and other groups locked in battle with the government of the day was strictly limited. The isolation of STC activists highlighted not only the weaknesses in the culture's ability to broker alliances, but also (more damningly) its lack of interest in making the kind of wider common cause that might extend the reach and range of the protestors' combined leverage.

There was greater militancy, a reduced identification with pacifism, and a greater sense of combativity and confrontation in evidence than before. Demonstrator Phil 'Hedgehog' Tonge observed that the previous year's sense of 'subversive glee' had been replaced by a 'brooding, threatening atmosphere'.[66] The tone of Crass's own exhortations had also changed, and with it the political language. One of the band's flyers spoke in strongly provocative terms about the City's occupants:

> Why should these rich scum be allowed to hold the world in bondage? As they suck on their fat cigars, we – the ordinary people of the world – are expected to beg for a living. [...] Stop the City... gives us the chance to let the wealthy scum know we're not going to let them get away with it.[67]

This was hardly the kind of rhetoric expected of 'peace punks'. Yet amidst the growing seriousness of STC, whimsy and humour remained in evidence (although little of it originated directly from within the ranks of anarcho-punk). A banner hung at the main assembly point which displayed anarchist Emma Goldman's celebrated insistence that 'If I can't dance to it, it's not my revolution'; a couple in fancy dress declared themselves to be 'Royals against the bomb';

---

66   Phil 'Hedgehog' Tonge, quoted in: Linda Peirson, "Stop the City Considered," *Peace News*, April 27, 1984, 10-11.

67   Crass. "Stop the City – London, March 29," [leaflet] 1984.

another activist in a simple bird costume sported a T-Shirt with the slogan 'pigeons against the pecking order'.[68]

Criticism of the initiative continued. At *Peace News*, co-editor Linda Peirson described her frustration with the lack of organisation, weak strategic and tactical clarity and the predominant atmosphere of 'chaos, confusion and confrontation'.[69] But while Peirson looked forward to improved 'effective and fun' STCs in the future, Dr Tony Weaver urged those 'whose concern is to reduce violence to have nothing more to do with this of protest', which delivered action, 'indistinguishable from hooligans on the rampage'.[70] Other militant pacifist demonstrators were struggling to reconcile the tensions raised through the demonstration's heightening polarity:

> There are so many fine distinctions in active pacifism; we have to find in work in the area between the contradictions: we must neither place ourselves as passive willing punch-bags under the boots of the frustrated policeman, nor must we 'confront' the guardians of the state simply for the *confrontation* itself, and then accept anything short of a near-riot as nonviolent.[71]

Others felt that the scruffy, punky tone of the demonstration was unfortunate: 'We need to express ourselves more tactfully, to use what is construed as good, responsible, and worthy to express our affirmation of peace, growth, and life. Consequently, I feel we should "clean up our act", so to speak,' suggested one demonstrator.[72] Others reaffirmed the righteousness of confrontational pacifism: 'Smashed windows belonging to banks which finance death is hardly anti-pacifist. [...] Pacifists want a better world through peaceful means. But the governments don't always play cricket, my dear chap, so sometimes you have to break the rules'.[73] This divergence in approach was

---

68    "STC – London," *Peace News*, April 13, 1984, 7.

69    Peirson, "Stop the City Considered."

70    Dr Tony Weaver, quoted in: Peirson, "Stop the City Considered."

71    Rich Cross, "Pacifism is Not 'Nice'," *Peace News*, May 11, 1984, 13.

72    John Kendall. "Clean-cut anarchy" [letter], *Peace News*, May 25, 1984, 9.

73    R Scanlon, "Reassess Your Attitudes!" [letter], *Peace News*, May 25, 1984, 9.

becoming more pronounced as the momentum and direction of the wider anarcho-punk movement itself shifted.

On 14-15 April, a follow-up weekend conference drew 60-70 participants to discuss the outcome of the event, arrange solidarity and support work, and to agree the outline for an autumn Stop the City, to be held on 27 September 1984. At the second event, there was growing evidence that the police were now adapting to what had previously been a novel experience. Despite the sense the numbers were growing and the temper of the demonstration was itself becoming more intense, it was just as clear that the police and authorities were learning more effective methods of containment, and were themselves becoming more fluid and flexible in their response. The balance of initiative was now shifting. The police had become adept in identifying the punks, peaceniks, and punk-identified militants liable to be the most 'troublesome', and the authorities seemed increasingly able to pre-empt these unruly agents' ability to act.

With a feeling that the net was closing around the protestors, some advocated a pro-active response. As a result a follow-up Stop the City event was organised by militants in London on 31 May 1984, taking advantage of short-notice and surprise, in an attempt to circumvent police efforts to contain the demonstration. This was to be a 'totally self-organised protest' without co-ordination meetings.[74] Flux of Pink Indians explained in their giveaway *Taking a Liberty* booklet:

> This time it is expected to be a 'low-key' event. No advertising has been planned and it is hoped that world of mouth will draw sufficient small active groups to cause havoc – and hopefully, because the action is less central[*ised*], the police won't be able to control it.[75]

The 'secrecy' of the event was immediately compromised, and it also proved difficult (in an analogue age) to publicise the demonstration. As a consequence, the numbers which were mobilised on the day were low and the police were able to prepare and deploy a sufficiently sizeable response.[76] The authorities' approach was a pre-cursor

---

74  "Stop the City," *Freedom*, 45:5, May, 1984, 4-5.

75  Flux of Pink Indians, *Taking a Liberty* [booklet], 1984.

76  Glimpses of the demonstration can be seen in footage shot by a Thames TV news

of the strategy which they would implement, more firmly still, that September. London Greenpeace reported that although several hundred people turned out, many of whom 'showed great courage in continuing to leaflet and protest', most 'were unable to do anything effective due to swamp policing'.[77] A Stop the City 'planning gathering' in London on 21 July acknowledged that the event had not lived up to the more optimistic expectations, and that clear lesson was that 'widespread publicity, preparation and co-ordination will be needed for September, as in March'.[78]

## THE FOURTH STOP THE CITY

The fourth Stop the City was a turning point event, and one which confirmed that the police's efforts at containment had reached an entirely new level of effectiveness. Anarcho-punk benefit gigs, which had the goal of raising money for the inevitable Stop the City 'Bust Fund', were held at Dickie Dirts on Coldharbour Lane, London the evening before and the evening after the demonstration. Their pre-emptive action, including the arrest and detainment of all identifiable demonstrators, roving patrols, and the fencing off of the Mansion House assembly point, effectively meant that the demonstration was scuppered; and in fact never properly got started at all.

The possibility of a police lockdown had been anticipated by some activists within the movement; who proposed a pro-active clandestine response. Writing in *Peace News* author 'B Sneaky', urged protestors to avoid detection and arrest by going in disguise:

> Go in a decent suit or dress and mingle with the businessmen, as commuters, as a tourist who wants to see St Paul's and got lost, as a press reporter, as a plain clothes policeman, whatever makes sense.[79]

film crew. Thames TV, "Demo – Stop the City – Thames News," http://youtu.be/kjQ6sFCssmA, accessed April 3, 2014; and Thames TV, "Protest – Stop the City – Thames News," http://youtu.be/J_2Li5-sKIM, accessed April 3, 2014.

77  London Greenpeace, "Let's Try to Reclaim the City, Sept 27 (Thurs)," [leaflet] 1984.

78  "A Brief Report on the Stop the City Planning Gathering, London 21st July," 1984.

79  B Sneaky, "Stop the City – Time to Be Sneaky," *Peace News*, September 7,

The article cautioned against 'people turning up with no plans, no actions, and very little forethought and parking their bums on the steps of the Corn Exchange.' At Dial House, Crass's Pete Wright produced an anonymous 'press pack' (including extracts from the Sneaky article, alongside leaflets describing how to build a police radio jammer), which *The Standard* used as the source for the front page preview it ran on the eve of the demonstration, warning that: 'City faces demo chaos'.[80]

Although the *Standard* piece quoted Sneaky's disguise proposal (giving it far greater prominence than it would otherwise have had), the reality was that few radical peace movement activists (and even fewer punks) felt able or willing to considering change their appearance, even temporarily, in this way.

The only demonstrators able to escape the attention of the authorities were those who had taken to heart the encouragement to conceal their identity. Those demonstrators were small in number and immediately came to the attention of the police when they sought entry to buildings, unfurled banners or began to protest. There were exceptions (the suits worn by members of Flux of Pink Indians, for example, were good enough to grant the band safe passage through police cordons), but most participants arriving in the City wore their normal attire, and were immediately identifiable.

> The steps of St Paul's were barricaded off and were patrolled by police on horses and the steps of the Royal Exchange (the main meeting point last time) were similarly sealed off. The police were stopping and searching everyone not dressed the part [*and*] immediately broke up any group that got larger than about six.[81]

Many banks had boarded their windows, and hired security staff to vet visitors at the door. Some actions were successfully executed despite the lockdown, including a 'people's party' in a Russian bank, and the hanging of a 'People Not Profit' banner from a building rooftop.

---

1984, 10-11.

80   Peter Gruner, "City Faces Demo Chaos," *The Standard*, September 26, 1984, 1.

81   Rich Cross and Linda Peirson, "Stop the City: Covering Our Tracks," *Peace News*, October 5, 1984, 5.

*The Standard* reported that the only recorded damage in the City was 'graffiti on the walls of the Stock Exchange where earlier windows had been smashed'.[82] Such events were exceptions. For the first time, counter-demonstrators felt sufficiently confident to set up pitches around the City, with one small group handing out pro-business leaflets urging employees to 'Aggravate an Anarchist'.[83] Displaced demonstrators rallied on Oxford Street, for an impromptu anti-apartheid action against South African Airways; and in Trafalgar Square, where the water in the fountains was briefly dyed red, but these were fringe, peripheral actions to a main event which simply did not take place.[84] A rundown of the actions:

> listed more of what the police had done and what they had prevented us from doing than it did of what we had ourselves achieved. [...] One of the things so obviously missing from this Stop the City was the feeling of togetherness and mutual strength – that positive shared feeling [*that*] inspires you and empowers you to act. Unable to meet together, it was impossible to act together.[85]

By the end of the business day, more than 470 arrests had been made; with most demonstrators being released without charge later in the evening. Police strategy had been to smother and snuff out the demonstration, rather than focus on charging participants with offences. Protestors were simply denied the opportunity to mount an organised response.

A detailed log of all the actions that did take place concluded with the stark observation: 'it is clear that we need to bring together *a lot* more people if we are going to be able to challenge the System'.[86] The

---

82  Standard Reporter, "City Demo: 251 Held," *The Standard*, September 27, 1984, 1-2.

83  Ibid

84  Cross and Peirson, "Stop the City: Covering Our Tracks"; Rich Cross, "London's Burning," *Freedom*, September, 2013, 11.

85  Rich Cross, "We Have Every Right to be Angry," *Peace News*, October 19, 1984, 10-11.

86  "Stop the City, Finsbury Sq, Log of Events, September 27 1984," October, 1984.

fragmented and fractured nature of the action reinforced the argument of critics keen to make the case that the idea of Stop the City was 'hampered by it being a rag-bag of autonomous action thrown together on a certain date' and lacking 'some form of real central co-ordination'.[87] It did seem that the initiative had reached an impasse. Chumbawamba declared that the idea's utility had:

> gradually become outweighed by the inevitable "gag effect" of the mass arrests; it has become just another twice-yearly demonstration... a chance for the State's bully-boys to flex their muscles.[88]

Crass's Rimbaud also conceded that the game appeared to be up: 'Aware that we had been out-manoeuvred, no further Stop the City actions took place in London'.[89]

Discussions at follow-up meetings, reflected the sense of uncertainty about where the initiative might be taken next. A debriefing meeting in Leeds heard 'mixed feelings about the London protest – some people felt we should wait until we have more support, and then return to the City better prepared. It was also suggested that there could be co-ordinated local demonstrations around the country in March'.[90] There was evidence too of growing concern with the 'isolation' of Stop the City's militants, and the need to connect and make common cause with other in struggle, particularly Britain's miners in the context of the Great Strike.

### AFTERMATH

After the fourth London Stop the City event few organisers or participants could deny that the time had come for a strategic as well as a tactical rethink (even if they did not use terminology of that kind). One option, which was already being tested out, was to attempt to replicate and decentralise, by taking the original initiative and recreating it in other city centres, where the focus could be on the operation of retail capitalism and conspicuous consumption as well as that of the

---

87  Paul Rogers, "Stop the Demo?" [letter] *Peace News*, November 2, 1984, 16.
88  Chumbawamba, "A Call to Act," [leaflet] 1984.
89  Rimbaud, *Shibboleth*, 246.
90  "Stop the City Discussion," *Peace News*, October 19, 1984, 3.

financial services industry. Several, far smaller, Stop the City events were held in cities across the UK, the largest of which took place in Leeds on 9 August 1984 (Nagasaki Day), and involved members of Chumbawamba, Passion Killers, and numerous other anarcho-punk activists. Timed to coincide with a local CND memorial vigil, and the arrival in the city of the Greenham Common women's Walk for Peace, hundreds of activists took part in actions:

> ranging from symbolic (showers of Monopoly money falling on shoppers from a roof-top) to more direct action – the Plaza porn cinema had its doors chained up, coats in fur shops were sprayed, and a large statue of the Lloyds bank black horse was daubed with red paint. Thousands of leaflets and booklets were given away to passers-by to explain the actions; and a pirate radio station transmitted for most of the day on and near local commercial and BBC wavelengths.[91]

More than 100 demonstrators were arrested, most were charged with obstruction, breach of the peace or 'using insulting words and behaviour'. What was notable was that: 'Many people who had planned specific actions were able to carry them out because they went "under cover": they went in disguise and stayed away from the main meeting point. People who turned up unprepared and dressed in black had a very rough time of it, and often a fruitless day'.[92] A smaller Stop the City action was held in Birmingham on 11 October 1984, and a number of similar sporadic (and often sparsely attended) days of action were held, usually at the initiative of local punks, in other cities.

Between 1985 and 1988, new variants of decentralised, locally co-ordinated 'action day' were organised under the rubric 'Stop Business As Usual' (including spin-off initiatives such as the 'Smash South African Business Day' called for 30 September 1985). Rather than a single city location, this initiative attempted to rally simultaneous protests in cities across the country. In stretching the numbers of those who were involved still further, the action proved harder to sustain even than the one-day events which were held in single provincial cities. In Norwich,

91    "Reaching Out," *Peace News*, August 24, 1984, 3.
92    Sneaky, "Stop the City – Time to Be Sneaky".

for example, a short-lived surge through the high street, targeting banks and other financial companies, ended abruptly with the arrest (and later prosecution) of around 20 local punks. In any event, by this time, the attention of the disarmament movement had refocused on the issue of the deployment of Cruise and the escalation of anti-nuclear activity at the USAF bases at Greenham and at Molesworth, while the anarcho-punk movement (no longer the innovative, agenda-setting force within the ranks of British anarchism) had begun to retrench and contract.[93]

## LEGACIES

Stop the City could quite reasonably be held up as the quintessential anarcho-punk political event: imaginative, inspired, subversive, and norm breaking, but politically polarising. Its world-changing ambitions were uncompromising, its list of social iniquities lengthy (in pursuit of 'a dazzling range of opinions and ideas'),[94] its politics inchoate and sprawling, and its hostility to 'institutional organisation' pronounced. STC's politics were not mapped by anarcho-punk, but shared a common lack of concern with strategy, and a fierce sense of outsider autonomy, which militated against the forging of common cause with others in struggle whose politics were not so absolute. *Freedom* acknowledged how, even at the height of Stop the City's powers:

> it was difficult to involve those who went on strike
> the same day to defend public services and the GLC,
> and also striking miners.[95]

It was a shortcoming which the organisers themselves acknowledged. Ahead of the final STC, activists articulated the urgent need to broaden and deepen support for the action by:

> linking up with Greenham people, and also the
> mining communities. [...] We can also encourage

---

93  Rich Cross, "British Anarchism in the Era of Thatcherism," in Evan Smith and Matthew Worley (eds.), *Against the Grain: The British Far Left from 1956* (Manchester: Manchester University Press, 2014) 133-152.

94  "Stop the City," *Freedom*, 45:5, May, 1984.

95  Ibid

people active in the women's movement, ecology, international solidarity groups, the labour movement, ethnic groups and everyone struggling in various ways for a better life... It's vital we continue to broaden out all the time and not allow the media to succeed in caricaturing Stop the City as a marginal protest.[96]

It was an agenda that proved largely beyond the activists' ability to deliver. Numerically speaking, Stop the City's continuing 'marginality' could scarcely be doubted. Weeks after the first STC drew some 1,500 radical oppositionists to the financial heartland of the capital, estimates suggest that as many as 400,000 (generally moderate) anti-nuclear demonstrators gathered in Hyde Park for the Campaign for Nuclear Disarmament's largest rally to date.[97] Weeks before, some 4,000 nonviolent peace activists (representing the radical current within the disarmament movement) attempted to shutdown USAF Upper Heyford by human blockade. While STC showcased innovative methods of mobilisation of action (demonstrating, in embryonic form, some of the collective political potential of anarchist punk, and its wilful, passionate utopianism) it also revealed many of the limitations of punk activism.

All movements and subcultures experience differing levels of engagement; separating an activist core at the centre and a less committed periphery beyond. But for anarcho-punk, premised on the principles of individual and collective self-activity, it is possible to see the levels of engagement with Stop the City revealing not the *strength* of the conviction driving anarchist punk culture, but its *fragility* and shallowness. Given the numbers of bands and fanzines that were active, the turnout at gigs across the country, the volumes of record and tape sales, and the animated postal correspondence all taking place under the rubric of anarcho-punk in the early 1980s, should not the scale of Stop the City been that much larger? On *Yes Sir, I Will* Crass had derided the numerous inactive consumers of punk culture, insisting: 'Passive observers offer nothing but decay'.[98] But ultimately

96 "A Brief Report on the Stop the City Planning Gathering, London 21st July".
97 "What Comes Next?" *Peace News*, October 28, 1983, 3.
98 Crass, *Yes Sir, I Will*, Crass Records, 1983.

Flyer advertising a Stop Business as Usual demonstration, circa 1985.

if 'there is no authority but yourself',[99] then the decision *not* to participate in active resistance to the 'existing order of things' must be accepted as no less valid a personal choice.

Strong echoes of the Stop the City initiative came to be discerned in more recent libertarian political mobilisations – including the anti-globalisation protests which emerged in Seattle in the late 1990s, the Reclaim the Streets protests which later followed them, and in more muted and contradictory form, in the worldwide Occupy! phenomenon. Rimbaud insists that the events: 'inspired actions throughout the world that continue to this day'.[100] Yet it remains questionable how *conscious* that sense of historical continuity really is. STC's currency in the minds of present day activists appears faint. For one participant, Stop the City, 'was one of those mythical events that if you weren't there it's almost as if it never happened [...] and it simply disappeared into the mists of history'.[101] Stop the City's opaque legacy is testament to the short-term memory which so often afflicts contemporary anti-authoritarian cultural and political movements.

Thirty years ago, its punk protagonists were clear about the wider significance of the explosive but short-lived experiment:

> The machinery of oppression thrives on appearing
> invincible, unquestioned and eternal, and our protests
> have begun slowly to break this spell.[102]

They sensed the actions' inadequacy too; at least when compared to the scale of the tasks which the movement had set itself. In the words of Subhumans' *Rats*:

> We fought the city but no one cared
> They passed it off as just a game
> The city won't stop till attitudes change
> Rats in the cellars of the stock exchange [...]
> The papers played the whole thing down

---

99   Ibid

100  Rimbaud, *Shibboleth*, 246.

101  Metzger, "The Original Occupy Wall Street: Stop the City, 1984."

102  "People Against Profits – in the City of London," *Children of the Revolution*, 6, 1984.

Said there was nothing to worry about
The rats have all gone underground
But we'll be back again next time round.[103]

One of the key organisers, Dave Morris, remained insistent about the profound long term repercussions of Stop the City. For him, the demonstrations ensured that: 'the secrecy and supposed invulnerability of the City was punctured for all time'.[104]

---

103 Subhumans, *Rats*, Bluurg Records, 1984.

104 Quoted in David Kynaston, *The City of London, Volume 4: A Club No More, 1945-1999* (London: Pimlico, 2002), 718.

MATT GRIMES

# FROM PROTEST TO RESISTANCE

## BRITISH ANARCHO-PUNK ZINES (1980-1984) AS SITES OF RESISTANCE AND SYMBOLS OF DEFIANCE

**THIS CHAPTER FOCUSES** on the role that alternative publications played in the cultural, political, and ideological practices of the British anarcho-punk movement between 1980 and 1984. I explore the way these zines[1] disseminated the central ideas of anarcho-punk and the

---

1    In this chapter I use the term zine rather than 'fanzine'. Although it is recognised that the term zine is a shortened term of the term 'fanzine' or magazine, the prefix 'fan' could imply that one is a 'fan' of a particular form of music, art, or culture. Many punks don't necessarily perceive themselves to be fans of punk rock but rather members of a subculture, scene, or movement that for many is a lived experience (way of life). The term 'fan' is, for many punks, associated with pop music and the commodified, mainstream music industry and is often explicitly rejected. See Matt Worley, "'While the World was Dying, Did You Wonder Why?' Punk, Politics and British (fan) zines 1976-84." *History Workshop Journal* 79/1 (2015), 76-106

way that the editors mediated a shifting notion of anarcho-punk. In doing so I seek to move beyond the simpler notion that zines acted simply as channels of communication, but to the idea that discourses of resistance and defiance are constructed and reinforced through the embodiment and undertaking of ideological work of zine editors as 'organic intellectuals'[2] and thus represent cultural work. This raises some interesting questions about the role of zine editors/producers as key agents in articulating the perceived central tenets of a subcultural movement. Previous studies on zines have alluded to the role of editors but little emphasis has been placed on the way that these zine authors take on leadership roles.

As punk emerged in the 1970s zines soon became one of the central methods of communicating the developing ideologies, practices, and values within this new musical and subcultural movement as they have historically been regarded as an alternative to mainstream publishing and being independently representative of the 'underground'. Early protagonists of anarcho-punk, such as Crass, sought to reinforce the personal politic of being responsible for one's own authority and actions, and the political agenda of anarcho-punk came to embrace notions of anarchism, peace, libertarianism, animal rights, feminism, anti-capitalism and anti-globalization. The analysis explores how these discourses of political position were mediated and the sense of an anarcho-punk movement that they constructed.

Firstly, I interrogate some of the key studies of punk zines in order to try to contextualise their role and importance within punk music culture. Secondly, I consider the role of zine editors as contemporary examples of what Gramsci termed 'organic intellectuals'. I draw on the work of Gramsci (1929-35), Lipsitz (1990), and Abrams (1995) to explore how these editors, through their publications, presented themselves as organic intellectuals, and in doing so, forged a link between the members of the scene and its construction. Thirdly, I draw on examples of the visual and textual discourses from of a selection of British anarcho-punk zines and examine how discourses of counter

---

2    I derive this term from Antonio Gramsci as intellectual leaders who emerge from
     a group, although I take it in terms wider than those discussed by Gramsci him-
     self in Antonio Gramsci, *Selections From the Prison Notebooks of Antonio Gramsci*,
     trans., Geoffrey N. Smith and Quintin. Hoare (New York: International
     Publishers, 1971).

hegemony and community are constructed. Finally, drawing on the work of Thornton (1995) and Duncombe (1997), I investigate how these 'organic intellectuals' discursively constructed notions of authority and identity through the articulation of specific and at times oppositional ideological positions, and how this contributed to the construction of the musical, cultural, and political boundaries of the British anarcho-punk movement.

## ZINES ARE PUNK[3]

Within punk music culture, zines, along with the variant emerging music styles of punk rock, are generally credited with being one of the main means that this new emerging subculture constructed and represented its style and ethos. The developing DIY culture of punk was embodied in the production and distribution of zines, which were seen to provide an alternative to mainstream publishing and therefore more representative of punk's underground and independent subculture, which both produced and consumed them. It is widely recognised that the first UK produced punk zine was *Sniffin' Glue* produced by Mark Perry in 1976[4] which, given its full title *Sniffin' Glue and Other Rock 'n' Roll Habits*, it could be argued positioned itself as having an intentionally challenging contentious and antagonistic stance in its editorial, toward the hegemonic culture. The strong link between the emerging punk culture and the zines that followed *Sniffin' Glue* was apparent by the amount of British punk zines being produced with, as Laing suggests, as many as fifty in 1977-78.[5] It could be argued however that Laing underestimated the number of zines which were in circulation in that period. Matt Worley's insightful work on the contextualisation of the political content of British punk zines from the 1970s into the 1980s also presents us with a comprehensive historiography of the rapid development and production of punk zines during this period and into the 1980s.[6]

---

3    Declaration by the editor of US fanzine *Hippycore* as quoted in Paul Rutherford, Fanzine Culture (Oldham: Springhead Books, 1995), 3.

4    Dick Hebdige, *Subculture: The Meaning of Style* (London: Routledge, 1979), 111. Dave Laing, *One Chord Wonders: Power and Meaning in Punk Rock* (Milton Keynes: Open University Press, 1985), 15.

5    Laing. *One Chord Wonders*, 14.

6    Worley "While the world was dying, did you wonder why?" 76-106

As I have discussed elsewhere[7], the existing literature on zines tends to emphasise the way that zines served as a medium for communication and propagation. Indeed for O'Hara the ideas which define 'punk culture and philosophy': anarchy, gender politics, community, environmental philosophies, and the politics of DIY punk business and entrepreneurship are still propagated in the zine which, he suggests, is the primary form of communication amongst twenty-first century punks.[8] This notion of zines serving as vehicles for cultural and subcultural communication is shared by Teal Triggs in her analysis of the visual design of zines. She asserts this position when she states that "fanzines became vehicles of subcultural communication and played a fundamental role in the construction of punk identity,"[9] whilst simultaneously "establishing and reinforcing shared values, philosophy and opinions."[10]

However, Triggs's analysis echoes the approach of many analyses of punk zines in that they tend to focus on the way that punk was symbolised through the visual language of these publications. The use of cut-and-paste, roughly and almost intentionally poorly typed or hand written narrative that was interspersed with swear words and misspellings that combined a mixture of music and art with personal and political ideology[11]. For Hebdige this signified the immediacy of a publication that was produced in haste from whatever limited resources were at hand[12].

Arguably Hebdige's seemingly overly deterministic and fundamentally structuralist approach, together with the subcultural discipline from which it emerged, tends to place accent on the meanings which

7   Matt Grimes and Tim Wall, "Punk zines – 'Symbols of Defiance' From the Print to the Digital Age" in *Fight Back: Punk, Politics and Resistance*, ed. Matt Worley (Manchester: Manchester University Press, 2014), 287-303.

8   Craig O'Hara, *The Philosophy of Punk: More Than Noise* (Edinburgh: AK Press 1999), 62-69.

9   Teal Triggs, 'Scissors and Glue: Punk Fanzines and the Creation of a DIY aesthetic' *Journal of Design History* 19/1 (2006): 70.

10  Teal Triggs, "Generation Terrorists: Fanzines and Communication," in *Communicating Design: Essays in Visual Communication*, ed. T. Triggs (London: B.T. Batsford, 1995), 34.

11  see, for instance, Phil Stoneman, *Fanzines: Their Production, Culture and Future*, (University of Stirling: MPhil dissertation, 2001).

12  Hebdige, *Subculture*, 111.

are anchored within the style, rather than the discursive practices of punk. Whilst I recognise the importance of the repertoires of visual design, political philosophy, and textual meanings that zine editors encode in their work, I want to accentuate the discursive practices of the zine editors in my analytical approach to examining zines. Indeed, Barker points out that discursive theory can be especially advantageous in pinpointing the 'micro processes by which people make claims about themselves'[13]– it also leads us out of various arguments surrounding the discourses of popular music culture to focussing on how they are actually manifest in varying texts and practices.

Laing's broader reading of punk as discursive practice arguably offers a much wider framework for investigating punk zines, though has been less often used as a foundation for such analyses[14]. Therein Laing locates, what he suggests as the productive power of the DIY culture that punk utilised, in a longer history and broader set of DIY practices. Similarly George McKay, in his cultural history of British counterculture since the 1960s, suggests that punk and its zines owe much of their oppositional idealism and DIY practices to the 1970s hippy counterculture and underground independent press such as *Frendz*, *OZ*, and *International Times*. McKay's hypothesis suggests that there has been a historical and cultural progression and connection between youth cultures of resistance since the 1960s.[15] He cites Stewart Home who points out, "in retrospect, punk also appears as a very straightforward progression from the sixties, whereas at the time it was perceived as a break."[16] In many of the traditional popular music histories punk becomes assimilated into the mainstream of the popular music industry but the significance of the punk critique is sustained through its DIY practices and ideologies[17] and a more self-conscious politic through the anarcho-punk movement.

Anarcho-punk as a subgenre and scene has a pivotal place within punk politics and music culture and anarcho-punk zines operated at

---

13   Chris Barker, *The SAGE Dictionary of Cultural Studies.* (London: Sage, 2004), 55.

14   Laing, *One Chord Wonders:*

15   George McKay, introduction to *Senseless acts of Beauty: Cultures of Resistance Since the Sixties* by George McKay (London: Verso, 1996), i-ix.

16   McKay, *Senseless Acts of Beauty*, 5.

17   Michelle Liptrot, "Beyond the Lifespan of a Scab: The Longevity of DiY Punk in Britain" (PhD diss., University of Bolton, 2011).

the juncture of DIY music criticism and political activism and therefore provides a useful way to think through zines as sites of resistance and symbols of defiance. I suggest that these zines helped establish an evolving philosophy of the musical, cultural, and political ideologies that were incipient within the nascent British anarcho-punk scene. Many British anarcho-punk artists proclaimed themselves to be the true voice of punk, taking The Sex Pistols sloganeering of 'Anarchy in the UK' towards its logical progression/conclusion. These artists pursued a DIY music ethos, allied themselves to different strands of anarchist philosophy, more self-consciously political positions, and a commitment to different forms of direct action.[18] Within these zines I also suggest that idealised notions of politics, music, and community were being constructed; that these zines and their editorials, inspired by the lyrical content of punk music, ordered the way in which readers and contributors became more politically and ideologically informed.

It could be argued then, that the role of anarcho-punk zines was central to the dissemination and reinforcement of these political and ideological positions. However I would suggest that many previous investigations of zines have tended to ignore or downplay the importance of the editors/producers of the zines in propagating and promoting those ideologies and in offering alternatives to the popular media's representations of punk. This is a position I wish to explore in the following parts of this chapter.

## ZINE EDITORS AS 'ORGANIC INTELLECTUALS' AND 'CULTURAL AGENTS'

A useful way of investigating the role and practices of zine editors/ producers is through the Gramscian concept of the 'organic intellectual.' Antonio Gramsci, writer, Marxist politician and philosopher, argued

---

18  For authors who articulate or explore this idea see, for instance, Rich Cross, "The Hippies Now Wear Black: Crass and the Anarcho-Punk Movement, 1977–84." *Socialist History 26 (2004): 25-44;* Rich Cross "'There Is No Authority But Yourself'": The Individual and the Collective in British Anarcho-Punk'. *Music and Politics* 4/2 (2010): 1-20; O'Hara, *The Philosophy of Punk,* 92-3; Ian Glasper, *The Day the Country Died* (London: Cherry Red, 2006), 8 and 104-9; George McKay, *Senseless Acts of Beauty: Cultures of Resistance Since the Sixties* (London: Verso, 1996), 87; George Berger, *The Story of Crass.* (London: Omnibus Press, 2006), 109-11.

that every social class forms its own group of intellectuals whose role is to develop and maintain a model or pattern of ideological thoughts, that functions as a means of directing and giving purpose to that class. He further posited that what emerges from society are two types or groups of intellectuals. The first are 'traditional' intellectuals such as teachers, priests, politicians; people who are bound to the institutions of the hegemonic order and serve to legitimate that current system or order. Although at times they articulate the voice of dissent, by asking probing questions of the existing hegemony and its functions, they can never lead the revolutionary class, for them there is no power for revolutionary change. The second type is the 'organic intellectuals', those individuals whom naturally emerge from a social group, or whom that social group extemporaneously creates, in order to advance its own self-awareness and to ensure the interconnectivity and cohesive unity within that social group. The 'organic intellectual' must break with the traditional intellectuals of the current hegemonic society and, in doing so, must form his or her own hypotheses to fulfil his or her purpose in providing a revolutionary ideology to that movement. For Gramsci then the 'organic intellectuals' are those individuals who

> ...took a collective character within a working-class social formation in which the role of theory was organically linked to the ebb and flow of daily proletarian life.... where ideological functions and intellectual tasks were .....centered within the proletarian milieu (factories, community life, and culture). In this respect intellectuals would be organic to that milieu only if they were fully immersed in its culture and language. Intellectuals therefore carried out universal functions that situated social activity within local and specific class struggles and in the defence of class interests.[19]

Although Gramsci is mostly concerned with the notion of the 'organic intellectual' in relation to class struggle, labour, and capital, Gramsci's

---

19   Gustavo.E Fischman and Peter McLaren, 'Rethinking Critical Pedagogy and the Gramscian and Freirean Legacies: From Organic to Committed Intellectuals or Critical Pedagogy, Commitment, and Praxis'. *Cultural Studies ↔ Critical Methodologies* 5/4 (2005): 433

concept has been successfully applied, in broader terms, to popular music communities. In his work on collective memory and American popular culture, George Lipsitz likens Chicano rock musicians in Los Angeles to Gramsci's 'organic intellectuals.'[20] In doing so Lipsitz develops a model of analysis that draws on some of Gramsci's concepts to demonstrate how those Chicano rock musicians functioned as 'organic intellectuals'. He discuss how those musicians are involved in the generation and circulation of subversive and counter hegemonic ideas that reflect the needs of the community which they are part of.[21] Through that process, of generating and circulating those ideas, they present texts and images that are subversive of the existing power relations and attempts to challenge the ideological and cultural hegemony of that society. This is supported through the process of connecting other oppositional cultures to create what Gramsci refers to as a 'historical bloc'[22], a collection of groups that are in some way connected to, or united around, those counter-hegemonic or subversive images and texts.

Lipsitz's application of Gramsci's concept is further utilised by Nathan Abrams[23] in his insightful analysis of US hardcore rap, where Abrams identifies

> four salient features that characterize these organic intellectuals. That they are members of an aggrieved community; that they reflect the needs of that community; that they attempt to construct a counter-hegemony through the dissemination of subversive ideas; and that they strive to construct a historical bloc – a coalition of oppositional groups united around these subversive or counter hegemonic images[24]

Using Abrams's framework I want to draw on those features of the 'organic intellectual' and apply them to zine editors of a small

20    George Lipsitz, *Time Passages: Collective Memory and American Popular Culture.* (Minneapolis: University of Minnesota Press, 1990), 133-160.

21    Lipsitz, *Time Passages,* 152.

22    Ibid

23    Nathan D. Abrams, "Antonio's B-Boys: Rap, Rappers, and Gramsci's Intellectuals." *Popular Music and Society* 19/4 (1995), 1-19.

24    Abrams *Antonio's B-Boys,* 2.

selection of anarcho-punk zines from the early 1980s as a means to explore, through their editorials and visual content, their role as 'organic intellectuals' within the 1980s anarcho-punk movement. I seek to examine how the discourses of these zine editors construct and reinforce discourses of resistance and defiance through the embodiment and undertaking of ideological work. Therefore to deal with both the broader orders of discourse and the singular moments of representation I will use Norman Fairclough's approach to discourse.[25] So whilst Fairclough focuses on the discursive practices of the community in which texts are produced he furthermore suggests that attention should also be paid to the production practices and conventions of the producers of those texts, as being representational forms, which generate relationships and identities.

## DISCOURSES OF ZINE EDITORS AS 'ORGANIC INTELLECTUALS'

Other contributors to this book offer detailed discussion on the emergence and continuation of anarcho-punk both locally and globally. British anarcho-punk emerged as a DIY music culture and subcultural scene during the late 1970s in a period that witnessed political upheaval/dissent and the marginalisation and repression of many cultural and political groups in British society. Matt Worley states that "Punk, by late 1976, was seen to reflect a breakdown in the post-war 'consensus'; it was typically portrayed as a product of crises that in its music, rhetoric, attitude, and style embodied Britain's deteriorating economic and moral standing".[26] This was eclipsed in 1979 with the election of a Conservative government, under the leadership of Margaret Thatcher, whose "strict monetarist agenda required significant cuts in government spending and the withdrawal of state subsidies, which triggered a sharp rise in unemployment. The Thatcher administration also directed additional funding (as well as assigning additional powers) to the police and law and order agencies".[27]

In 1983, on the back of a military victory, against the Argentinians in the Falkland's war, Thatcher's Conservative government was

---

25   Norman Fairclough, *Media Discourse* (London: Arnold, 1995)

26   Matt Worley 'Shot By Both Sides: Punk, Politics and the End of 'Consensus' *Contemporary British History* 26/3 (2012), 1-22

27   Cross 'There Is No Authority But Yourself,' 1-2

re-elected on a draconian anti-union, pro-nuclear, and pro-state platform that sought to expand its power both domestically and internationally. Demonstrations against wage cuts, rising unemployment,
and numerous public and private sector strikes followed, riots took
place in inner city communities across the UK as "youth reacted
against police harassment, endemic racism, and worsening living conditions. The political atmosphere was one of overwhelming confrontation, polarization, and uncertainty".[28]

So to enable me to explore the Gramscian concept of the 'organic intellectual', through Lipsitz's and Abrams's frameworks I will use
selections of the editorial content from a number of examples of anarcho-punk zines. *Pigs for Slaughter* (1981-82), was produced and edited by Ian (Slaughter) Rawes and other contributors who were associated with the Anarchist Youth Federation and Autonomy Centre in
Wapping, London. Its content regularly advocated direct action and
revolutionary violence, which challenged the attitudes of the otherwise pacifist anarcho-punk scene at that time. *Intensive Care* (1980-
81) was also a London based zine which was produced and edited by
Kevin and Cram. *Toxic Graffitti* (Graffitti/Grafitty/Grafity/Graffity),
the spelling of the title changing with every issue, (1979-82) was one
of the more thought provoking zines to come out of London. It was
produced and edited by Mike Diboll who had previously produced
and edited *No Real Reason* zine which developed into *TG. Essentielles
Pour La Bonne* (1982), which also came out of London and *Cobalt
Hate* (1979-80) produced and edited by Timbo in Stevenage followed
a similar approach as TG in that they contained more politically focussed essays and articles.

Similarly *Acts of Defiance* (1981-83), which was produced and edited by Raf, Russ, and Mike in Sunderland, increasingly gave over
more space to politics than music with each issue, whilst reflecting
the local punk scene in the North East of England and was associated with The Bunker, a music venue and social centre in Sunderland.
*Anathema* (1982), emerging from Stockton-On-Tees and produced
and edited by Lee, also reflected the scene in the North East.

For many producers and consumers of zines, music, band interviews, and gig reviews would remain the mainstay of the zines content. However where earlier zines had started to discuss the political

---

28    Cross 'There Is No Authority But Yourself,' 2

meanings and impact of punk rock, many of the later anarcho-punk zines developed a more focussed political initiative in their content. Partly influenced by seminal anarcho-punk band Crass their instructive fold out record sleeves, pamphleteering at gigs, and the lyrical content of their songs exposed "articulate dissections of religion, geo-politics and social relations…" that "…provided a template for combining visual and textual assaults against 'the system"[29], zine producers began to explore the notion of anarchism as a political pathway to challenge the established political system and the polarised left and right wing factions.[30]

In his analysis of rap artists as organic intellectuals, Abrams notes that an important function of Gramsci's notions of organic intellectuals is to subvert the existing power relations: "Organic intellectuals endeavour to undermine the legitimacy of the dominant ideology that the traditional intellectuals seek to uphold".[31] As Gramsci argued, the domination of a culturally diverse society by the ruling class is upheld by the manipulation of that society's culture, so that the ideology of the ruling class is imposed and accepted as the norm. The dominant hegemonic ideology would be perpetrated and reinforced through societal institutions such as the church, academia, and the mass media where the media served the public as a distraction from the realities of the dominant ideology. Critiques of the machinations of the mass media appeared in a number of anarcho-punk zines, for example;

> …most of the shit dished out by the BBC and ITV is designed to brainwash you (the consumer ha ha). Can't you see they are just using you to make money. They churn out biased bigoted programmes that do nothing to entertain you or give you information…[32]

---

29  Worley, *"While the World was Dying, Did You Wonder Why?"* 94-99.

30  For a more detailed discussion on punks relationship with anarchism See Worley, *"While the world was dying, did you wonder why?,"* 30-36; Jim Donaghey, 'Bakunin Brand Vodka: An Exploration into Anarchist-Punk and Punk-Anarchism' *Anarchist Developments in Cultural studies, 1, (2013).138-70.* Cross, 'The Hippies Now Wear Black,' *25-44;* Cross, 'There Is No Authority But Yourself, ' 1-20.

31  Abrams, *'Antonio's B-Boys',* 3.

32  *Intensive Care* #1, 7.

we are attacked continually, the violence doesn't just come Police or the army, but also from the spineless degrading 'culture' forced daily down our throats by the media.[33]

Indeed, as Worley suggests, the mass media were "recognised as forces of control that reinforced social moralities, stifled dissent and distracted from the iniquities of everyday life."[34] What zines offered was an independent and DIY /self-produced alternative to those forms of media[35] wherein a space for the exploration, development, and dissemination of counter hegemonic ideas could take place. Many of the anarcho-punk zines would include short statements, poems, and at times extended essays as well as visual attacks against, and critiques of, what was perceived to be the ruling classes domination over the individual through a number of institutions and hegemonic ideologies that were often referred to as 'the system'.

The ruling classes have had it their way for too long, its time to take back what's ours. Its our world not theirs, there is enough for us all to live, there is no need for people to be denied of what they need. The Rolls Royces and the sick fur coats are symbols of our oppression, symbols of a system which places money before people. It's time to fight back.[36]

Other common motifs and points of critique, in many anarcho-punk zines and their editorials, included government and the political system coupled with the imbalance of wealth and power in society, where the state forces of oppression, such as the police and military, were employed to protect and defend both the owners of the capital and the politicians and institutions that supported them. "The law is for the rich, for the elite…for property."[37] and "the police

---

33   *Pigs For Slaughter* #1, 3.

34   Worley, "While the World Was Dying, Did You Wonder Why?" 88.

35   Stephen Duncombe, *Notes From The Underground. Zines and the Politics of Alternative Culture.* (London: Verso, 1997).

36   *Fight Back* #1, 1.

37   *Toxic Graffity* #3, 11.

protect money and property, fuck human beings, the filth only look after the rich, money is your passport to protexion (sic)."[38] The relationship between the government and the police is similarly expressed in the editorial of *Cobalt Hate #3*;

> The government and the police run our country and they run it wrong....the methods that Thatcher and her gang are approving for the police to use are getting more violent and oppressive... The government have their own morals and if we don't like em they got the police force to beat us into submission or their institutes (sic) to fuck our minds.[39]

Similarly marriage and the role of 'the family' was challenged both visually and textually, as it was perceived to exist "as a site of conditioning through which gender roles, patriarchy, and hegemonic values were imposed and further reinforced via the education system...."[40] and similarly via the mass media in its commodification and objectification of those gender roles. Visual representations of happy couples in domestic family settings juxtaposed with images of pornography and/or bondage were accompanied by caustic treatises on the illusion of marriage and lifelong happiness, domestic slavery, patriarchy, misogyny, and gender stereotyping. "Daddy goes out to earn the bread. Mummy does the cleaning – is the man's slave. Likewise Jill finds out how she should look after the kids and spend a life of drudgery slaving for her husband."[41]

The church and religion in general, was also understood to be part of 'the system', an institution that demonstrated oppressive powers by controlling and subjugating people through religious and moral indoctrination. Often the hypocrisy of the church would be revealed and challenged over its role in the 3rd world and its support of 'just' conflicts, past and present.

> The church is the ultimate structure working for, with and part of the ultimate system, they co operate

---

38  *Toxic Graffity #3*, 2.

39  *Cobalt Hate #3*, 21.

40  Worley, "While the World Was Dying, Did You Wonder Why?" 98.

41  *Precautions Essentielles Pour la Bonne #1*, 9.

to keep control…The church is built upon corruption, the pope does not divide his wealth among the victims of year zero, the starving babys(sic) swollen with severe malnutrition, the famine struck nations…Religion has been used for wars too long. Your pope and your white christs are as much to blame as the oppressive governments.[42]

Many other anarcho-punk zines included extended essays on religion and exposing its complicity in perpetuating the ideologies of the hegemonic culture. For example *Acts of Defiance* #3 dedicated two pages to the subject titled "This is religion"[43] where the editor verbally dissects a number of religious dogmas and describes what he sees as the failings and contradictions of religion, including patriarchal oppression, the wealth of the church and its response to poverty and famine underpinned by an agenda of oppression through fear, employed by many faiths.

The education system was also perceived as part of the state apparatus of control and conformity of the masses, which divided a society in which private education was seen as an instrument for the wealthy to be schooled in ways of retaining and maintaining power and wealth.

The educational system is the largest instrument in the modern state for telling people what to do… Contemporary critics of the alliance between national government and national education would agree and would argue that it is in the nature of public authorities to make stronger social inequality and to brainwash the young into the acceptance of their particular slot in the organised system.[44]

Abrams also identifies, in Lipsitz analysis of Chicano rock musicians, that the organic intellectual is someone who reflects the needs of its community and attempts to build a "historical-bloc" with other

42  *Anathema* #1, 19.
43  *Acts of Defiance* #3, 15-16
44  *Acts of Defiance* #5, 23.

oppositional groups united around counter-hegemonic ideas.[45] The construction of these counter-hegemonic alliances is formulated by the appeal of common points of reference and similarities of experiences between the groups. As the political debates within the editorial content of anarcho-punk zines were further unpacked and explored, so issues around war and violence, state oppression, squatting, vivisection, animal rights, drug use, veganism/vegetarianism, consumerism, Third World poverty, and gender politics started to appear regularly within the zines both textually and visually.

Anarcho-punk's relationship with national movements, such as CND and similar pacifist anti-war organisations, Hunt Saboteurs Association, and the Animal Liberation Front, also became a common component of the cultural and editorial language of anarcho-punk zines. This included articles giving advice to readers on how to deal with the police when stopped and searched, how to set up squats, produce fanzines, organise events and protests, sexual health, direct action and political activism, animal liberation and anti-vivisection, among a multitude of DIY practices deemed important to the developing scene. It could be argued that the sharing of information about, and from, other groups, who were also challenging the hegemonic culture, warranted inclusion into the zines by the editors as a way to coalesce these oppositional groups into a historical-bloc, united around counter-hegemonic images and texts of subversion. Indeed some groups that reflected the needs of the anarcho-punk community developed out of and/or were supported by some of the zine editors/producers.[46]

---

45   Abrams, 'Antonio's B-Boys', 2.

46   For example, some members of the Kill Your Pet Puppy (KYPP) collective, who produced the zine *KYPP*, were active supporters of, and participants in, the Black Sheep Housing Co-op based in Islington, London which continued to operate as a housing co-op until 2002. http://greengalloway.blogspot.co.uk/2014_02_01_archive.html (accessed 5/13/2014). Other zines such as *Pigs For Slaughter, Book of Revelations, Enigma, Paroxysm of Fear, Scum and Precautions Essentielles Pour La Bonne* whose editors/producers gathered in and around the Centro Iberico (1982-84), an anarchist squat and social centre in Westbourne Park, West London and the short lived Autonomy Centre (1981-82) in Wapping, East London. The Sunderland based 'zine *Acts of Defiance* were aligned with, and involved in, The Bunker in Sunderland, a venue for live music

## DISCOURSES OF ZINE EDITORS
## AS AUTHORITATIVE REPRESENTATIVES

These 'needs' of the community are also reinforced by the notion of authority that is at times embodied within the discourses of the zine editors/producers. To demonstrate this I will draw on the editorial content from four fanzines. *Incendiary* was a London based fanzine produced and edited by John Slam in 1984. The three further examples I utilise, *Acts of Defiance*, *Cobalt Hate*, and *Pigs for Slaughter*, I have contextualised in the previous section of this chapter. As I stated earlier Hebdige's focus on 'style' and the seeming 'immediacy' of their production seems to discount the effort and time involved in the cut and paste techniques of zine production. This commitment to production and the clearly articulated positions of the editors, I would suggest, represents cultural work and that the editors were key agents in defining what anarcho-punk was or should be. Because of the passion and commitment that is necessary for zine production, I suggest that the editors, through this cultural work, stake a claim in warranting, the authority to assert specific ideological positions.

Sarah Thornton suggests that media is instrumental in defining and circulating cultural knowledge and authenticating cultural practices through a process of 'enculturation' where these practices are considered integral or essential to that subculture[47]. When attempting to understand the cultural practices of zine producers/editors one has to consider notions of authority. In the process of selecting, presenting, and displaying a set of knowledge or opinions to define and speak for a group, belief or value, the zine producer/editor simultaneously fashions their own identity and the identity of the group that they see themselves as representing 'out of the experiences and values of the subcultures of which they are part.'[48]

---

and a meeting place for political and community groups. Worley, *"While the World Was Dying, Did You Wonder Why?"* 96 and 98. *Knee Deep in Shit (KDIS)* began as a zine for Bradford's 1 in 12 club, a social space and members club and collective based on anarchist principles and values. The 'producers of *KDIS* went on to form the 1in 12 Publication Collective. http://www.1in12.com/publications/mail/about.htm

47   Sarah Thornton, *Club Cultures: Music, Media and Subcultural Capital* (Cambridge: Polity. 1995), 29

48   Duncombe, *Notes From The Underground*, 37.

Duncombe suggests that this creation of identity in the editorial and pages of the zine is both a reflection of the larger world of reality and representation and a search for an authoritative self[49] where that level/degree of personalization by the zine producers/editors is a way of seizing authority[50]. He further argues that the punk discourse that is often found in zines is a combination of a way of defining oneself as being against society as an individual but simultaneously defining 'yourself as being part of a group, adhering to community standards where the mix of authentic individuality and communal solidarity is a rough one'[51]. What Duncombe considers important in the discourses of zines is that the individual and personal narratives are of and by real individuals, where self-expression is what zine producers and consumers consider being authoritative, authentic and where importance is placed on the expressivity of doing rather than the effectiveness of the end result.[52]

So in this context the verbal language of anarcho-punk zines represent a discursive practice that produces and articulates important notions of what it was to be an 'anarcho-punk,' an anarchist, a pacifist, vegan, et al; what role music, symbolism, and the scene had in its construction and the role that the zine editors had in this activity. Many of the zines allude to a form of opposition, defiance, and activism that is anchored in the title of those zines[53]. The editorial content attempted to define what it was to be a member of a scene that increasingly constructed a discourse of defiance, anarchism, and anti-authoritarianism. These personal responses are also clearly articulated in the editorials of a number of anarcho-punk zines where a consistent and solid philosophical and ideological discourse is centred on the idea that the fanzine is a site for identity creation, ideological engagement, and action. So for example, the editorial of *Acts of Defiance* #6 critiques perceptions of what being an anarcho-punk constitutes and attempts to define it through the discourse of individual responsibility and anarchism.

---

49   Ibid., 40.

50   Ibid., 30.

51   Ibid., 62.

52   Ibid., 33-35.

53   For example, *Acts of Defiance; Fight Back; Raising Hell; Subvert.*

Its funny isn't it, how many people who have got anarchy signs all over themselves and claim to know what
its all about-peace and love and all that isn't it? And yet
despite this how many act as if they actually meant it-
not bloody many... People who claim to believe in anarchy but let us down on the most basic thing-trust...
they say that anarchy begins with the individual but its
still right, you always complain that your mistreated by
'society' but unless you fulfil peoples trust in you your
going to remain isolated and unless you can learn to
trust fully then we are going nowhere.[54]

This theme continues in the editorial of the following issue of *Acts
of Defiance*,

Now its time to become more involved, to really get
down to things seriously. So all you 'punks' out there
who thought that you were helping the revolution by
buying records on Crass label and spraying anarchy
signs all over think again. There are loads of things really worth doing... you can always start with yourself
(I said this in the last issue and probably the one before
and I'll keep saying it until someone listens). If you are
going to go around calling yourself an anarchist then
at least try and act like you mean it.[55]

What comes through in the discourses of the editorial from these
two issues of *Acts of Defiance* is how strong and forcibly the identity
of being a 'punk' is articulated. In particular, a distinction is made
between those who use the signs of being a punk – critique of the
status quo; sporting anarchy signs; and 'buying records on Crass label'
– and those who take personal responsibility to act. Here the editors,
through their seeming frustration and anger, are using the editorial
to remind and reinforce what they think anarcho-punk is about and
how it is down to individual responsibility to make it work as an ideological practice. The punk discourse of doing rather than just one of

---

54  *Acts of Defiance* #6, 2.

55  *Acts of Defiance* #7, 37.

pretentious posturing is evident in many earlier punk zines, however in some anarcho-punk zines the importance of the notion of personal responsibility for engagement and action seems to become more prominent and the lack of it critiqued more. The editors reinforce, in their minds, what they believe constitutes and defines anarcho-punk and anarcho-punk identity through the discourses of DIY ethics, anarchism and individual responsibility. It could be argued that through this process there is an attempt to elevate their position, within the scene, as more authoritative and superior.

The editorial of *Cobalt Hate* #3 takes a similar stance in its critique of what the editor thinks constitutes anarchy and interestingly what could be seen to be a struggle with the ideological boundaries of anarchy, by putting their own take on who anarchy is for;

> yeah sure you want anarchy its good fer (sic) the brain and allows free expression and free enterprise etc, but its so easy and yet so hard to have, but only if you are considering it at face value, its about people its about freedom and the way we relate to one another, its individuality"… "you might say ANARCHY FOR THE UK but why?? do you really want everybody free to do whatever? NO ITS ANARCHY. FOR US. NOT THEM WE LOOK AFTER OURSELVES. THEY DID IT THEIR WAY AND IT DIDN'T WORK SO WE'LL DO IT OUR WAY AND LEAVE THOSE CUNTS ALONE….FOR A WHILE. I could say I got anarchy now well I aint. even poxy things like dole, tinned food, t.v is defying the meaning.[56]

Some of the zine editors expanded on the editorial 'space' by producing treatises and 'manifestos of action,'[57] 'declarations of intent',[58] and a 'call to arms' to challenge the hegemony of society but also to challenge the anarcho-punk scene and what they perceive to be its failures and contradictions[59];

---

56   *Cobalt Hate* #3, 3.

57   *Incendiary* #1, 2.

58   *Incendiary* #1, 3.

59   *Pigs for Slaughter*, produced by Ian (Slaughter) Rawes, was a more militant

This and every issue of 'Incendiary' is the "we do what we fucking want to" issue. After all, that's the only way to do anything. I don't concern myself with any sort of compromise. UNFORTUNATELY many do, and everything gets diluted"... "We've been accepting this for far too long. Accepting that there are 'correct' ways to do things, accepting there is 'right' and 'wrong', 'good' and 'evil'. Open your mouth for a minute and they will ram their morals down it! And at the other extreme (ie the same place) you get the anarcho gestapo forcing their morals onto you"... "DANCE TO YOUR TUNE ALONE, AND NO OTHER"... "there i go, preaching on. Who am I to tell you what to do? Well im going to regardless because your reactionary values deserve a good hard kicking.[60]

Indeed in the first issue of Pigs for Slaughter, where its cover declared it as "AT LAST... A PRACTICAL PAPER FOR THE MILITANT ANARCHIST PUNK!! FAR OUT,"[61] the editorial took a more politically hard line approach to anarchism. Occupying the first three pages, the editorial contained a searing critique of Crass and the anarcho-punk movement that developed in their wake. It highlighted the failures of its pacifist approach, lack of commitment to direct action and confrontation with the system and all its agents. Similar zines[62] also took a hardline anarchist approach that promoted and encouraged direct action against the state, the owners of capital, military defence and arms companies, animal laboratories. Thus the editorials became a site not only of authority but one of debate and contestation where, as Worley suggests[63], charged disagreements ensued between those who took a pacifist position and those who advocated direct acts of physical confrontation, and similarly those who perceived anarchism as the responsibility of the

anarchist zine that was representative of the Anarchist Youth Federation and produced searing critiques of the anarcho-punk movement, especially the pacifist element who they perceived to be incapable of direct action

60 *Incendiary* #1, 3.
61 *Pigs for Slaughter* #1.
62 For example *Cardboard Theatre, Fight Back, Paroxysm Fear, Enigma* and *Scum*.
63 Worley, "While the World Was Dying, Did You Wonder Why?," 96

individual and those who perceived it as a collective movement committed to smashing the 'system'.

However, despite these polarities, by the mid 1980s there existed an abundance of anarcho-punk zines each propagating their perceptions of the system and its homogeneous culture. As the anarcho-punk scene developed the music content for many fanzines lessened with available print space taken up by more political and cultural counter-hegemonic discourses. A look through a large selection of those anarcho-punk zines also brings forward a sense of homogeneity in their production practices and editorial discourses, which could be interpreted as being naively idealistic and utopian. This sense of homogeneity is critiqued by the editors of *Acts of Defiance:*

> Well there has been an increase in the number of zines knocking about recently, and although this is good from the point of view that at least people are doing it themselves, its really disappointing to see the same old things coming up, the same old interviews, the same old anti bomb, anti religion articles coming up, its all been done so many times before. Where's that originality gone?[64]

As the anarcho-punk scene developed so the visual and textual content of the zines also shifted to accommodate the scenes that were emerging out of the punk milieu that followed in the wake of anarcho-punk[65]. Indeed Liptrot argues, many of the practices of the 1980s British anarcho-punk scene have over the last twenty years been absorbed into a wider contemporary DIY punk and hardcore punk scenes across the world. In these scenes the anarcho-punk DIY ethic is still prominent and the print fanzine still remains one of the key means of ideological communication within the subculture[66]

## CONCLUSIONS

In this chapter I have aimed to consider and analyse the role of anarcho-punk zine editors as organic intellectuals and authoritative

---

64   *Acts of Defiance* #7, 37.

65   D.Beat, Crust punk, Hardcore, Goth and Industrial.

66   Liptrot, "Beyond the lifespan."

representatives who engage in the construction of anarcho-punk as a sub-cultural/political movement. In doing so, I have aimed to encompass the usual emphasis on zines as channels of communication and symbols of wider punk practices, but recognising that it was the zine which was one of the key ways in which anarcho-punk was made meaningful through the discursive practices of their editors. I would argue, then, that simply focusing on the characteristic visual design of the zine, as in previous analytical approaches, limits our understanding of its cultural role and the position of its editors as organic intellectuals. More importantly, perhaps, we need to understand that it is not only in their iconography and symbolism that the zines were relevant and meaningful but also the discursive practices which were employed by the editors. The zines' visual design was an epiphenomenon of the discursive practices of the editors who produced the zines in a manner which indexed their DIY nature, a practice central to the ethos of anarcho-punk, and the investment of time and effort which were attributed to their construction and distribution by the editors. It could be argued then that the time, effort, and commitment involved in aiding and supporting the development and understanding of the scene, positions the editor as organic intellectual and authoritative voice.

PETER WEBB

# DIRTY SQUATTERS, ANARCHY, POLITICS, AND SMACK

## A JOURNEY THROUGH BRISTOL'S SQUAT PUNK MILIEU

*The four years we were in Bristol we were mired in the mud... just
increasing despair, really, we had something going for us and we
had the band but we were going deeper and deeper in to this sludge.
The image I use is of a dead city; everyone is asleep, everyone is
gauged out, drugs pulling the soul out of the whole place. The whole
creative impetus of the Bristol scene just getting drained away by this
perpetual fucking erosion of drugs, of smack culture, of the selfish
fucking nihilism of the whole thing. I don't have much sentimentality
towards Bristol at all. It was a very, very hard time; there was
constant insecurity, constant trouble.*[1]

---

1    Rob Miller, singer of the Amebix, quoted in the unreleased film *Risen: A History
     of Amebix.*

*I was a functioning drug addict... A long time of depressing shit
really. Even through those times I kept a guitar and an amp... I never
lost faith in the power of music, I never stopped wanting to do music
but I was never together enough to put together a proper band...
Methadone, valium, speed and then all the drinking on top of that...
You never really quite realize that you feel straight on drugs, even if
you are not off your face you feel that you are functioning, you are
functioning fine but there is so much that you miss.[2]*

**THE FIRST QUOTE** above comes from Rob Miller of the band
Amebix talking about his time in Bristol during the early period of the
band when they went from hanging around with a group of squatters
and drunks to becoming a highly influential and important band.
The period of the early 1980s, the development of the second wave of
punk and the centrality of anarcho-punk (for want of a better term at
this point) to it were evolving in a period where punk was becoming
a huge underground and DIY culture. It was becoming political in a
real sense, getting involved in campaigning over animal rights, declaring itself anti-war, anti-state, anti-oppression and trying to present
positive lifestyles. But at the same time elements of it were mired in
uncertainty, drug dependence, chronic alcoholism and the darker side
of squatting where insecurity, the threat of violence, and homelessness
were always in the minds of members of this milieu. Many writers,
including several in this collection, have written about the positive
impacts of anarcho-punk. I have done this too in previous and continuing work.[3] But here I chart and discuss the side of anarcho-punk
that was prone to self-destruction, even while maintaining a sense of
collectivity and to some degree camaraderie. The second quote above
gives a sense of the price that a number of people paid for letting the
drug, alcohol, and more self-destructive side of this milieu take over
their lives for a period of time. This, in a sense, is the flip side to the
positivity of this type of punk and gives us a clear picture of those
countervailing tendencies within it.

2    Anonymous, interview with author, October 2014.

3    See Peter Webb, *Exploring the Networked Worlds of Popular Music: Milieu Cultures*
(London: Routledge, 2010).

When looking at the state of the punk milieu from 1980 through to 1986 there seemed to be some key themes that informed the trajectories of the different groups and individuals within the 'community' of punk. The bands that this chapter concentrates on namely: Disorder, Amebix, and Lunatic Fringe were part of a wider social milieu in Bristol that populated some of the cities squats and cheap rental accommodation in central Bristol and who were frequent users of the central squat venue and café The Demolition Ballroom and Diner. These people and bands all linked Bristol to an international milieu interwoven with a growing movement that became framed as anarcho-punk. Penny Rimbaud, one of the founders of the band Crass who were central to this new wave of punk, said this of the motivation and momentum of the idea of anarcho-punk:

> Crass, the anarchist punk band of which I was a founder member, drummer, lyricist and big mouth, can reasonably claim to be the initiators of anarcho-punk. We saw Johnny Rotten's 'no future' ranting's as a challenge. We believed that there was a future if we were prepared to fight for it, and fight for it we did. Following the release of our 1978 album, *The Feeding of the Five Thousand*, we spearheaded a radical protest movement that had no parallel in late-twentieth century Britain. Crass and fellow anarchist bands put words into action, and encouraged a whole generation to do the same.[4]

The anarcho-punk or anarchist punk milieu developed as a 'second wave' of punk alongside and often completely intertwined with post-punk, positive punk, and gothic punk which at the time weren't named or as genre coded as they have been in more recent history. In his PhD thesis, Mike Dines outlined the development of punk in its first wave around bands such as The Sex Pistols, The Damned, The Clash, X Ray Spex, The Slits, Adverts, Generation X, etc., and suggested that this first wave used the tropes of 'anarchy and chaos', 'nihilism', 'destruction' whilst also building on genuinely critical groupings

---

4   Penny Rimbaud, *The Last of the Hippies: An Hysterical Romance* (Active Distribution, 2009), pp. viii to ix.

such as the Situationists, CND, the London squatting campaign, and the Angry Brigade but presenting copies of those groups political messages in terms of musical and sartorial expression.[5]

The anger was genuine but the scene soon fell prey to the co-option and commercialisation of a record industry that could throw money at something new and controversial and get a profit out of a new 'fad', as they would see it. The Pistols became the nation's *bête noir* and made loads of money in the process. The Clash became a stadium rock band, bands like the Buzzcocks, Siouxsie and the Banshees, The Ruts, The Damned all signed to major labels and appeared regularly on *Top of the Pops*.[6] Dines then suggests that the second wave of punk and in particular groups such as Crass, Discharge, The Subhumans, Poison Girls, etc. took that idea of 'anarchy' seriously and directed efforts into positive social protest and lifestyle movements. These groups and the punks who were associated with them started to get involved in political initiatives such as support for squatting, animal rights, anti-war campaigns, vegetarianism and veganism, and anti-state rhetoric. The second wave of punk turned against the first wave's commercialism and vacuity and presented something more tangible, DIY, and coherent.

When analysing the three main bands that are the focus of the piece and the many individuals who were a part of the Bristol scene at this time (i.e., 1979/80 onwards) you get a sense of some of the similar characteristics that these people shared. There seemed to be a set of events that had triggered a reaction of incandescent rage at the unfair treatment of someone (often at the hands of the state), or an individual's own experience of maltreatment and social exclusion, or equally a quest for something that challenged and disrupted the chaos of the Britain of the period. These people all felt angry and despairing at the same time but also keenly excited and engaged with the idea of punk.

There has been a lot of recently (2000 – 2015) published and self-published material from people involved in punk who were born in the early 1960s. These people were too young to be fully involved

---

5    Mike Dines, "An Investigation into the Emergence of the Anarcho-Punk Scene of the 1980s" (PhD diss., University of Salford, 2004.

6    British TV chart show that ran from 1964 to 2006 and showcased the top 40 selling singles in the UK charts with mainly mimed performances and sometimes videos from the leading artists.

in the first wave of punk in 1976 in England but were excited by it, attracted to it, and developed into key members of the punk milieu in their late teens and early twenties. When thinking about the individuals who formed the key Bristol bands I noticed that a similar set of narratives began to appear. I was a part of that milieu and being born in 1964 had similar reference points to these individuals. However, I grew up in Yate, a sprawling 1950s housing estate on the outskirts of Bristol and would travel in by bus to gigs and events until I moved into the city centre at the age of 18. So even though I felt like I was a part of this milieu when I moved into the city itself, I felt that I had a newcomer's lens to view the scene through. Although I know a lot about this period I felt that I needed to interview a number of people who were involved in order to get their retrospective understanding of that time and also to attempt to unravel what that particular milieu represented.

This chapter then presents a series of reflections from participants in the three bands and some other individuals who were heavily involved in Bristol's punk milieu and some analysis of the groups musical, artistic, and lyrical output and how that reflects on the key elements and focus of the culture of punk in Bristol. The key themes which are explored here are the drug use, alcoholism, and more destructive elements of this group of people rather than the more positive cultural and political ones. That is not to say that the destructive elements were dominant but that they were an equally important part of this milieu at this time (i.e., 1979 through to the late 1980s). I will start by situating Bristol as the location of this part of the punk milieu and then go on to discuss the three bands and reflections from some key people who were involved at that time. I will finish by suggesting that Punk represented a milieu that was incredibly creative, very intelligent, and full of active people who were existing in often very difficult social situations with little financial resource but who managed to make things work. They existed in a maelstrom that could easily veer into serious drug and related social problems to do with housing or health but that was a key component of the chaotic and creative world that they lived within.

Bristol is a relatively small city (population of around 450,000) but in a small geographical area it had an interesting and diverse mix of communities and people. Very diverse housing areas surround the city centre where the river Frome flows from East of the city, then under the streets and into the docks or Harbour side as it is now known, and then eventually out into the Bristol Channel. To the north of the Centre there is Cotham, Clifton, and Redland; historically they have been the more affluent areas of the city but areas that are also peppered with bedsits, flats, and multi-occupancy homes which have often housed students and also a more transient population of musicians, artists, middle-class bohemians and the casual workforce. To the East of the centre there is St Pauls, Montpelier, Easton, and St Werburghs. These areas have a more predominantly mixed ethnic community: Jamaican and Afro-Caribbean immigrants who have been in Bristol for four or five generations, Pakistani, Bangladeshi, Indian, Irish, and more recently Somalian people, live mixed in with a White Bristolian working class which also has a slightly bohemian and student mix.

To the South of the centre are the big working class areas of Bedminster, Southville, Totterdown, and further out Hartcliffe, Knowle and Knowle West. To the West of the centre there are the open fields of Ashton, Ashton Court, and the countryside that leads to the county of Somerset and the South West of the country. In 1980 Bristol had a major riot in the St Pauls area of the city, one of the first in a series of urban disturbances in the early 1980s. Punks were just as much tied into the milieu of the inner city as they were to the subculture of punk and knew how the events had unfolded. Some of them were involved and they clearly saw connections between the policing of the inner city, the attitude of police, and the Council to squatting and minor drug use in the area, and the attitude towards a mainly Afro-Caribbean community, members of whom were involved in the initial 'trigger' event around a drugs raid at the Black and White Café in the centre of St Pauls.

These events had a lasting impact on the city and were influential for many of the later music scenes including punk, hip hop, trip hop, dance music, etc.[7] Two members of the band Vice Squad and Simon Edwards; an owner of an existing record label in the city (Heartbeat Records) formed the punk label Riot City records using the city's infamy as a calling card. Vice Squad released their first single on the label as did Chaos U.K. and Chaotic Discord, two other Bristol punk

7    Harris Joshua, Tina Wallace and Heather Booth, *To Ride a Storm: The 1980 Bristol 'Riot' and the State* (London: Heinemann, 1980).

bands. Disorder was given the privilege of setting up their own label: Disorder Records through Riot City.

Disorder was a group whose members were all squatting in the late 1970s and early 1980s in Bristol. They had a settled line-up for a short period of time but then developed a fairly unstable membership that changed frequently but that was drawn from a distinct layer of punks who were all involved in the squatting scene. Locally they were known as 'crusty punks'. This term was used in a variety of forms nationally and internationally and Ian Glasper has two sources for the inception of the term; the band HellBastard from Newcastle and Norwich's Deviated Instinct who spoke about the idea of 'crust punk' and crusty guitar sounds:

> 'Rippercrust' is widely regarded as the first time the word 'crust' was used in the punk context, and hence the specific starting point of the whole crustcore genre, although some would attribute that accolade to the likes of Disorder, Chaos UK and Amebix several years earlier.[8]

In Bristol from around 1980 onwards the group of squat punks that gathered around the city centre squats in St Pauls, Montpelier, Cotham, and Redland became known as 'crusties' due to their appearance which often was characterized by shredded trousers that were often worn for weeks on end, hair spiked with dried soap which often later turned to dreadlocks, ripped t-shirts, and a range of second hand clothes that often didn't conform to typical punk fashion. As Chris Neill, the second and most well-known singer of Disorder, said; the period of punk that they were a part of had a slightly different set of aesthetics and cultural reference points to earlier forms of the milieu. There was often a clearer political agenda around this time of punk, but a politics of rage against the authorities and the oppression of the system that expressed itself through animal rights, vegetarianism, squatting, anti-nuclear protest, women's groups and politics, and a more environmental approach to things. Within Bristol, the squat scene was incredibly important but also the influence of travelling

---

8    Ian Glasper, *Trapped in a Scene: UK Hardcore 1985-1989* (London: Cherry Red Books, 2004), 185.

bands from other parts of the country that would come and play in Bristol and Bath at some of the more unusual, squatted or hired venues. Crass, Flux of Pink Indians, The Mob, Dirt, Zounds, Poison Girls, Subhumans, all played some interesting venues in Bristol and Bath and the individuals who were involved seemed to be developing a very similar set of ideas and were motivated by very similar things to this segment of the punk community in Bristol.

Punk as a subculture, scene, milieu, or category[9] had and still has various entry points, places, and times where people engage with it and start to interpret and understand it in their own way. Neill remembers his 'entry' point into the punk scene after he had been to a concert by Bristol bands Vice Squad and the X Certs in 1979:

> By this time I was very much entrenched in the Bristol punk scene and the squatting movement. This in itself separated us from the 'traditional punks' in Bristol at that time, that was the old school who were a bit older than us and who were around in 1977, which seemed to have some sort of emblematic significance for them. The standard gear was, blonde spikey back-combed hair, leather jacket with studs and some sort of album cover or name of a band painted elegantly on the back, in fact some jackets were authentic works of art.
>
> This seemed like a uniform to me at the time, and within our squatty group we began to dress anti-punk. We would wear dresses bought from charity shops and any old rags that we found; including mutton clothes, which is a type of material slaughterhouses used to wrap around the carcasses of animals. We would ask for these from the butchers and cutting three holes in them would serve as T-Shirts, complete with the fat and blood from the dead animal.
>
> It wasn't just aesthetically that I felt distance from the traditional punk scene, but also musically. While most people were listening to Slaughter and the Dogs

---

9   These terms are all loaded with theoretical significance and academic baggage but this chapter is not the place to elaborate on this. For a full discussion of the see the first two chapters of Webb, *Exploring the Networked Worlds of Popular Music*.

or UK Subs, I was more intrigued by groups like Black Flag, The Killjoys and started listening to more foreign punk music like Wretches from Italy or Gism from Japan.[10]

Neill makes clear reference to the differences between his group of friends as squatters and people who were thinking beyond the style of punk but who were taking its energy and openness to new areas. 1977, he says, seemed to have an 'emblematic significance' to the older punks. When people who were involved with punk discuss punk, or any music-based subculture for that matter, the issue of authenticity or being involved at the inception of the form has clear subcultural importance. Several punk documentaries[11] or written accounts such as Jon Savage's *England's Dreaming* and[12] Greil Marcus's *Lipstick Traces*[13] concentrate on describing and charting the early days of punk rock's inception in the UK and its development mainly in London. As well as the important early bands, these accounts tend to concentrate on key individuals such as Vivienne Westood, Malcolm Maclaren,[14] John Lydon, Siouxsie Sioux, Joe Strummer, Sid Vicious, Dave Vanian, Viv Albertine, etc. The early adopters of punk were seen as being the more knowledgeable, more sophisticated in their understanding and more au fait with the stylistic signifiers of the scene. Neill and the group of squatters who became the key bands of the early 1980s in Bristol entered the scene at a later point, they were younger, and their understanding

---

10 Chris Neill, interview via email with the author, 30 July 2014.

11 For example: Don Letts (director), *Punk: Attitude* (London: Fremantle, 2005); Julian Temple (director), *The Filth and the Fury: A Sex Pistols Film* (London: Channel Four, 2007); Zillah Minx (director), *She's a Punk Rocker* (London: Ultra Violet Punk Productions, 2011).

12 Jon Savage, *England's Dreaming: Sex Pistols and Punk Rock* (London: Faber and Faber, 1991).

13 Greil Marcus, *Lipstick Traces: A Secret History of the Twentieth Century* (London: Faber and Faber, 1989).

14 Owner of a shop on the Kings Road called Sex, which became a focal point for punks. Here he worked with Vivienne Westwood one of the key designers of punk fashion. He was also the manager first of the New York Dolls and then of The Sex Pistols.

was different and interpreted through a very different lens. This difference can be seen partly through the description of the type of clothes that Neill's group wore.[15] Neill and the people around him bought or stole the clothing they wore from charity shops, wore butchers mutton clothes (which they often got free); their trousers were often so dirty and so worn that they were a patchwork of holes and shreds. The style was different to the older punks and as we shall see the music and attitude showed a very different side too.

It wasn't just the clothing, aesthetic or musical references that were different for Disorder. They were developing at a time when their immediate contemporaries were seemingly more overtly political than the earlier generation of punk bands. Disorder were not on the surface of things a 'political' band. Their music and lyrics were often as much about drinking to excess, fighting, and having fun as much as about squatting and attacking the establishment. But Disorder was actively involved in key movements and causes as a group of individuals and the band didn't always reflect that. Neill said that:

> By the time I was singing with Disorder and we were playing and touring a lot in the UK underground squatting scene, we played a lot with Chumbawamba from Leeds, who, apart from being a great band, were also part of a well organized squatting movement in Leeds. This inspired us to start the same movement in Bristol and we got involved more and more in the squatting movement, animal rights and hunt saboteurs. All of these seemed to me to be noble causes and worth defending, but at the time I was incapable of looking after myself never mind defend the rights of animals.[16]

So the groups of people within, and around, the band were all getting involved in these areas even if the music didn't always reflect that. Neill used to wear a T-Shirt that had his own message scrawled on it

---

15   One such shop was Paradise Garage, another gathering point for Bristol's 'fashion punks.' It sold brothel creepers, bondage trousers, mohair jumpers and Johnson's boots that were coming into fashion in the late 1970s.

16   Chris Neill.

saying 'Eat soya protein motherfucker' emphasizing his veganism and the wider trajectory within this group of punks for veganism or vegetarianism. Disorder was different from the emerging bands like Crass, Zounds, Poison Girls in that the presentation had an insecure element about it. They didn't present the certainties that Crass did in their lyrics or graphics. They did write about injustice, were very anti-state, and aware of mental health issues in their songs such as 'Rampton' on the *Mental Disorder* EP. Taf, who is the Disorder bassist and the person who continues the band to this day, suggested that they had some experience of mental health issues and the provision in the health service. He talks about Steve Robertson and Neill both having been through parts of the system.[17] The sleeve of the single also presented a stark contrast between a hand drawn picture of a punk drinking and saying 'fuck the system' and a second image of a suited man holding a sweeping brush and saying 'I'm happy, sweeping is good, where's my medication, I'm better now'. This juxtaposed the alcohol soaked punk being nihilistic against the medicated society conformist. When you also look at some of Disorder's lyrics you can see the rage and anger but also the nihilistic inevitability that they seem to see in a future that is bleak:

> Condemned at birth, when they give you a slap
> Their gonna steal your mind & there's no worse crime
>    than that
> Condemned at birth, you might as well cry
> You're gonna be condemned till the day that you die
> Condemned at school, you don't like that
> But there's worse to come
> Condemned to work, you can't stand that
> So you're on the dole 'cos you got the sack
> Condemned to boredom, worse than before
> No money so you steal and you're messing with the law
> Condemned to the cell, you learn how to hate
> Stamp on your pride, try to fight the state
> Condemned to be sent down or learn to settle down
> They don't care; it's going to hurt

---

17  Ian Glasper, *Burning Britain: The History of UK Punk 1980-1984* (London: Cherry Red Books, 2004).

Dragging your pride through the fucking dirt
Condemned to have kids, you might even have a
mortgage.[18]

Neill commented on the insecurity that the band and he felt in
comparison to some of the other bands at the time:

> Groups were becoming more and more political as
> bands like Crass and Flux of Pink Indians were emerg-
> ing and becoming more prominent. I can remember
> feeling jealous to a certain extent about how they
> seemed to be so certain about everything and have a
> clear political discourse. I was unsure about everything
> and looking back I can see how this was a projection
> of my own inability to 'get my shit together' as other
> bands seemed to do. My own insecurity in myself re-
> ceived its highest manifestation when I finally became
> addicted to heroin. That was when I really didn't give a
> fuck about anything or anyone.[19]

Disorder's music had an incredibly thick, compressed, oppressive,
chaotic, and furious sound to it. Their first EP that was released on
a label was set up for the band by Simon Edwards of the previously
mentioned Bristol based Riot City label. The EP *Complete Disorder*
showcased four tracks that were fast, frenetic, and a blur of distortion
and half-screamed half-shouted vocals. 'Complete Disorder', 'Violent
Crime', 'Todays World', and 'Insane Youth' all seemed to have lyrics
that mainly repeated the titles, punctuated by observations of fighting, agro, violence, and the occasional warning of prison. Disorder re-
peatedly state that they 'don't care' because we are all 'gonna get blown
up', a statement of the fear of impending nuclear war that was palpa-
ble amongst a lot of young people in the early 1980s. Disorder were
political in that they lived a life of squatting, supporting animal rights
activities, and hunt sabbing but were also nihilistic in the extreme,
and were forever singing the praises of cider. In the mid-1980s some
members of the band got heavily into heroin. The music did parallel,

18   Disorder, "Condemned," *Perdition*, Disorder Records. 1983.
19   Chris Neill.

to a degree, the emergence of an early 1980s scene of bands with a similar approach to their music and some shared lyrical and presentational motifs: bands such as Discharge, The Disrupters, Special Duties, Insane, and Demob. But Disorder had the anger, nihilism, and hedonism that illustrated another side of the anarcho-punk scene: its focus on drugs, alcohol, and getting wasted tied-in with the lifestyle of living in squats and facing all the problems which were associated with an almost vagrant lifestyle. Disorder's fellow squatters included two brothers who had moved to Bristol from Devon in 1980 and who would form another band which would become central to the Bristol and surrounding areas scene: Amebix.

Amebix were a group whose driving force were the brothers Chris (Stig) and Rob (The Baron) Miller. They had grown up and lived in Devon before moving to Bristol in 1980 to develop what initially had been a group called 'The Band With No Name'! They couldn't play very well and had no idea how to tune their instruments so did a number of gigs in and around Devon with strangely tuned songs.

Stig had been sent to a school for maladjusted kids when he was 13 and it was there where he heard The Sex Pistols album *Never Mind the Bollocks, Here's the Sex Pistols* (1977) being played by a school friend. He immediately related to the sound of the record, what he had read about the group, and the sense of rebellion that the Pistols seemed to engender. The young brothers had then met a local character who looked like a tall Sid Vicious. Martin Baker came from an eccentric but well off family who lived in a large mansion on the edge of Dartmoor near the village of Peter Tavy, which in turn is near to Tavistock. His parents had gone away travelling and had left him in charge of the house, which was called The Glebe and was described as a gothic mansion by many who saw it. Martin's parents were students of esoteric writing and rumoured to be involved in the occult. Martin was very influenced by Alistair Crowley and had many books and works that had given him a strong knowledge of the occultist who had also fascinated many previous musicians and artists such as the Rolling Stones, Led Zeppelin, Black Sabbath, Kenneth Anger, Killing Joke etc.[20]

---

20   See Gary Lachman, *Aleister Crowley: Magick, Rock and Roll and the Wickedest Man in the World* (New York: Tacher Press, 2014) and Tobias Churton, *Aleister Crowley: The Beast in Berlin: Art, Sex and Magick in the Weimar Republic*

Stig and Baker were introduced to heroin and a branded version of methadone called Physeptome by a visitor to the Glebe, a well off middle class friend of Martins called Kay. From that point on late night rehearsals at the Glebe and heavy drug use characterized the Amebix. The Glebe was on the edge of Dartmoor and it was suggested that it had been built on top of a Saxon burial site, various bits of imagery started creeping into what the Amebix did. An Austin Osman Spare drawing became the key visual image for the band. Spare was an English psychic, occultist, and artist. He spent time with Crowley but developed his own path.[21] These elements were being drawn upon by the Amebix partly because of their proximity to the moor, Glebe house itself, and an interest developed through Baker's parents and apparently the brothers' father who also had an interest in esoteric literature.

When they moved to Bristol they met and moved into a squat with members of the Bristol punk band Disorder. Through Disorder they met and started to do gigs with other similar Bristol bands such as Lunatic Fringe, Chaos U.K., Vice Squad, and Baths Smart Pills. The Amebix had a different sound and approach to the other bands; the hedonism seemed more controlled, the politics were there but there was also some kind of mystical calling to an ancient, seemingly Celtic or pagan past. The artwork for the first single *Who's the Enemy* featured a drawing of a banner displaying the words 'Who's the Enemy' being held up by a seated skeleton. The reverse side of the cover featured drawings of the band looking as though they were warriors at the top of a desolate hill, with one of them holding a pike or spear; nearby is a gibbet and some broken fencing that all gives the impression of a previous generation of warriors and a broken social order.

The music has echoes of Killing Joke but also of the more hardcore punk that they were surrounded by in Bristol. The second track 'Curfew' features an intro with a wasp synthesizer making a low bass rumble and Rob Miller talking over the top possibly through a megaphone or distorted mic reading a narrative of finding dead bodies, a house that was completely destroyed, and then walking to the town square to find… and then he screams. The lyrics hint at an army take

(Rochester, Vermont: Inner Traditions, 2014).

21   See Phil Baker, *Austin Osman Spare: The Life and Legend of London's Lost Artist* (London: Strange Attractor Press, 2012).

over and possible nuclear war leading to the curfew. The next two tracks are both anti-religious and clear about the bands antipathy to organized religion. 'Belief' shows disgust at the giving up of body and soul to religion. Rob Miller sings about people giving away their freedom and the excellent line that: 'The church is just like the bondage of the brain.' The title and lyric of the final track on this EP became the Amebix's signature slogan and is always used in conjunction with a discussion of the band: 'No Gods, No Masters'. The track again has a choppy, distorted guitar riff that lays the foundations of what became known as 'crustpunk', but the lyrics of the track have taken on a life of their own and appeared on many painted leather jackets and t-shirts as a mantra of anarchist punk:

> Your god is your chains
> Reject your god reject your system
> Do you really want your freedom?[22]

'No Gods, No Masters' is emblematic of the Amebix's thematic centrality to the blossoming of anarcho-punk in the early 1980s. This theme of anti-religion and their complete distrust of authority tie them in with Crass, Poison Girls, Subhumans, and many other bands that delivered similar statements. It is almost like the anarchist punk version of the Trotskyist left's mantra 'neither Washington nor Moscow but international socialism', it has been used in a similar way by anarchist punks. The importance of a hatred for religious dogma has been expressed within the milieu from Crass's first single 'Reality Asylum' to the Subhumans's 'Religious Wars E.P.' and countless other tracks.[23] The themes of anti-religious dogma, anti-organised religion and a hint of either paganism or the occult were ones that Amebix carried through their work but which were often submerged in amongst songs about alcohol, drugs, and despair like 'Sunshine Ward'[24] or 'Drink and be Merry' or 'Largactyl'.[25] Their second single 'Winter' had an adapted image from the artist Frantisek Kupka, a Czech

---

22 From Amebix. *Who's the Enemy*, Spiderleg Records, 1982.

23 Crass *Reality Asylum*, Crass Records 1979, Subhumans *Religious Wars EP* Spiderleg Records 1982

24 From Amebix, *No Sanctuary*, Spiderleg Records, 1984.

25 All from Amebix, *Arise*, Alternative Tentacles, 1985.

abstract and cubist painter, on the cover. This image, 'The Black idol', a huge Egyptian sphinx-like sculpture looking menacingly down on a barren environment, continued the very esoteric looking imagery that the band were using.

The track 'Winter' feels like a very controlled scream against the harshness of winter probably echoing experiences of the band during this squatting phase of their lives. The music is a very choppy but flowing set of distorted chords with a tom-tom drum pattern and a very distinct accentuated snare drum every second beat of the bar. Rob Miller's voice gives the whole track a very heavy, bass baritone sound that conveys the extremity of the conditions that the band were living in at the time across to the listener. As their music developed it got more sophisticated but that raw atmosphere still pervaded every release. The esoteric undercurrent, the drug and nihilistic references, the anti-religious element, the anti-authoritarian stance, and an un-settling sound carried through to the 12" mini album *No Sanctuary*, and the albums *Arise* and *Monolith*. Amebix moved away from the anarcho-punk scene, moved cities to Bath in 1985 and eventually moved more towards a type of metal sound with the last album but their key developmental period was Bristol's anarcho-punk squatter milieu and all that went with it. Recently in 2009 they returned to do a series of gigs and ended up recording a new album *Sonic Mass*. This work firmly accentuates the bands interest in pagan and Celtic themes and mythology and really does showcase that side of the band more than anything else.

Other Bristol bands like Lunatic Fringe and Chaos U.K. represent-ed a continuation and parallel world with Disorder. They developed at the same time and had that same attitude of being uncertain about themselves, of enjoying being punks, drink and drugs, and possessed of a comedy streak that showed up in the Fringe's EP *Who's in Control* on the track 'Bristol Buses'. There was a political strand to what they did as well and this was expressed in a similar way lyrically to both Amebix and Disorder. John Finch, the band's guitarist, explained how they felt as a group of young punks forming a band in 1979-1980:

> There never seemed to be any question about lyrical inspiration. We were all becoming socially aware, and were angered and frustrated at the hypocrisy, brutality, injustice and racism that we perceived our society to

be founded upon, and it made sense to articulate this
frustration through our songs. In addition, many will
recall that at the time adopting a punk lifestyle meant
living with the constant threat of physical and verbal
aggression, not least from the police, as well as blanket
banning from pubs, cafes and music venues. Situations
we were encountering on a daily basis would therefore
also influence our lyrics, as was the case with many of
our contemporaries.[26]

Lunatic Fringe had started playing cover versions of well-known
punk songs from the likes of the Buzzcocks, Sex Pistols, and Stiff Little
Fingers but soon started to develop their own repertoire and fed their
experiences into the lyrics and ideas for the band. Riot City records
released a compilation in 1982 called *Riotous Assembly* and a Fringe
track called 'British Man', which was an anti-racist anthem, was included. They recorded a debut EP called *Who's in Control* (released on
their newly founded Resurrection Records, which was set up and run
by another Bristol band Vice Squad, who were getting a lot of success
and national airplay) which paralleled themes in Disorder's first release.

The EP, also like Amebix's first *Who's the Enemy*, had a political
edge to it as the first two tracks 'Who's in Control' and 'Mail Order
Rebels' were about peer pressure, authority, control, and manipulation. The third track though showed the humorous side to the band.
The track 'Bristol Buses' made fun of the local bus company and has
gone down in Bristol punk folklore as an enduring mantra. The ironic
delivery of the lyrics and the melody of a real advert for Bristol buses
start the track perfectly with the lyric: 'You've got friends when you go
by bus, take a trip on Bristol omnibus'. There then follows a vitriolic
attack on the service provided by the bus company but laced with
Bristolian irony. The cover of the single had a picture of a cat that was
clearly being experimented on as part animal testing and was a sign of
the band's links to the growing vegan and animal rights strand within
the Bristol punk milieu. The band was also constantly thinking about
what they should do commercially as this didn't chime well with the

---

26   John Finch, "History of Lunatic Fringe," Bristol Archive Records, http://www.
     bristolarchiverecords.com/bands/Lunatic_Fringe_History.html, accessed 14
     December 2014.

band's anarchist stance. They even had debates about whether they should produce t-shirts and decided in the end that the least commercial thing to do, and of course the funniest, would be to produce Lunatic Fringe underpants.

It took three years and a line-up change before the band released their second EP titled *Cringe with the Fringe*. This was released on another new Bristol label called Children of the Revolution Records or COR for short. Tim Bennett had set up the label in 1984 as Riot City records had begun to wind down its activities. COR released Lunatic Fringe and Chaos U.K. from the local scene but became an international hardcore punk label as it released material from Italy: Negazioni, Declioni, CCM, Vicious Circle form Australia, Heibal from Belgium, and the Accused from the USA. British bands such as the Stupids, Concrete Sox, Onslaught, A.O.A., and Sacrilege also found a home on the label. Again the release had a mix of tracks that reflected the political anger (and also the humour) that the band had. 'Whose War?' and 'Conformity (Face the Truth)' had the social commentary whilst 'Curse of the Bog People' had the humour. The band called it a day in 1986 as they were all pulling in different directions and a variety of tensions had emerged within the group. When discussing the last couple of years of the band's existence, Finch describes the context of the period in relation to drugs, and the devastating affect that their use was having on this particular group of musicians and the associated punks within the milieu:

> One of the downsides of this period was that it coincided with and provided a ready network for the sudden availability of hard drugs, most significantly heroin. Lunatic Fringe did not escape the harmful fallout from this drug, although it would be unfair to lay all of the bands' problems at its feet.[27]

So just like Amebix and Disorder, Lunatic Fringe expressed a similar set of ideas about their work. The political which was combined with the hedonistic and mixed with a later realisation of the huge impact of hard drugs, especially heroin, on a scene that was trying hard to mean something and that was wrapped up in strands of political

---

27   John Finch, "History of Lunatic Fringe".

activity from animal rights, veganism, squatting, anti-state, and anti-imposed authority. There are many individuals who would recount similar stories about this milieu. Justine Butler, a punk who grew up in Hertfordshire but who ended up in Bristol in the early 1980s, discusses her take on the Bristol scene after returning from a trip away to hear of one friend's death from heroin and then learning of another:

> Not long after that another friend with a taste for heroin died but he was murdered. Something to do with a deal that had gone wrong and an argument followed and he was stabbed and died. Again, I am not sure he was ever going to make it as an old man. He had '99% is Shit' tattooed on one side of his face and 'goats breath' written on the other.[28]

Justine's account echoes many others in this milieu and presents the history and cultural elements of it as a reality that was all to keenly felt by many of the participants. The creativity, politics, and energy of punk often had to fight with the nihilistic, drug or alcohol focused elements that constantly provided a chaotic and frenzied environment that these individuals actually thrived upon. For some of them, like Justine's friend, the chaos of the milieu ended in death and despair.

Bristol's second wave of punk was very productive and creative and was active around a number of serious political concerns. The Bristol milieu admired Crass, Flux of Pink Indians, Poison Girls, Zounds, Rudimentary Peni, etc., for their seemingly committed and clarified politics. They admired this strand of politically engaged and active groups but felt themselves uncertain about what they were doing and their own future. The Bristol milieu had a strong squatting scene, was prone to supporting animal rights' activism, class politics, and took vegetarianism and veganism very seriously. When we look at later developments in Bristol the Animal Liberation Front, Hunt Saboteurs, and Class War all had huge support and a number of activists. Wholefood companies like Essential and Harvest had bases here, often built and staffed by punks from this period. They had differentiated themselves from the first wave punks and disliked the

---

28  Justine Butler, "Disgustin' Justin," in *Tales From the Punkside: An Anthology*, ed. Greg Bull and Mike Dines (Portsmouth: Itchy Monkey Press, 2014), 85.

fake, fashion consciousness, and seeming lack of sincerity. This group of punks took everything very seriously, but then had to have a sense of humour because they couldn't decide whether what they were doing was right or wrong and also faced a lot of battles in terms of street politics, squatting issues, and general harassment. All the time the hedonistic and nihilistic elements were also keenly felt. Drug and alcohol use were a key part of this milieu and eventually in the mid-1980s caused havoc in terms of key individuals becoming addicts, dealers becoming violent, and money playing a central role in destroying a number of lives that were key to this milieu through having to pay for the drugs.

Anarchist punk in Bristol had many aspects to it. This chapter has concentrated on one of the darker and more negative areas as the more widely political and activist elements of this national milieu have been charted in some detail and some of the chapters in this book also do this very well. The darker more uncertain and fragile side of the milieu also needs recognition if only to provide a warning to all who are involved in these scenes and those who are to come. It, still for me though, is one of the most creative and important milieu to have developed in the last 40 years. Many of the music scenes around anarchist punk have been just as creative, and musically and sonically more interesting, but there was a clear attempt within this one to change wider social practice, lifestyles, and politics. In some respects this was very successful but in others we had a collapse of the creativity and a sharp descent into hardcore drug use. These elements can be seen to have gestated in the drug dealing and taking underbelly of this very fertile milieu and should be understood as a part of the very difficult social and political period. The various responses and actions of individuals towards those processes within a very committed and creative group of people yielded conflicting and often contradictory ends but that is the nature of this truly unique and motivated milieu and we need to understand all parts of it to truly know its power and affect.

MICHAEL MARY MURPHY

# ANARCHO-PUNK IN THE REPUBLIC OF IRELAND

## THE HOPE COLLECTIVE

**THE HOPE COLLECTIVE** operated in the 1980s and 1990s in Dublin and drew inspiration from anarcho-punk bands including Crass, Flux of Pink Indians, and Poison Girls. Before examining the Collective it is worth remembering that all culture, including music subcultures, depends on social and technological factors for its transmission. In Ireland, early anarcho-punk was often transmitted by letter writing and was frequently associated with zines, record shops, and tape trading by post. These factors have all diminished since then. What has not changed is how music and its culture can lead to social bonds. Friendships can be made via an interest in music genres; and in some cases this interest can be encouraged by family members. Occasionally, music choices can lead to conflict with parents. The recollections of two of the leading musicians from Dublin's current vibrant punk scene highlight the personal impact of their youthful interest in anarcho-punk.

Both of these musicians recalled writing letters to addresses provided on records from the Crass Record label. These led to very different, yet formative, events. P.A. Jesu from Paranoid Visions remembered being invited to his 'first punk rock gig', while Dave Linehan from street-punk band Hooligan, received a visit from Ireland's Special Branch, a section of the police force that deals specifically with subversion and extreme activities:

> The first punk rock gig I would have been to was Poison Girls on the Total Exposure tour, 1981. I got a letter from Richard Famous, 'cos I'd been writing to Poison Girls and I got a letter from him saying: 'just letting you know, we're playing in Dublin, in the Lourdes Hall, Sean McDermott Street – love to see you there.' Personal invite! I couldn't get any of my mates to go, Wednesday night on a school night. I was fifteen. So my sister very nicely volunteered to drive me to Sean McDermott Street which was very fuckin' rough at the time, and she parked up on the side of the road and was knitting me a black and red stripy mohair jumper. She brought her knitting along and she knitted me the jumper while I went to see Poison Girls. I came out utterly and completely elated because I'm standing there watching this gig. This is me. This is where I belong. I fit in this. And then Richard Famous comes walking by. I stopped him and expected him to go 'oh yeah, whatever.' He stopped and chatted to me there for about twenty minutes, giving encouragement, 'you should try and get a band together', 'the feeling of playing in a band is just astonishing'....It was organised by something called the Dublin Anarchists who I didn't know existed either.[1]

Dave Linehan described being twelve or thirteen in 1980:

> ...I had the first Crass single by then, 'Reality Asylum,' and I bought into the Crass thing very fast because I was so young. It was mind-blowing: you remember all the literature? You'd open the sleeve and

---

1    P.A. Jesu, interview by Michael Murphy, July 26, 2009.

they'd tell you about writing to anarchist bookshop, Just Books, in Belfast. I actually had a visit from the Special Branch because they found my name in an address book...my parents were stunned but they gave....them tea and biscuits and they [the two Special Branch officers] said...they don't usually get that kind of reception. And also I had to surrender.... Just Books had just sent me a load of anarchist literature you know some of the original anarchists like Bakunin, just bits of photocopied stuff like that, I had to show it to the Special Branch and they took it all you know...it stopped me writing off to those places.[2]

## THE HOPE COLLECTIVE

If the anarcho-punk movement inspired some people to form bands, or not to write to anarchist bookshops, it inspired others to get involved behind-the-scenes in Dublin's music community. Taking its cue from Crass, the Hope Collective, operating between in 1988 and 1999, was governed by an ideological decision to promote only international music acts unaffiliated with major record labels. The operation of the Collective appears to fit with some of recent calls for independence in culture and resistance to homogeneous commercial forces.

In a series of articles and public addresses which were written between 1999 and 2001 the French theorist Pierre Bourdieu explicitly advocated a response to what he claimed was 'misleadingly called "globalization"', a process he believed instead to be '...the imposition on the entire world of the neoliberal tyranny of the market.'[3] In some respects, the Hope Collective demonstrates how the music industry field can also be a site of political and social engagement. The Collective certainly fits Bourdieu's definition of culture. To him, culture, 'presupposes investment for no financial return or for uncertain or often posthumous returns.'[4] He depicted a struggle between dominant forces and individual choice and wrote of a,

2    Dave Lineham, interview by Michael Murphy, May 20, 2010.

3    Pierre Bourdieu, *Firing Back: Against the Tyranny of the Market 2* (London: Verso, 2003), 9.

4    Ibid., 70.

'...ruthless war being waged not only on the economic ground but also within the realms of culture and, particularly law through all the agreements typified by the...GATS...WTO...through the great concentration of the means of productions and distribution of cultural goods those agreements tend to foster...'[5]

Of specific relevance to the music industry are his quotes from Jean-Marie Messier, then head of Vivendi-Universal, parent company of Universal Records, the world's largest record label and Thomas Middlehoff, then CEO of Bertelsmann, the parent company of BMG Records. He cited Middlehoff's demand that the firm's three hundred and fifty profit centres should achieve a 10% return on investment within two years.[6] To Bourdieu this pursuit of short term profit represents 'the very negation of culture.'[7] Messier, who headed Universal Records, advocated American-style cultural industry deregulation in France. He claimed this should be done for, amongst other reasons, 'the employment of our children' and would, he claimed, 'open wide the doors of competition and creativity.'[8]

Bourdieu countered these arguments, which he represented as 'the mythology of the extraordinary differentiation and diversification of products.'[9] Instead he identified the production of increasingly uniform cultural products nationally and globally, and concluded: 'competition breeds homogeneity.'[10] Even more alarmingly for Bourdieu, 'competition regresses continually with the concentration of the apparatus of production and...distribution;' the result of this process being a 'veritable censorship by money.'[11]

## THE HOPE COLLECTIVE AT WORK

The Hope Collective is an example of a music promoter, challenging this 'censorship by money' by creating a culture within the framework

5    Ibid., 9.
6    Ibid., 70.
7    Ibid., 68.
8    Ibid.
9    Ibid.
10   Ibid.
11   Ibid., 69.

of 'investment for no financial return.' The Dublin-based Collective presented one hundred and seventy public music events between 1988 and 1999. Despite their anti-corporate methods and principles (the majority of these events generated limited publicity and attracted small attendances), the Collective was capable of filling larger venues to capacity. For example, they sold 1,300 tickets for their ACT UP benefit concert with Fugazi, Chumbawamba, and In Motion at the St. Francis Xavier Hall on 11th May 1992.

The collective worked with acts which originated from Ireland, Wales, Scotland, England, the Netherlands, the Basque region, Germany, Norway, the U.S., and Canada. The DIY ethic maintained by the organisation meant that gigs were undertaken for reasons other than making a profit, and many were benefit gigs. While not all of Hope's gigs were financially successful, or intended to be, they provided performance opportunities to acts that either lacked appeal to commercial promoters, or held beliefs preventing them from working with those promoters. Lacking their own venue, the Collective promoted gigs in a series of different venues, as was remembered by a member of the Californian band Green Day:

> It was in this tiny room above a bar, which even by the standards of the places we'd been playing in the States was a bit of a dive. Anyway, we were about to go on when somebody, the promoter I guess, told us: 'no one's allowed to pogo or jump around 'cause if they do the floor's going to collapse.....It's the first and last time I've told a crowd to 'go fuckin' crazy...but can you do it standing still please.....[12]

## THE BOUNDARIES OF THE 'INDEPENDENT' MUSIC FIELD.

This chapter builds on a series of interviews which were conducted with individuals who associated with the Hope Collective. A number of the interviewees used the words 'independent' and 'indie'

---

12   Stuart Clarke, "Smells Like Green Spirit," *Hot Press* Vol. 33 Number 22, November 18, 2009, 35.

interchangeably when discussing music and commercial activity.[13] Therefore, the meaning of the word 'independent' must be established in the context of this Irish music scene micro-history. It was clear that the interviewees attributed to the word 'indie' the values of independent in the sense of being unaffiliated to major firms in the music industry. This definition is contested in practice; the 'slipperiness' of the meaning both causes confusion and demonstrates how power struggles occur over language and meaning.

Wendy Fonarow's survey of the defining characteristics of 'indie' music highlights some of these difficulties. While acknowledging arguments over the definition of 'indie' music exists, her characterization of 'indie' appears to include discourses which surround aesthetic conventions ('music with particular sound and stylistic conventions'), as well as 'a category of critical assessment.'[14] To Bourdieu, these classification struggles are significant. They literally define the field: 'the struggles over definition (or classification) have *boundaries* at stake (between genres and disciplines, or between modes of production inside the same genre)…'[15] The meaning of the word 'independent' within music industry discourses has evolved in the past four decades. Historically the industry identifies the term with the collation of a specific music chart that excluded major record labels. To the industry as constituted by the sales charts it is an instrumental not an aesthetic

---

13  These interviews took place between 2009 and 2013. For example, Jim Carroll, an *Irish Times* journalist used the term ten times when discussing the Hope Collective and the Irish music scene with the author.

14  Wendy Fonarow, *Empire of Dirt: The Aesthetics and Rituals of British Indie Rock* (Middletown CT: Wesleyan Press, 2006), 27. Indeed, Fonarow highlights the commoditization effects of the industry. A word that formerly defined countercultural practice, the act of refusing to engage with major music firms, has been emptied of that meaning and re-purposed by those major firms as a marketing category

15  Pierre Bourdieu *The Rules of Art: Genesis and Structure of Literary Field* (Cambridge: Polity, 1996), 225. To Bourdieu these classification struggles resulted in hierarchies. As an illustration, if the genre 'independent music' includes all products issued by major labels (with their attendant resources) which those firms market under the term 'indie' or 'independent.' The system of hierarchies in the field would be very different from a field where the modes of production specifically excluded all major label products.

category. Recent discourses have both acknowledged the industrial definition of the term (non-major firm)[16] and positioned the independent firms as a site of opposition to major label practice: 'it's proof that you don't have to be backed by a multinational to be successful. I guess it's kind of the flip-side to the likes of the X Factor and The Voice.'[17] In the case of the Hope Collective 'indie' or 'independent' coincides with this definition, specifically excluding artists contracted to a major record label. It is not a category based on aesthetic considerations or one that accommodates self-definition. In its absolutism it is closer in definitions used by anti-capitalist social movements.

## BOURDIEU'S CRITIQUE OF 'GLOBALIZATION'

In his conclusion on how power-groups dominate any field or society, Bourdieu argued that the progress towards professionalization in the cultural industries and sports had diminished the role of the amateur. The latter were now engaged merely in 'passive and spurious participation which is merely an illusory compensation for dispossession by experts.'[18] Bourdieu's citation of Gramsci's conclusions; 'the worker tends to bring his executant dispositions with him into every area of life'[19] can be interrogated with reference to the Hope Collective. The micro-history of the Collective can be read as challenging hegemony. By active participation in the field of independent music production, Hope Collective members shared experiences which were not typically available to audience members at commercial rock or pop concerts. They simultaneously occupied the space of 'fan' and 'producer.' After promoting his first concert Timmo recalled '…I've never had anything else that made me feel [equivalent] achievements, especially that one Fugazi concert, because there were a thousand people there.'[20]

Bourdieu lamented society's convergence of self-esteem with occupational status and educational capital and Timmo, quoted above,

16  For example see Nick Clark in the *Independent* newspaper: "Artic Monkeys Make History as Firth Album AM Enters Chart at Number One," http://independent.co.uk/arts-entertainment/music/news/arctic-monkeys-make-history-as-fifth-album-am-enters-chart-at-number-one-8818013.html.

17  Ibid

18  Pierre Bourdieu, *Distinction* (Oxon: Routledge, 1984), 387.

19  Ibid., 387.

20  Timmo, interview by Michael Murphy, June 28, 2010.

indicated how the Hope Collective provided an opportunity to breach the causal relationship between self-esteem and education or traditional occupational status:

> I was actually going to leave the country at the time. I was going to move to America with a girl I was going out with. But I'd never had a job. I don't have my Leaving Cert[21] and I'd never been to college. And certainly putting on Fugazi – it was the first time that I'd had a sense of achievement that didn't come from completing a video game. So I wasn't going to walk away from it. And I just clung really tightly to it ever since.[22]

The place of Fugazi in the Irish independent music scene recalls another of Bourdieu's aspirations. He addressed the implications of increased concentration in culture-for-profit and identified the United States as a dominant force in the process. Yet he also felt that North Americans could participate in challenging the process. He acknowledged the paradoxical role of nation states in the process. He felt they were 'endorsing the very policies that tend to consign them to the sidelines,'[23] instead calling for individual and collective non-state action; specifically welcoming action from fellow scholars and activists in the struggle. In one respect, the relationship between the Hope Collective and the Washington D.C. band, Fugazi, matches Bourdieu's desire. The band's mode of activity within the music scene is frequently described as the operation of a group of activists.[24]

Fugazi's principles, ethics, and work practices have been well documented within the punk subculture. For example Daniel Sinker (2008) summed up many opinions when he wrote: 'Fugazi is perhaps most influential because of the manner in which [singer Ian] MacKaye and company have chosen to conduct themselves as a

---

21  This is a national exam taken in Ireland at the end of the Secondary school cycle.

22  Timmo, interview by Michael Murphy, June 28, 2010.

23  Bourdieu, *Firing Back*, 14.

24  In some respects, their engagement with the Hope Collective continued the support of and investment in the Irish music field by Diane Hamilton who had funded the early recordings by pivotal folk-group, the Clancy Brothers and Tommy Makem.

band.'[25] A statement substantiated by Michael J. Iafrate (2013), who has provided a comprehensive list of the band's distinctive commercial practices.[26] Furthermore, Bourdieu described politically engaged 'artists, writers and scientists' (who he collectively termed 'intellectuals') as 'indispensable to social struggles' due to the current configuration of power-groups in society.[27] Fugazi appear to provide a strong example of the practice of a politically engaged artist.

## ZINE AND TAPE TRADING CULTURE

The Hope Collective must be understood within the specific social and cultural context of Dublin's independent music scene. The country's relatively small population was combined with a historical pattern of emigration to England. Young fans of independent music and those seeking careers in the music industry were amongst those leaving. The market for independent music was also small, so realistic prospects of artists making a living solely from the Irish market were limited. Jim Carroll, now a music journalist, was one of those who emigrated to London to advance his career. He reflected on the Irish independent music scene at the time of the Hope Collective:

---

25   Daniel Sinker, *We Owe You Nothing: Punk Planet: The Collected Interview* (Chicago: Punk Planet Books, 2008), 4.

26   Iafrate lists practices such their self-owned record label, Dischord Records, which exists to document the local Washington, DC scene, eschewing music industry contracts in preference to friendship and trust, the label maintaining low product prices and advertising only with independent music magazines and fanzines. As a band, Fugazi demonstrate local community commitment by participating in benefit shows other activities; they allow audience members to sit or stand on the stage during their performances; they shun elaborate rock lighting systems; they book their own shows;are self-managed and prefer to play in non-standard music venues; this ensures most of their shows are accessible to all-ages. This encourages local community participation and bypasses the commercial music promoters. The band also keeps ticket prices low; do not make or sell merchandise like T-shirts and do not sell CDs or records at concerts to emphasize the shared experience of punk. The band actively prevented 'slam-dancing' at their shows and participate in debates about lessening 'punk rock's macho tendencies' with the aim of making the music environment more inclusive.

27   Bourdieu, *Firing Back*, 20.

We had a small indie press you know. We had fan-zines at that stage. *Hot Press* was covering it. It was covering it; those on the scene would probably say 'they should have been covering it more.' The newspapers weren't covering it.... But the other parts of an infrastructure just weren't in place. Bands weren't prepared to go with indies for longer than one single. There weren't people, the non-playing members of the scene, prepared to do labels.[28]

Independently promoted gigs in Dublin took place prior to the Hope Collective activity. A series of these were organised by the members of the band, Three Ring Psychosis, whose members were from the Dun Laoghaire and Glenageary suburbs of Dublin. One of the members, Tommy Trousers, described his introduction to zines and tape trading:

Then Deko[29] was selling fanzines one day and I bought a fanzine off him.[30] It introduced me to fanzine culture. I didn't realise these things existed. There was a whole network of people. You'd buy records by mail order; you'd buy fanzines by mail order. And you'd start writing to people, and inevitably meet other people who did fanzines as well and you'd start trading tapes. Tape trading was a big thing. It was all done in the mail, through the post. I started trading tapes, 'cos there was nothing on the radio, nothing much in Ireland beyond a few bands wanting to make a racket.[31]

---

28  Jim Carroll, interview with Michael Murphy, June 26, 2010.

29  Deko is the singer in the band Paranoid Visions. He lived in a flat above Tommy when Tommy moved to Dublin.

30  'It was called *Ten Years On*. It was a guy called Graham from Northumberland. The other weird thing about fanzines: they weren't from big cities. They were nearly always people from smaller towns and more obscure places. They probably didn't have much else to do. It was an outlet.' Tommy Trousers, interview by Michael Murphy, June 20, 2011.

31  Tommy Trousers, interview with Michael Murphy, June 20, 2011.

Niall McGuirk from the Hope Collective described his introduction to zines when he won a cassette tape from a pirate radio station and met the disc jockey:

> ...he told me he did a fanzine and then I saw his one, *Alternative Sounds*, and then I went 'anyone really can do this fanzine lark; it doesn't have to be like *Vox*'[32]. And then it was like 'you know there is so much good music...my friends don't even know it.' I just thought 'why not just write about the good music?' And to be honest, at that stage I was big into animal rights as well, and thought more people should know about that as well, so there was that dimension to it.[33]

Through reading English zines, Tommy Trousers became aware of the Warzone Collective in Belfast. He made contact with the Collective and Petesy Burns from Warzone asked the band to promote concerts in Dublin for bands that were playing in Belfast. Between June 1988 and March 1989 Tommy and his friends in Dublin promoted approximately twenty concerts. He recalled:

> [Petesy] just said to us will you do the gig? And we were like seventeen and when you're that age nothing standing in your way. OK we'll get a venue and we'll put on the gig. How do you put a gig on? You get a PA and you get a venue and you figure out how much that costs compared to how many people you think are going to come in the door and away you go. So literally, with the pure naivety of teenagers, we just walked into McGonagles.[34]

At the same time, Niall McGuirk was publishing his own fanzine, *Whose Life Is It Anyway?* The articles were initially hand-written, with

32  *Vox* was a Dublin fanzine, with a more professional layout in operation in the early 1980s. Anto Dillon provides more information on Vox and other early Irish fanzines: http://loserdomzine.com/earlyirishfanzines.htm Accessed 24 May 2014.

33  Niall McGuirk, interview with Michael Murphy, March 21, 2011.

34  Ibid.

some later typed by the girlfriends of McGuirk's two brothers, one of whom also photocopied the issues at her workplace.[35] He used two means of distribution: 'I sold them to friends and left them in town, Base X and Freebird, [Dublin record shops] and sent them over to Crass or whoever else was in it.' Additionally he participated in a network of other fanzine writers:

> [In a short] period I got to know other people selling fanzines. I used to send some over to them. *Ripping Thrash*, written by Ger Reid who was in [the band] Dawson in Scotland: he would have taken a couple. Then at that stage it was 'I'll send you a couple of mine if you'll send me a couple of yours.' Trades were then done....and I swapped fanzines with James Brown who's now editor of *Loaded* magazine.[36]

Zines were often a space for addressing political and social issues. McGuirk questioned the artists about their principles, including issues such as animal rights and their political ideals, noting that,

> for me music was never just about entertainment. It was a way of maybe affecting change. So it just made sense to ask those kinds of questions. And also around that time the miners were on strike, so it was quite a political time. It would have been soon after the riots in England. A lot of bands were political anyway. That would have been the kind of stuff I was interested in knowing about. It just seemed the right thing to do.[37]

This was small-scale production; zines had print runs between fifty and five hundred copies. In the zines, artists were challenged about their commercial practices. McGuirk did not exclude acts on major labels from his publications (as he would subsequently do with the Hope Collective) yet he questioned their business decisions:

---

35   Ibid.
36   Ibid.
37   Ibid.

I remember writing to New Model Army because they played in the TV Club and I was giving out to them because it was £5 to see them: 'this is disgraceful.' Then they wrote back and said 'well maybe we can talk about it when we're in Dublin.' And then [I] went and interviewed them and asked them the question. They gave a perfectly reasonable answer I suppose, but it's not something I would dream of doing now.[38]

## 'I'LL ASK FUGAZI':
## DIRECT COMMUNICATION IN THE MUSIC SCENE.

Letter writing and tape trading were also important to Tommy Trousers. This was how he first heard about the band Fugazi:

[I first heard them] just from swapping tapes. It's really funny because when you started writing to people regularly, you would give them a list of stuff you had on tape. I'd say 'oh yeah I've got this if you write back to me I can copy x, y and z.' Someone had a demo from this band Fugazi, and it's Ian McKaye. 'Oh yeah I'd love to hear that.' It was strange; it was all done by letter you know.[39]

At approximately the same time, McGuirk heard about the band and invited them to play in Dublin. Examining how the Hope Collective worked in practice makes it apparent how much of its activity was based on direct person-to-person communication. This is very removed from the expensive advertising and promotional campaigns undertaken by major labels on behalf of their 'priority acts.' Niall McGuirk recalled how

They were doing a European tour and a friend of mine, Alan Sherry was over in England and he heard, he used to work for Aer Lingus, so he got a flight to London to see Hüsker Dü. And at that gig he heard that

---

38   Ibid.

39   Tommy Trousers, interview with Michael Murphy, June 20, 2011.

Fugazi were doing a tour. And we were: 'Fugazi who are they?' Alan said 'Minor Threat, Rites of Spring they were in those bands.' So I went 'OK we should and get them to come over to Ireland.' So I rang up Southern Studios who distributed the Dischord Records in the UK and got taking to someone in Southern Studios and said 'could they play?' and they put me in touch with this fellow Jabs who was organising the tour and he said 'I'll ask Fugazi.'[40]

The densely networked independent music scene provided one of the other bands on the bill:

> Three Ring Psychosis got on the bill because they were a local band from Dun Laoghaire and in the lead up to the Fugazi gig I was talking to them and said: 'Do you know this band Fugazi?' And their bass player Tommy, Tommy Trousers, had a tape of Fugazi and he posted me the tape, it was Fugazi's demo. Because of that I said: 'Oh, well do you want to play with them?'[41]

After a subsequent concert in McGonagle's by Fugazi, and when the money was counted, a profit of £1,400 was realized. McGuirk presented this sum to Fugazi's Ian McKaye. The American singer refused to take the full amount, saying: 'how about we take £550 and you use the rest to do other things.'[42] The money was used to start a 'Hope' fund, which covered expenses on gigs that failed to break even. Thus the Collective was able to invite acts to Ireland even if they felt the concert was likely to lose money.

## THE HOPE COLLECTIVE AS COUNTER CULTURE

The Hope Collective philosophy and practice was initially influenced and inspired by a number of music acts, including English bands Crass and Flux of Pink Indians, local Dublin band the Pleasure Cell, and subsequently by Washington D.C. DIY advocates Fugazi. Therefore

---

40 Niall McGirk, interview with Michael Murphy, March 21, 2011.

41 Ibid.

42 Niall McGuirk, *Document: A Story of Hope* (Dublin: Hope, 2002), 21.

it must be interrogated in light of the sociological discourses about punk rock and counterculture. The success of the Hope Collective has also to be placed in the context of Dublin between 1988 and 1999. The sense of community which was fostered by the Collective within the music scene was enhanced by the lack of perceived alternatives. Their events became an opportunity for socialisation; for young bands, introducing themselves or getting involved with the Collective could lead to performance opportunities in concerts which support-visiting artists.

For audience members, the gigs were often 'something to do.' Niall McCormack from the band, Jubilee Allstars, recalled:

> ...the venues were clubhouses for groups of people to share fanzines, swap records, form new bands, argue about music, meet the few girls that actually were into music... But then when a big band came over, even a small band, any band that got in a van and came to Dublin and got out and set up their gear, everyone would be there: goths, punks, crusties, the pop kids. It was a diverse mix of people. But I think the core of it was this punk DIY notion.[43]

The way in which the Hope Collective connected with politics can be described as 'countercultural.' First noted by Theodore Roszak in his 1973 volume *The Making of a Counter Culture,* the author defines the countercultural as an embodiment for 'the young, in their desperate need to grow up sanely amid an insane environment, who hunger for lively alternatives.'[44] Sarah Thornton described how a number of theorists in the field, including Young and Hebdige, presented youth subcultures as inhabiting the 'progressive side of the political arena.'[45] A number of the Hope Collective members articulated a similar stance.

One member, Anto Dillon, who is the co-author of a recent fanzine *Loserdom,* recalled his introduction to the Hope Collective:

---

43  Niall McCormack, interview with Michael Murphy, May 25, 2011.

44  Theodore Roszak, *The Making of a Counter Culture: Reflections on the Technocratic Society and Its Youthful Opposition* (London: Faber, 1973), 183.

45  Sarah Thornton, *Club Cultures: Music, Media and Subcultural Capital* (Hanover NH: Wesleyan, 1996), 164.

I first came across Hope and the Irish DIY scene through the local free sheets and zines that I used to pick up in Freebird Records: *Gearhead Nation* and *React*. And, I just remember reading about the gigs through that. The first Hope gig I was at was Bikini Kill and Team Dresch in Charlie's Rock Bar. And I just really enjoyed the experience....Just a great atmosphere. I remember getting a flyer at the gig about Hope and all these tapes they had available...a kind of manifesto. I thought it was brilliant. A while down the way I started my own freesheet or 'zine.[46]

Anto now runs the fanzine, *Loserdom*, with his brother Eugene. They interviewed members of the Hope Collective for one issue and became involved with the collective:

And my brother Eugene in one of our issues...[got] in touch with Derek Byrne and Derek Byrne said 'do you want to come along to a Hope meeting? Then me and Eugene started going along to the Hope meetings and became involved that way...We used to have cups of tea and vegan biscuits...Braycott biscuits from the factory out in Bray. They were lovely...at the time I was only learning about stuff. I became a vegetarian shortly after. I used to hear about stuff like this. Derek Byrne used to talk about John Pilger and political stuff, Noam Chomsky.[47]

## HOPE AND PUNK

Dave Laing identified two aspects of the social construction of punk ideology and practice which were particularly relevant to the Hope Collective. He sought a geographically inclusive narrative for punk to explain the musical diffusion, the input of cultural consumers, and producers outside England to be addressed: 'what did Scots, Welsh, Irish, and North American people have to do with the process?[48] He

---

46   Anto Dillon, interview with Michael Murphy, January 12, 2012.

47   Ibid.

48   Dave Laing, *One Chord Wonders: Power and Meaning in Punk Rock* (Milton

also acknowledged, in the early punk movement, the influence of the band Crass in propagating a 'self-proclaimed anarchist politics' as more 'significant' than the 'fascist' leanings of some early punk groups.[49]

The first issue of McGuirk's fanzine *Whose Life Is It Anyway?* contained an interview with Crass. This is consistent with Clark's representation of the English anarchist group as pivotal in the DIY movement. The band's Penny Rimbaud supplied hand written responses to McGuirk's questions via post. Other acts interviewed for the zines included Flux of Pink Indians, The Damned, New Model Army, Billy Bragg, The Housemartins, The Redskins, The Men They Couldn't Hang, The Pogues, and The Wedding Present. *Maximum Rock 'n' Roll* magazine's editor Tim Yohannan put a forty five minute tape recording of his answers into the post. Dublin acts like Paranoid Visions and The Pleasure Cell were interviewed face-to-face.

Dylan Clark also engaged with the punk subculture. To him, punk advanced a 'do-it-yourself' practice where 'culture could be produced with less capitalism, more autonomy, and more anonymity.'[50] According to Clark, punk achieved this when it abandoned some iconography and symbols objectionable to members of the periphery.[51] Both Laing and Clark identify inherent contradictions of punk subculture, a subject Helen Reddington encapsulated in her study of women in the Brighton punk scene, noting 'the variety of views of people in punk cannot be overestimated.'[52]

This echoes the statements of some members of the Hope Collective. For McGuirk the perspective of Crass proved an inspiration, echoing the views of Clark who also acknowledges the influence of Crass in other punk scenes globally. Their work was part of what he described as 'a vast litter of anarchism' advancing 'a social form which

---

Keynes: Open University, 1985), vi.

49    Ibid., 112.

50    Dylan Clark, "The Death and Life of Punk, The Last Subculture," in *The Post-Subcultures Reader*, ed., David Muggleton and Rupert Weinzierl, (Oxford: Berg, 2003), 231.

51    He specifically named 'Dog collars and Union Jacks' (Clark, 2003, 229). The early ephemera of punk were often interpreted in different ways outside England.

52    Helen Reddington, *The Lost Women of Rock Music: Female Musicians of the Punk Era* (Hampshire: Ashgate, 2007), 165.

anticipates and outmanoeuvres the dominance of corporate-capital-ism.[53] While Hope may not comply with this definition complete-ly, most of its practices belong within Clark's framework. Many of Hope's modes of operations derived from its founder, Niall McGuirk's background in the DIY fanzine subculture. Reddington's conclusions are matched very closely by Ian McKaye, the singer from the band Fugazi, 'What was attractive to me about it [DIY culture] was the idea of creating something. Just to create your own community. We'll make it ourselves. We don't need anybody to approve it. We're just going to do it DIY.'[54]

## THE DIFFERENCE WITH HOPE

Most conceptualisations of the music industry concentrate on the ac-tivities of commercial concerns. Frith cites *Music Week's* designation of the UK industry as a journey from 'glorious amateurism' to 'multi-bil-lion-dollar corporations.' He also represents the increasing importance of live music for both social intercourse and the negotiation of collective identities. He depicts the commodification of the live music experience as somewhat inevitable: 'where there are social desires, there will be entre-preneurs – promoters, ready, at a price, to meet them.'[55] Irishman Feargal Sharkey, advanced the claim that aspiring artists are still typically support-ed by: 'the "traditional" music industry, whether in the shape of a man-ager, a label, a publisher, or a combination of the three' (his emphasis).[56]

The Hope Collective was distinctive in its removal of the profit aim. It differed from standard profit-driven promoters in a number of practices: it attempted, where possible, to provide alcohol-free and all-ages entertainment; artists were hosted in homes rather than in paid accommodation; no contracts were issued, all deals were made on the basis of trust; bands were selected purely on the criteria that they requested help from Hope in playing shows in Ireland; shows were not promoted by acts from the Republic of Ireland: they were

53   Clark, "The Death and Life of Punk, The Last Subculture," 224.

54   *Roll Up Your Sleeves*, DVD, directed by Dylan Haskins, (Dublin: Project Arts Centre and DCTV, 2008).

55   Simon Frith, "Live Music Matters," *Scottish Music Review* Volume 1, Number 1 (2007): 14.

56   Feargal Sharkey, "Let Musicians Play," *The New Statesman*, supplement, February 21 2011, 6.

only invited to participate in gigs to raise money for charitable caus-es;[57] the cooperative refused to work with artists on major recording labels; the members of the cooperative paid admission like everyone else attending the gigs. These practices should not be viewed as utopi-an even if they deviate from standard music industry practice. Because Hope did not control its own venues it depended on commercial es-tablishments and the types of compromises they entail.

These types of compromises have received strong analysis from Dylan Clark. He is explicit in his conclusion on the operation of punk collec-tives reliant on alliances within standard modern neoliberal economies. He described them as 'parasites on capitalist business', dependent and at times compromised by this dependency. Commercial music venues and their standard practices are anathema to subcultural resistance. 'When a subculture is bathed in alcohol at a club, centered on reverence for musicians...its ability to resist and be autonomous is in jeopardy.'[58]

McGuirk experienced this compromise when his band Not Our World played in Trinity College Dublin. An advertising banner for Guinness hung in the stage area; McGuirk wanted it removed. When an argument ensued which he didn't win, he resolved: 'I don't ever want to be involved in a gig that has an alcohol industry banner.'[59] When the Hope Collective presented a gig by Bis, Bikini Kill, and Team Dresch in Dublin they encountered the marketing campaign of a major alcohol company.

> Well it was Heineken Music Week or something in Dublin. But we'd booked Charlie's [venue] separate-ly and we walked in and in the venue there was just bunting with Heineken. And we just thought 'what's this got to do with Bis, Bikini Kill and Team Dresch on a Saturday afternoon?' That was an all-ages gig. So I went around and took the bunting down. The man-ager of the bar was like 'what are you doing man? I

---

57  The causes for which money was raised included Stop Animal Experiments, M.E. Association, The Rape Crisis Centre, Vegetarian Society of Ireland, and the ISPCC.

58  Dylan Clarke, "Walker Cells and Subcultural Resistance," *Peace Review* 16 (2004): 1.

59  Niall McGirk, interview with Michael Murphy, February 14, 2011.

said 'it's not sponsored' and if it had been sponsored we wouldn't have put on the gig. So we took it down.[60]

The standardised tropes of live music presentation meant that distinctions between the Hope cooperative shows and commercial gigs were relatively small. One major difference was in their approach to the sharing of knowledge and the encouragement of participation from groups often under-represented in music promotion. When financial gain is not the sole reason for an organisation, the discourse can involve community and life skills can be highlighted. The philosophy of the organisation was stated with hindsight 'as enthusiasm for what you wanted to do, the will to do it yourself, the ability to learn as you went, and the capacity to share with other like-minded people.'[61] Niall McGuirk described the Hope practice:

> ...it was: 'always address people coming in' and when they were leaving, 'always say goodbye to people and thanks.' And try to even...we went through a phase where we'd give out popcorn and sweets and stuff just to make it seem like: 'listen, you aren't just consumers at the gig – we're not promoters, we're all just people together.'[62]

For Miriam Laird it was important for attendees to know that Hope was a collective not-for-profit concern:

> We were aware even at that time of letting people be aware where the money was going or not going and that there wasn't a profit being made by us. It didn't go to our pocket. So we always put it out there where the money was going.[63]

The practice of live music presentation emanating from not-for-profit collective activity for 'contribution' rather than 'profit' has a long history. When the collective goal is not solely dedicated to

60  Ibid.
61  McGuirk, *Document*, 21.
62  Niall McGuirk, interview with Michael Murphy, June 26, 2010.
63  Miriam McGuirk (né Laird), interview with Michael Murphy, July 2, 2011.

making a profit, social reasons can explain the perseverance of the enterprise. Mavis Bayton for example found that friendship was highlighted rather than a focus on output for women musicians in her study. The conspicuous absence of women in the music industry has been documented by authors including Reddington. This can be seen in her her interview with Caroline Coon, who described how to young women 'it doesn't enter your head that the reason you don't see women guitarists is a political issue.'[64]

The Hope Collective contained a significant number of women. There was a conscious effort to be inclusive. Members of the collective saw a possible outcome of their promotion of all-female group Inside Out. It was an opportunity to inspire female musicians. McGuirk stated:

> If Inside Out could be used as an influence for more women to get involved…great. Doing the main organising of 'Hope' gigs at this stage were four people: two men + two women. Quite a few women went to the gigs but it seemed they played a less active role (if doing more than listening makes one more active of course).[65]

## FUGAZI IN THE ST. FRANCIS XAVIER HALL, MAY 1992

The May 1992 visit by Fugazi challenged the Hope Collective's organisational abilities, for by then, the band were able to draw significant numbers to their concerts. For commercial promoters, and bands, this would be an opportunity for increased profits. Niall McGuirk explained the situation for the Collective:

> We kind of sat around and said 'right Fugazi are coming back, this is going to be a pretty big gig. We're going to need a lot of help'…. we said we'd meet at the Winding Stair [a Dublin book and coffee shop] and see what we could come up with ideas for the gig…To be honest when we realised that Fugazi were going to play

---

64    Helen Reddington, *The Lost Women of Rock Music*, 174.

65    McGuirk, *Document*, 46.

a venue bigger than McGonagles we realised then there was going to be a lot of money. And because Hope as a promotion, as a group of people, we had no interest in getting any financial gain from what happened, we knew that there was going to be money made.... This fellow Brian, he used to just come along to gigs and he said 'can we do this as a benefit for ACT UP'? And we said 'sounds good.' At that stage ACT UP were pretty active with events around the world....[66]

The Hope Collective also lacked the resources and cultural capital to make the concert happen. They required another alliance. McGuirk explained:

And in the course of those discussions Colm [O'Dwyer, Trinity College Entertainment's Officer] came in...and he said: 'want to have it with Trinity? It's Trinity's anniversary; Trinity 400.' Because we thought it was the perfect size for Fugazi, obviously everyone had been to gigs at the SFX and had no idea how to book it or anything. So Colm took the booking of the SFX on, so he booked it through the Jesuits.[67]

In addition to advancing money for the deposit on the venue and booking the venue from the Jesuits, O'Dwyer also agreed to pay for an additional act, Chubawamba from England, to travel to Ireland. They appeared in Trinity College as well as at the SFX hall. Because their expenses had been covered by Trinity College, and they performed without a fee for the Hope Collective concert, a larger sum was raised for ACT UP. While Fugazi were reliant on the host promoters, and were happy to see the concert proceeds donated to ACT UP, they maintained a sense of control over the proceedings. McGurik recalled: 'Fugazi

66  Niall McGuirk, interview with Michael Murphy, February 14, 2011. ACT UP (AIDS Coalition to Unleash Power) was a 'direct action' lobby group founded in 1987 in New York. Its aimed to draw attention to the AIDS crisis and the lobby for a solution to the disease. For a history of the group see: http://www.actupny.org/documents/capsule-home.html.

67  Niall McGuirk, interview with Michael Murphy, February 14, 2011.

wanted to know everything: Where's the gig on? How much is it going to be in? Who else is playing? They wanted to be involved with the whole running of their gig.'[68] The Trinity Entertainment Officer also engaged lawyers when an attempt was made to break the venue rental agreement. Objections were raised when the concert ticket provided information about birth control and AIDS. It is unlikely Hope could have covered such legal expenses. Without this socially constructed alliance, the cultural capital of Trinity students and the institutional reputation of the college the event may have been cancelled.

The notion of inclusiveness was part of the Hope Collective philosophy. Alliances were formed with cooperatives in Belfast as well as small independent promoters in Cork, Kilkenny, and New Ross. In the initial stages of Hope (1988-1994) McGuirk played a leadership role in the organisation. During the second stage of the operation (1995-1999) the group functioned as a co-operative. The Collective encouraged attendees to become involved. Their intention was to de-construct the divisions between artist, promoter, and audience. The Hope practice placed them in the gift economy. Their relationships involved a network rather than the organisation structure which would be found in the purely commercial music industry field. While McGuirk selected the bands purely on the basis of them asking for help to perform in Ireland, his social network from his fanzine writing acted as a filter of sorts.

Hope's lack of its own venue (in contrast, the Belfast gig collective Warzone controlled its performance spaces) required fostering alliances with club managers. This involved relationships ranging from veterans of the Irish music scene, a biker gang, the semi-state bus company, the Communist Party, Dublin colleges and universities, as well as both the Church of Ireland and the Catholic Church. Yet their alternative practices and contestation of values did not lead to complete isolation from Ireland's field of power or overall social space. For instance, they profited from an Irish State grant to visit Belfast and reinforce their alliance with the Warzone Collective. They also benefitted from both the institutional reputation of Trinity College and the cultural capital of its students. In addition, most of the venues they used had emerged from a history of providing leisure for clients with a closer relationship to mainstream social mores.

---

68    Niall McGuirk, interview with Michael Murphy, January 18, 2010.

Similarly, their activities clearly benefitted both artists and individuals who, subsequently or at the time, participated fully in the mainstream music industry. The Hope Collective's ideological decisions placed them within a subfield of the overall field of cultural production, an area of 'restricted production.' Yet this did not confine the impact of their activity to that subfield. They hired venues, equipment, and skilled professionals (sound engineers). Additionally, a number of acts who worked with the collective subsequently enjoyed career success with major labels, for example Green Day on Reprise/Warner,[69] Quicksand on Polydor, Richie Egan (Jape) on V2, Babes in Toyland on Reprise/Warner, and Chubawamba on Universal. Perhaps they did not share the Hope Collective philosophy, yet they enjoyed the benefit of playing in Dublin at a time when other local promoters were apparently uninterested in them. In addition, a number of the individuals were involved with the collective later because they were full-time professionals in the music industry as booking agents, managers, and record label owners.

## THE END & LEGACY OF THE HOPE COLLECTIVE

The Hope Collective was in operation for just over eleven years. It did not provide income for its members, yet it did engage with the production of culture. This in turn had an impact on Dublin's mainstream music production of culture. Ultimately the Hope Collective wound down as other promoters began to cater for the growing market for independent and alternative music. Additionally, the Collective members found other priorities in their lives. Two of the members reflected on the ending of the Collective:

---

69 Green Day have seven albums which were certified by the industry for sales of at least one million copies each in the United States. When interviewed in 2013 their manager cited their early DIY European tour, which included the concert with the Hope Collective, as one of the reasons why he decided to work with them: '…if there was a text book of how it happened: they got in a station-wagon and played 1,000 shows. Got themselves to Europe on their own and spent three months touring Europe in a station-wagon, doing 62 shows in Germany. They booked that all themselves…I say to new bands: "if you are waiting for someone to help you – just go home and get jobs." Interview with Pat Magnarella, published January, 26 2013 at https://www.youtube.com/watch?v=J_tQWjhb1TQ.

**NIALL MCGUIRK:** I think then towards the end bands did start looking for money, to make sure that they weren't going to lose money. Which I can understand from their point of view, but then I think that ended up taking the fun out of it for ourselves. Because then, we became another promoter.

**MIRIAM LAIRD:** And there were plenty of promoters out there who would do it for money, who are coming from the same angle, which wasn't ours.[70]

The Hope Cooperative produced two artefacts in addition to its live performances. One was a 12" vinyl single featuring four Dublin bands; the other was a book. This volume featured the history of the cooperative as recalled by Niall McGuirk as well as vegan recipes from many of the artists who performed at Hope promotions. One copy was bought in a record shop in BrayCounty Wicklow by a teenager on his way home from school. He recalled his impression:

So I took the book home with me and I read it and a lot of it just resonated – like this is: 'wow I can do the gigs myself.' I had kind of been at gigs in Kilcoole [a town in County Wicklow with a DIY scene] already. But this was seeing – it was a step-by-step guide to how somebody did it and their starting points and how it grew. And literally how I put on my first gig was doing exactly what Niall had written about, which was ringing up every venue in *Hot Press* yearbook.[71]

Dylan Haskins described the process as a 'direct arc from reading the book to wanting to organise an event, to meeting the people that helped me organise the event and then asking Niall to be a part of that.[72] The idea of collaborative action appealed to him in particular:

70  Niall McGuirk and Miriam McGuirk (né Laird), interview with Michael Murphy, July 2, 2011.

71  Dylan Haskins, interview with Michael Murphy, January 22, 2010.

72  Ibid.

> It was definitely a big inspiration, just to see that
> people were doing this in Dublin, and to think 'that
> would be great.' And especially the idea of collective,
> that was probably where I first read about a 'gig collec-
> tive' and stuff like that.[73]

In turn, Haskins set up a DIY label and also produced another self-published artefact, a documentary about DIY culture entitled *Roll Up Your Sleeves*.[74] This documents the DIY scenes in Ireland and other European countries, interrogating the philosophy and ethic. The trailer for the documentary features a voice-over from McGuirk: 'if you've got something to complain about, then you've got something to do. There's no point in complaining about something if you're not going to do something about it.'[75]

The field of limited production intersects with the larger field of cultural production. The cultural capital (networks, alliances, reputation) can transition from the smaller field in a number of ways. The means by which Paul 'Timmo' Timmony became a professional booking agent in the large field of the Irish music industry demonstrates the permeability between the two fields. He recalled:

> And I mean being able to go and say 'oh I've pro-
> moted a Fugazi concert and you can ring their agent
> and see if he thinks I'm worth dealing with' it made a
> lot of difference. And the fact, even more so, that Niall
> had recommended me.[76]

## CONCLUSION

The specific nature of labour, working conditions, and career possibilities of the music industry mean the cultural capital acquired in the field of limited production can be transferred to the larger field. It can provide an entry point that may not be available for new entrants,

---

73   Ibid.

74   *Roll Up Your Sleeves*, DVD, directed by Dylan Haskins (Dublin: 2008)

75   "Roll Up Your Sleeves: A Documentary About Do-it-Yourself Counterculture," accessed February 24, 2011. http://www.youtube.com/watch?v=alOex97EIRY.

76   Timmo, interview with Michael Murphy, June 28, 2010.

lacking that capital, in the larger field. Both Fugazi and the Hope Collective need to be placed within their specific sociological contexts. Alan O'Connor invoked Bourdieu's concept of *habitus* to situate the ideology of Fugazi's record label: it should include 'the personal and the social geography' of Washington, DC. He quoted Ian McKaye who was encouraged by the early 1980s hometown scene: 'I think it's great what is happening right now, this kind of local or regional scene, as opposed to the nationwide music we've been living through all these years.'[77]

The co-operation between the Hope Collective and Fugazi demonstrates how local scenes can interact with each other. By empowering and supporting the Hope Collective, Fugazi helped to sustain an element of the Dublin independent music scene. They also provided an illustration of the activity which was advocated by Bourdieu: activists from the United States engaged with challenging the 'imposition on the entire world of the neoliberal tyranny of the market.'[78] The Hope Collective suggested possible alternative modes of, and outcomes for, live music production. This represents 'innovation,' especially if we accept the characterisation of the music industry as inherently 'conservative' as Dave Laing asserts.[79] The Collective proved Ireland's small open economy, with a limited music market, could sustain alternative practices. The members of the collective both lacked, and were uninterested in, knowledge of that standard industry practice and its evolution. They indicated the vital role 'amateurs' could play in that field of production. In some ways the Collective, by their inclusive approach and demystification of the separation between 'fan' and 'participant' appear to embody Bourdieu's demand: 'the relatively autonomous microcosms within which culture is produced must... ensure the production of both producers and consumers.'[80] It is fair to conclude that the Hope Collective, in its distinctive way, achieved that objective.

---

77  Alan O'Connor, "Local Scenes and Dangerous Crossroads: Punk and Theories of Cultural Hybridity," *Popular Music* 21 (2002): 227.

78  Bourdieu, *Firing Back*, 9.

79  Dave Laing, *Sound of the City* (Chicago: Quadrangle, 1970), 30.

80  Bourdieu, *Firing Back*, 71.

ALASTAIR GORDON

# THEY CAN STUFF THEIR PUNK CREDENTIALS CAUSE IT'S THEM THAT TAKE THE CASH

## 1980S ANARCHO-PUNK: ETHICAL DIFFERENCE AND DIVISION

*The name is Crass, not Clash!*
*They can stuff their punk credentials*
*'cause it's them that take the cash!*[1]

**THIS CHAPTER OUTLINES** the general, divisional aspects of anarcho-punk ethics. It explores what is involved in the production of
an ethics from a UK DIY perspective. Attention is drawn to divisions
*within* and *between* punk scenes. In developing this focus I do not
mean to rule out the question of international influences – what Ulf
Hannerz called 'transnational connections' – or the impact of large
scale social and political events. Nor do I wish to suggest that the

---

1     Crass, "White Punks On Hope," *Stations of the Crass*, Crass Records, 1979.

methods espoused by punk bands such as Crass and later US hard-core punk influences provide the sole model for punk *or* present the only authentic punk way to proceed. There is no such model, and no one, true, absolute way. The existence of scene divisions and dualisms attest to this. Punk generates a conflicting, reflexive, and relatively internal dynamic with regard to what it actually is, *how* it is conducted, how it is authentic, and how it conducts and presents its ethical discourse. Through its intersection of music and political practice, DIY punk discourse employs a definite rhetorical strategy which involves competing claims that are specific to the identity and values of any particular subcultural variant. It is on the basis of these claims that the main tenets and principles that collectively add up to something approximating to an ethics of punk can be outlined.

The five main areas below sketch the ethical standpoint of punk and are chosen for their direct and specific relevance to both the ethnographic subjects and the subcultural practices which were observed in field-research by the author. They are the initial inception of punk in the 1970s, the anarcho-punk legacy and the incorporation of American hardcore from the mid-1980s onwards.

## PARASITIC PUNKS AND MEDIA PARASITES

Declaration of the emerging DIY punk ethic was first set out in the 1976 *Sideburns* zine: 'This is a chord, here's another! Now form a band!'[2] Such expressions signalled a cultural sensibility in keeping with the alienation and sense of frustration at thwarted creative energies of working-class youth in the late 1970s. Gray articulated the early punk spirit of DIY: 'if you're bored, do something about it; if you don't like the way things are done, act to change them, be creative, be positive, anyone can do it.'[3] At that time there was a significant gap between pop music aesthetics and the everyday experience of unemployed and low-paid youth. This was registered as an extension of the previously existing DIY ethic of the British counterculture. Influences from this period fed into punk. In ethical terms it has since been manifested in terms of being and remaining authentic. The ethical imperative

---

2    Jon Savage, *England's Dreaming: Sex Pistols and Punk Rock* (London: Faber and Faber, 1991), 281.

3    Marcus Gray, *The Clash: Return of the Last Gang in Town* (London: Helter Skelter, 2001), 153.

of authenticity has directly informed DIY punk values and practices, sometimes in quite divisive ways.

Once established in the vernacular of punk culture, those who sell out, ignore, transgress, or just step over the mark of historically located punk ethics are met with the moral discipline of those deemed (by themselves and/or others) as authentic members of the scene. Joe Strummer referred to the punks in general as 'being infected with the kind of Orwellian revisionism and doublethink that was guaranteed to deny personal freedom.'[4] Gray also cited Tony Parsons as viewing punks' new ethics as 'Stalinist.'[5] This approach however obscured the internal division's ethical tensions and transgressions which were produced in the scene, as for instance those based around support for or refutation of such bands as The Clash.[6] The early period of UK punk revealed the first sinners and transgressors of a putative punk DIY ethic. The Sex Pistols and The Clash are perhaps the most obvious, though similar sell-outs, subversions of the commodity form and trade-offs, were met with equal subcultural venom in the subsequent years of punk's emergence.[7]

After the initial outrage and censorship of punk, the UK record industry signed up significant numbers of punk bands in order to stave off the general recession which resulted in the decline of record sales in the late 1970s.[8] This incorporation by the industry was viewed by the Epping punk band Crass as an utter travesty – a complete 'sell-out'. The term 'sell-out' here refers not only to seduction by the lures of commercial success, but also to compromise or even abandonment of punk ethical principles and values, or what, rather less kindly, we might call an essentialist sense of punk propriety. This was the first significant example of a punk critique of ethical infraction. Rimbaud stated that:

---

4    Gray, *The Clash*, 163.

5    Ibid

6    Ibid

7    See Matthew Worley's "One Nation Under the Bomb: The Cold War and British Punk to 1984," *Journal for the Study of Radicalism* 5:2 (2011).

8    See Dave Laing's *One Chord Wonders: Power and Meaning in Punk Rock* (Milton Keynes: Open University Press, 1985) and Alex Ogg's *No More Heroes: A Complete History of UK Punk from 1976 to 1980* (London: Cherry Red Books, 2006).

Within six months the movement had been bought
out. The capitalist counter-revolutionaries had killed
it with cash. Punk degenerated from being a force for
change, to becoming just another element in the grand
media circus. Sold out, sanitized and strangled, punk
had become just another commodity, a burnt-out
memory of how it might have been.[9]

This blanket ethical censure gave rise to the offshoot anarcho-punk scene with its associated claim of moral and political authenticity in the face of what was considered to be a 'bought-out'
and sterilized punk subculture. Rimbaud and Crass were in many
ways responsible for first voicing the concerns that UK punk had
become watered down and politically inert. For Crass the core ethic
of DIY had been overtaken by executive managers, records deals,
contracts, and money which diluted the subversive and political
edge of punk. Such sentiments were articulated in their first twelve-
inch record, *The Feeding of the Five Thousand* (1978) on the track
"Punk Is Dead":

> Yes that's right punk is dead, it's just another cheap
> product for the consumers head. Bubblegum rock on
> plastic transistors, schoolboy sedition backed by big
> time promoters. CBS promote The Clash but it ain't
> for revolution it's just for cash. Punk became a fashion
> just like hippy used to be it ain't got a thing to do with
> you or me. Movements are systems and systems kill.
> Movements are expressions of public will. Punk be-
> came a movement 'cause we all felt lost, but the leaders
> sold out now we all pay the cost.

The anger in this quote at the 'leaders' (Rotten, Strummer) in their
'selling out' of punk rock stood as a lyrical and ethical centrepiece
which was crystallised in the anarcho-punk scene. The development
of this scene constituted a significant political turn in punk culture.
To quote Rimbaud on the beginnings of Crass again: 'When Rotten
proclaimed that there was "no future," we saw it as a challenge to our

---

9    Penny Rimbaud, *Shibboleth: My Revolting Life* (Edinburgh: AK Press, 1998), 74.

230

creativity – we knew there was a future if we were prepared to work for it.'[10] The influential effect and legacy of this political and musical turn on my fieldwork interviewees (2001) was substantial. Under the threat of the Cold War and the economic and social decline of the UK at the turn of the 1980s, Crass was organized as a band which provided accessible and authentic conduits for the anger, and political concerns of young people who found themselves disenfranchised by both sell-out punk and organized political movements. Crass arose out of Rimbaud's response to the mainstream challenge which posed against punk creativity.

After falling foul of censors over the pressing of the 'Reality Asylum' track on the Small Wonder version of their first 1978 record *The Feeding of the Five Thousand*, they began their own label, Crass Records. This venture was a clear crystallization of uncompromising DIY ethics. Recording contracts were shunned; complete creative-control of the uniform artwork was retained by the Crass label. Bands had records released at an affordable price (the 'pay no more than' notice on records becoming operative here[11]), thus ensuring access and showing sympathy with many of the unemployed, low income, and younger pocket-money punks. The band lived on wages which were derived from record sales. Promotion and information were only granted to DIY zines and they only played benefit shows.[12] Under its own momentum, the band established themselves as both Situationist jokers – through a series of pranks on a number of unsuspecting establishment targets – and more importantly as the *ironic* ethical figureheads of the early anarcho-punk scene. They found themselves able to release records and compilation albums of other bands with a political edge.[13] While the political actions and music releases of Crass are too numerous and wide ranging to document here, their subsequent influence and legacy have acted as a blueprint

---

10  Rimbaud, *Shibboleth*, 62.

11  Derived from the Desperate Bicycles earlier DIY record covers with a 'pay no more' note on the cover.

12  Rimbaud noted that the two shows the band were actually paid for were the infamous Roxy gig and a Rock Against Racism appearance in 1979.

13  The actions and activities of the band Crass and their now huge legacy are too detailed and wide-ranging for the scope of this research. See: Crass *Best Before 1984* sleeve notes (Crass Records, 1985).

for the operation of subsequent DIY scenes.[14] The DIY ethical example which Crass pioneered in their groundbreaking early releases had a marked impact that inspired large numbers of political punk bands during the late 1970s and early 1980s.

## COMPILATION RECORDS
## AND ANARCHO-SCENE NETWORKS

The iconoclastic anarcho-punk compilation which demonstrated the spread of DIY ethics was the 1980 Crass Records compilation, *Bullshit Detector*. Featuring twenty-five DIY bands from across the UK and retailing at £1.35, this record achieved a consolidation of the early underground band network, not least through such practical devices as the publication of contact addresses for the bands. The second *Bullshit Detector* album, which was released in 1982 and retailing at £2.75, contained 38 bands who were mostly from the UK. The spirit of DIY was clearly present in the sleeve notes to this double LP:

> The tracks on this album express the real punk spirit of protest, independence, originality and refusal to compromise, even if some of them do not conform to the media idea of what punk 'should be'. Punk is about 'doing it yourself' and *Bullshit* is a compilation of bands and individuals who have done exactly that – it isn't going to get anyone on *Top of the Pops*, but, because it shows that there are people who want more out of life than personal gain it offers HOPE that there's something the parasitic punks and media parasites will never give us (*Bullshit Detector Two* sleeve notes).[15]

There are two observations to make here. Firstly, the ethical, rhetorical position of anarcho-punk becomes explicit in the phrase the '*real* punk spirit,' while the 'originality' and 'authenticity' of anarcho-punk resistance are registered as an alternative to the presence of

---

14   See George Berger's *The Story of Crass* (Oakland: PM Press, 2008).

15   In 1997 Chumbawamba signed to EMI and appeared on *Top of the Pops* the same year: the subsequent chastisement of the band turned into one of the most famous ethical transgressions of the 1990s punk scene. For more details see the band's self-produced video *Well Done, Now Sod Off!* (2000).

'media punks': those out for personal gain and fame, those deemed to have become the very things punk came along to challenge. The latter are presented as a target of resistance, and othered as 'parasites' in order to provide a benchmark for where the anarcho-punk alternative should establish its initial foothold: *not to aspire* to the mainstream of *Top of The Pops, but to inspire* in the anarcho-punk conception of a political freedom built upon bottom-up hope, trust, and solidarity. In broad terms the ethical position is couched in clear and definite boundaries of 'them' and 'us'.

Secondly, by the early 1980s, the Crass DIY ethical blueprint had clearly established its activities within a growing anarcho-punk sub-genre in the UK. Its roots were firmly set in a rigid and uncompromising reading of the core ethics of DIY punk. The 'anyone can do it' ethos led to inspired 'spin off' projects that both cemented political links and reinforced geographically dispersed anarcho-punk scenes[16]. The *Bullshit* compilations were mentioned by Danbert Nobacon as an influential DIY blueprint for Chumbawamba's first compilation of bands known as *The Animals Packet*, a tape that was released in 1983 of bands which made animal rights statements. He stated in 2001 that Chumbawamba had a track on the second *Bullshit Detector* and had already made a number of contacts from this:

> The first thing we did was a compilation mail order tape which was called *The Animals Packet*. We did a tape of our songs and then we did other bands like the Passion Killers, we did everything, we wrote and re-corded all our own songs. We did the artwork, we put the label on the cassettes and sent them out to people. And from that I mean the time was about 1983 we were in touch [with other bands] partly though Crass's *Bullshit Detector 2* which we had a track on and the Passion Killers had a track on. We wrote to everybody asking if they wanted to be on the *Animals Packet* and that brought us in touch with the whole scene around the country which we weren't really aware of or weren't part of. And from that we went to Crass's squat gig in

16   See Ian Glasper's *The Day The Country Died: A History of Anarcho Punk: 1980-1984* (London: Cherry Red Books, 2006).

London and that inspired us to go on in Leeds and
we got invited to play other anarcho gigs around the
country. And for three or four years we were part of
this anarcho-punk underground.[17]

Stemming from the inspiration of the *Bullshit* albums, the above
quotation demonstrated how the early networks of anarcho-punk
began to congeal. It illustrated how such projects were inspired and
developed around political issues and DIY ethical principles with the
above inclusion of animal rights as a new ethical site of resistance.[18]
These recordings are a document of early UK DIY punk scenes,
demonstrating the far-reaching impact of the DIY ethic between
1980-84. In total 103 bands and individual performers were included
on these records, though this does not accurately index the total number of bands active in the UK at the time.

UK anarcho-punk held sway with Crass and London band Conflict
at the helm until 1984. In previous years Crass as a label began to
release records by other anarchist bands such as The Snipers, Dirt,
Sleeping Dogs, Zounds, Anthrax, Omega Tribe, Captain Sensible,
The Alternative, Hit Parade, Lack of Knowledge, Honey Bane, The
Cravats, Anthrax, and MDC. The latter Texan band, MDC, alongside their predecessors from San Francisco, The Dead Kennedys,
made one of the first transnational connections with the UK punk
scene in 1980. This is the period when the main anarcho-punk bands
Poison Girls, Flux of Pink Indians, the Amebix, the Subhumans,
Rudimentary Peni, and Conflict achieved popularity and began to
form labels of their own. For example London based Mortahate,

17  Danbert Nobacon, interview with author, June, 2001.

18  First raised as an anarcho-punk issue on the *Stations of The Crass* record with
track "Time Out" where comparisons are made to human and animal flesh.
Animal rights became a central ethical theme over the next decade. Around the
time of the *Animals Packet* there were numerous anarcho records voicing animal
rights issues such as the promotion of vegetarianism, anti hunting and anti vivisection themes. See for example Flux of Pink Indians (1981) *Neu Smell* EP and
the track "Sick Butchers." Conflict (1982) *It's Time To See Who's Who*, (1983)
*To a Nation of Animal Lovers*; Amebix, (1983) *No Sanctuary* ep. Subhumans,
(1983) *Evolution* EP; Antisect (1983) *In Darkness, There is No Choice*, in particular the track "Tortured and Abused."

Spiderleg, Corpus Christi, and Outer Himalayan records: maintained a stable output, while the South West gave rise to Bluurg and All the Madmen Records. These were the main labels which supported the large number of anarcho-punk bands who were not on the Crass label in addition to the growing international tape-trading network.[19] Anarcho-punk was not the only subgenre to continue and extend punk culture beyond the 1970s. Many of the original bands such as The Clash and The Stranglers continued through this period, alongside the street-punk that included bands such as UK Subs, GBH, Vice Squad, Discharge, The Adicts, The Varukers, and Chaos UK, to name just a few[20]. The other subgenre of Oi! combined the earlier working class skinhead fashion and politics of the late 1960s with punk's uncompromising position. Bands such as The Last Resort, The 4-Skins, Sham 69, and The Cockney Rejects stand as examples of this and also as testimony to the plurality of competing subcultural distinctions within the wider definition of punk rock.

Such subgenres and subcultures didn't co-exist in peaceful harmony. There were numerous clashes between the various scenes. Divisions between them are emblematic of the competing conflicts over *exactly* what constituted the real, basic, and durable punk ethic. This period germinated numerous examples of violent conflicts, most notably between punks and skinheads and street-punks against anarcho-punks.[21] Throughout the 1980s many shows were marred by violence, conflict, and fighting between the various scene-factions within

19    The Crass imprint record label Corpus Christi is also important here, though not technically separate from the Epping Forest/Southern Studio projects of the time.

20    For a detailed account of UK street punk and a select number of Oi bands of this period see Ian Glasper's *Burning Britain: The History of UK Punk 1980-1984* (London: Cherry Red Books, 2004).

21    This is perhaps an understatement: attacks on what were perceived to be 'lefty' peace punks were often committed by skinheads and punks against anarcho or hippie punks as they became known. Some of the most famous examples of the inter genre venom were the war of words between the Edinburgh band The Exploited and Crass in addition to the Special Duties' (1982) 7" record 'Bullshit Crass,' on Rondolet Records. The documentation of the skinhead violence is captured on the sleeve notes by Andy T's 'Whine and Broken Noses' and content of the Crass live Perth 1981 CD *You'll Ruin it For Everyone*, Pomona (1993).

punk. Many street-punks and skinheads viewed anarcho-punks as middle-class hippies and so legitimate targets of attack. In ethical terms anarcho-punk was defined against the values underlying such threats. Sned, guitarist of the Northeast anarcho band Blood Robots, recalls one occasion of attack:

> A load of skins came one time when the Subhumans played in '83 in Durham and randomly beat the fuck out of the peace punks. As peace punks we weren't very united. It was quite a new scene and we were all a bit dippy you know we didn't really know how to cope. The cops busted the wrong people and all this shit happened.

The right wing, and often racist, perspective of the skinheads was in vehement opposition to the anarcho (or peace) punks of this period. Right wing forces and tendencies have proved to be a constant threat to those who were involved with the DIY politics of the punk left[22].

Broader contextual factors were also highly formative in producing the anarcho-punk ethical compass. The political menace of the cold war and the threat of nuclear annihilation were constant, almost thematic political concerns in anarcho-punk. This is a central point in relation to the formation of punk ethics. Rather than examine the complexities regarding the cold war and nuclear weapons and the general recession western capitalist societies were experiencing during the 1980s, I argue that the subcultural reactions to such macro-factors had a timely effect on the anarcho-punks' ethical conduct. This would have been most acute in terms of subcultural members' social class, ethnicity, gender, and geographical location in addition to their age and standing within a given subcultural grouping. As an example, Crass made connections with CND in the late 1970s and wrote a number of anti-war songs. The most notable example was the 1980 'Big A Little A' b/s 'Nagasaki Nightmare' single featuring detailed sleeve notes on cold war issues and the threat of nuclear catastrophe. As the above quote shows, anarcho-punk became known

---

22  For a lucid historical and contextual account of punk and Oi politics see Matthew Worley's "Shot By Both Sides: Punk, Politics and the End of Consensus," *Contemporary British History* (2012).

as 'peace punk' as a result of these anti-war activities and the political sentiments of the bands and their followers. Russ[23] noted that there was a sense during this period that the world was at risk from nuclear weapons of mass destruction. The only solution was to protest against this through any means possible:

> There was a real sense that things were fucked up back then. People actually thought the world was going to get blown to fuck. I mean we can all laugh at it now, but people actually believed it. I believed it. I was going on CND rallies, I was in CND and we believed that these people had all this power taking all our fucking money off us and our parents to build these fucking weapons, putting us all at risk.

Crass voiced similar sentiments. Through a series of statements, actions and pranks they created a countercultural climate of refusal and dissent which resulted in the numbers at anti-war demonstrations swelling. In 1982 Crass released a series of records condemning the 1982 Falklands war: "Sheep Farming in the Falklands," "How Does it Feel (To Be the Mother of a Thousand Dead)?" and *Yes Sir, I Will.* During 1984 the miners' strike and the heavy tactics of Thatcherite policing provided visible targets for anarcho-punks to protest against. The main events encapsulating such protests and also demonstrating the size of the anarcho-punk movement were the 'Stop the City' actions of 1983 and 1984. Rimbaud describes them:

> Half riot, half carnival, they attracted thousands of people who in their own ways protested against the machinery of wealth and the oppression that it represented. Windows were smashed while groups danced in the streets to the sounds of flutes and drums. Buildings were smoke bombed while jugglers and clowns frolicked amongst the jostling crowd. People linked arms and blockaded access roads and bridges,

23   All participant names have occasionally been replaced with pseudonyms in respect of their ethical anonymity. Some are cited under their actual name post permission.

while others staged spontaneous sit-ins on the steps of offices and bands. City workers were handed leaflets and told to take the day off, phones were put out of action, locks were super glued, wall were graffitied and statues adorned with anarchist flags.[24]

One of the interviewees, Steve, attended a 1983 Stop the City action and found the protest served as an ethical meeting ground for people. An arena for protest that was outside of the punk concert, this helped to strengthen the UK network of anarcho-punk along common ethical lines of concern. Stop the City actions were just one of many acts of refusal which were bolstered by the anarcho-punk networks. CND benefit concerts and marches, hunt saboteuring, direct action animal-rights protests, prisoner bust-funds in addition to the picket support of the miners' strike of 1984/5, were all political activities mentioned by the interviewees of my 2001 research.

What can be established thus far is a crystallization of an ethical counterculture that had its scene roots in anti-commercialist autonomy, social protest, and independence from related, wider punk subcultures of the time such as street-punk and Oi!. Here the presentation of anarcho-punk music as a vehicle of *authentic* punk resistance was set up, with their characteristic practices which managed to enshrine and integrate themselves into punk culture throughout the 1980s. However, as I have pointed out, this was not without a sense of ethical irony in that it left the non-anarcho-punk feeling unworthy of subcultural inclusion. That the presentation of anarcho-punk was predicated on a rhetorical claim of authentic autonomy presented other forms of punk resistance as dishonest *poseurs* incapable of conducting real punk resistance. For anarcho-punk adherents, theirs was nothing but a fashion parade. The real/contrived oppositional discourse worked as a mode of cultural self-authentication and moral exclusion, whether this was directed at accommodative leisure habits or oppressive gender politics. As the band Rudimentary Peni made abundantly clear on their 1983 Corpus Christi record, *Death Church*:

> The "Punk Scene" is just a big farce. Gigs are pretty much a total waste of time. It's not even as they serve

---

24   Rimbaud, *Shibboleth*, 255-6.

to create a warm and creative atmosphere. All that is created is an atmosphere of indifference and isolation. The average "punk" still wastes his or her time indulging in the same old macho, sexist crap. It's just boys and girls out for the night "getting pissed".

There's nothing I find more tedious than the rows of identical painted leather jackets – how moronic. Nothing changes at a gig. It is still just the same old world where men are big and tough and women are just their "birds", with the sickening habit of plastering themselves with make-up because they want to look nice and pretty for the boys.

No doubt by now, if you've bothered to read this, you'll be nodding your head in agreement as if it's someone else that I'm talking about – well it isn't, it's you. You are a part of all this shit. Why don't you try using your brain and help yourself for once, not just a pratt masquerading as a stereotype (Rudimentary Peni 1983 *Death Church,* sleeve notes).

Here the boundaries between street punk and anarcho-punk scenes are clearly drawn through evocation and severely ironic use of the stereotype concept that street punks are portrayed as a narcissistic monkey parade, a sexist gallery of 'peacock punks' who are incapable of authentic, real rebellion. In ethical terms the traditional punk show from this band's point of view has collapsed into 'the same old world' of social conformity that offers nothing in terms of an authentic punk alternative. This is one of a number of examples where ethical splits between anarcho-punks and other, perceived, inauthentic punks are drawn out and reinforced. The rhetorical position adopted is that you can only become authentic if you accede to and confirm the thinking of anarchist punks. A major intersection for such thinking rests on debates over punk, money, and authenticity. It is to these that I now turn.

## MONEY AND MUSIC

Autonomy, independence, and freedom are ethical watchwords of anarcho-punk. Attempts to manipulate, control, and exploit bands by those outside them are strongly resisted. They are resisted in the name of the DIY ethic that is central to anarcho-punk practice. It is germane to such practice that it generates a sceptical, if not downright hostile view of the multinational recording industry, especially where labels such as EMI had links at that time with armament manufacture or other ethically reprehensible concerns. This example combines two targets of opposition: the capitalist exploitation of music for the sake of profit, and the capitalist production of military hardware for the sake of profit. Making money out of punk rock was ethical anathema to the anarcho-punk scene. Making money out of death and suffering was equally a source of political ire.

Anarcho-punk made music central to the dissemination of its moral and political critique. The central aim was to make this as accessible as possible. Such accessibility is itself based on ethical principle. For this reason participants have always tried to make all their products and concerts either free or as cheap as possible. The majority of anarcho-punk gigs in the early 1980s were benefits for political causes. All my interviewees stated they were unemployed during this period. This enabled them to participate fully in punk music and punk politics. One of the most striking critical statements came from the band Conflict on the 1984 "The Serenade Is Dead" single on their London label, Mortarhate:

> A message to all the parasites, such as agents, record companies, and managers etc: FUCK OFF!
> We don't need you, you need us. We can function without you, but you cannot without us and when all people realise this all your shitlink racket will become extinct. Punk is not a business, it meant and still means, an alternative to the shit tradition that gets thrown at us. A way of saying no to all the false morals that oppress us. It was and still is the only serious threat to the status quo of the music business. Punk is about making your own rules and doing your own thing. Not about making some pimp shop owner rich. Realise the con in the punk shops, fuck them up, they're only businessmen exploiting me and you. I look around at the so called punk bands at the moment and ask this question:- "What the fuck are they up to?" I see major headlines in kids magazines, wall

pinups of some of the latest punk rockers hair style.
They play in shitholes like the Lyceum for £3 a time,
and they claim to be punks, listen the people who play
for £3 a time are conning their own people, taking the
piss out of their own supporters. Think. Keep playing
in places like that and the system wins....Shove your
contracts where you shit.

The language of this piece, in similar terms to the Rudimentary
Peni hostility to street punks, is obviously explicit in its venom towards mainstream promotions and record companies that create a
'false' punk geared towards exploitation rather than political resistance. The uncompromising style of the writing and its underlying
ethic illuminates the ideal of authenticity of anarcho-punk and also
simultaneously authenticates the band in the light of this ideal. The
underlying ethical message is that anarcho-punk is *the* correct method of resistance. Participation in the mainstream, or in street-punk
subcultures, signals an inauthentic subcultural member. The 'system'
is in league with the 'business' man; they are the peddlers of 'fake
resistance'. They dilute the *core* ethics of the punk scene as they claim
them to be (resistance, revolution, and political change) through the
presentation of street punk as a politically inert subculture. This is
a central point in this chapter. Those aspects that are deemed to be
subcultural (those aspects concerned with fashion, style and identity
politics, those that consume punk culture rather than creating it) are
deemed anathema to the anarcho-punk scene, which presents itself
as a *counterculture* set up in criticism against those members of punk
culture who pursue agendas that are not explicitly political.

Once again we should resist the representation of punk in ethical
terms as a *unified bloc* which is void of internal disputes and differences. We can pursue punk's historical narrative in order to offer further
illustrations of this. The anarcho-punk genre set itself a time limit:
1984. Indeed all of the Crass record releases, apart from being accompanied by a 'pay no more than' price tag, had a catalogue number
counting down to 1984. As promised by Crass, the band split up
during this year, playing their last show as a benefit for striking miners
in July, 1984. What anarcho-punk had created during the preceding
seven years was a feeling amongst its followers that some kind of real
social change would be the logical outcome of its various efforts. The

aim was that the structures of power would feel, and indeed *be*, challenged by its presence. Russ noted that:

> You felt part of something, you would go on demos and there would be fucking loads of punks there. Like the CND demos there would be two hundred and fifty thousand people there. I mean the first gig I went to was a CND benefit. I mean I wasn't involved in CND but that got me thinking about things certainly.

The Orwellian prophecy, with its famous dystopian date, provided the sense of urgency that fuelled the spirit of revolutionary change which was prevalent in anarcho-punk at this time. The demonstrations and benefit concerts were a central part of the anarcho-punk struggle. Both Crass and Conflict began to push the direct-action line, though bands remained ethically divided between the methods of pacifism and violent direct-action. On their 1984 album, *Increase the Pressure*, the band Conflict stated: 'Conflict are not pacifists and have never claimed to be, we believe and strive for peace and freedom but will not let people destroy what little we have.'[25] Crass made similar statements on their last single "You're Already Dead" and made token concessions towards Conflict's position while undermining the solidarity of the band's position. Russ commented on how he had once believed in Conflict's direct action approach to social change, although he is now sceptical of their claims of authenticity:

> Conflict were fooling people, they were raising people's hopes in that they could change a lot and that there would be a fucking revolution. They weren't to be believed. I saw through them.

While Russ was doubtful about the validity of Conflict, Sned also observed that a lot of punks took both Crass and Conflict at their word:

---

25  See Conflict *Increase the Pressure* (1984) for a succinct, sincere and angry lyrical account of the Cold War, animal exploitation, political apathy and the escalation of the arms race.

People took them on and I was just that bit older and Crass were the ones that did it right. I think
punks, anarcho or otherwise, were looking for a leader;
they wanted something to follow and so Conflict filled
that gap. And then the backlash against them was the
same thing. It's like build up, smash down. The thing
is this thing goes on through society and that we, as
anarcho-punks should know a bit better really.

After splitting up in 1984, Crass left the legacy of anarcho-punk
open to Conflict and this resulted in a backlash against them that occurred mainly during the later 1980s. Shortly after the event, Penny
Rimbaud ruminated in the sleeve notes of *Best Before 1984* on the
ethical minefield involved in maintaining rigid political views. The
fun was removed:

> [*During the first couple of years of Crass's existence*]
> for all the chaos it was immense fun, no one bitched
> about leather boots or moaned about milk in tea, no
> one wanted to know how anarchy and peace could be
> reconciled, no one bored our arses of with protracted
> monologues on Bakunin, who at that time we proba-
> bly would have thought was a brand of vodka (author's
> italics).

This quotation illustrates the long-standing legacy of divisions of
the unified subcultural grouping. As ethical alternatives crystallise
into daily scene-practices, transgressions become frowned upon. This
statement is one of the first acknowledgements of *intra*-group tensions within anarcho-punk. Crass ended their activities with a series
of poems which were set to avant-garde jazz compositions, *Acts of Love*
and *Ten Notes on a Summers Day*, that pushed them out of favour with
fans of the musical anger that was produced in their previous work.
Conflict continued playing benefit concerts and advocating violent
revolution as a theme. Indeed, though the subject of a huge amount
of criticism (including some from my own interviewees) and the target of general accusations of hypocrisy from the last two generations
of punks, Conflict remain active, still playing benefit concerts, running their record label Mortarhate. Their work has become such a

long-standing emblem of anarcho-punk ethical refusal that they deserve a book to themselves.

## ALTERNATIVE MEDIA

One of the most popular means of musical reproduction, alongside vinyl, was the tape machine. Through such methods of mechanical reproduction, punk music was able to be inexpensively copied, traded, and shared. Cassette-tapes were central to underground DIY punk during the early 1980s and through the postal system, bands, ideas, and lyrics were mutually traded and shared. They were traded between friends and were (and still are) a useful tool for making contact with people, establishing acquaintances, and developing alliances. Zines which were sold at gigs contained reviews of tapes and records, and carried adverts and addresses for band tapes. Chumbawamba used this mode of production and distribution to produce the *Animals Packet*. Sned reproduced his band's demo-tapes for mail-order in a similar fashion. He recalled that one of the earliest examples of record distribution stalls was tape not vinyl-based. When he played a Leeds squat gig in a garage in 1984 with The Ex, The Three Johns, and the Instigators tapes were sold at the back of the venue. It should be emphasized that this was not a money-spinning venture; the price was intended to cover the costs of production only. The main form of income for most of the participants during this period were unemployment and housing benefits. Sned spoke of how he was able to channel benefit money to fund anarcho-punk tape projects:

> They used to give you money for bedding grants and I put that with my giro and spent a hundred quid on a crappy double tape. So I would copy my band's demo tapes on it day and night. And from that my band had a demo [tape out].

From this tape Sned's band, Blood Robots, established firm connections with the anarcho-punk scene, leading to more gigs and culminated in the collectively run Station venue in Gateshead, Newcastle.

The break-up of Crass, the centrepiece of anarcho-punk in the UK, may suggest that the practice of DIY suffered a similar demise. The end of Crass was certainly a blow to DIY culture. The end of Crass should *not* be read as the end of DIY countercultural ethics and values, despite views and intimations to the contrary from writers such as George McKay.[26] The continuation of the post-Crass DIY ethic was stimulated by the introduction of US hardcore. Its subsequent assimilation led to new forms and took on the original anarcho-punk genre in musical, aesthetic, and political terms.

Bands such as Dirt, Doom, Deviated Instinct, Extreme Noise Terror, Electro Hippies, Extinction of Mankind, Health Hazard, Suffer, and One By One are just a small example of the bands that continued the political issues initially raised by anarcho-punk into the 1990s and beyond.[27] Such tapping into European touring networks which were run by the blossoming political squat scene and government subsidised youth houses (Jugenhauses). They all played Bradford's 1in12 Club with some relocating and become centrally involved in the organization of music and general club activities. These structures of experience and sensibility which underlie anarcho-punk music intensified as a result of the diminution of political change and the continuing political drift to the right. For Sned, the music of anarcho-punk was characterised particularly by its ethically fuelled anger. The fast, furious, and hectic singing, which was central to britcore of the mid to late 1980s, traded and developed the anarcho-punk styles and aesthetics which equally drew upon US hardcore thus making the scene even more abrasive, fast, and angry. Indeed, many saw this newer style of music as a clear expression of the frustration at anarcho-punk's lack of political and cultural achievement. The ethical principles of DIY were sound but nothing seemed to have changed: 'As you go on you just get more manic and more fucking furious and you get angrier as you get older, you know and that's shit!'

So although the UK anarcho-punk scene may have been in a state of slow decline around the mid-to-late1980s, this did not mean that its informing ethos had expired. Quite the contrary. Its ethos spread, either through anarcho-punk music or in combination with related musical forms such as American hardcore, not only in the UK but also, during the latter part of the 1980s and early 1990s, all over the

---

26   For instance, George McKay's *Senseless Acts of Beauty: Cultures of Resistance Since the Sixties*) London: Verso, 1996).

27   For detailed accounts of the continuity of the UK anarcho-punk scene during this period and beyond, see the UK scene reports in *Maximum Rock 'n' Roll* fanzine 1984 – present.

continent and the US. A notable illustration of the spread of anar-cho-punk was the Minneapolis label and zine, *Profane Existence*, es-tablished in 1989.

## HARDCORE FOR THE HARDCORE

In *American Hardcore: A Tribal History* (2001) Stephen Blush sum-marised the ethics of the American version of DIY punk, known as hardcore, in his first chapter on DIY hardcore. At a tangential point in time to the emergence of anarcho-punk in the UK, its hardcore counterpart came to the fore in the US. The two genres share a num-ber of similarities and also foreground the irresolvable argument of punk's origins: UK or US? In spite of this, with the UK and US punk scenes having mutual head-of-state hate figures in Thatcher and Reagan, the politics and methods on both sides of the Atlantic had a number of mutual points of intersection. Andersen and Jenkins recognized the degree of convergence between the DC hardcore punk scene and UK anarcho-punk.[28] For example, how Crass had managed to galvanise thousands to gather in London for the 'Stop the City' protests of the early eighties was taken as a benchmark for similar anti-Reagan protests in DC in 1984.[29] Of course there were differences. American hardcore dealt with personal and social issues in equal measure to political statements, while UK anarcho-punk concerned itself with instrumental, political critiques against the cold war, the capitalist state and animal exploitation. In addition to the more experimental forms of punk such as Black Flag, hardcore was also characterized by a faster tempo and a more energetic stage presence. Apart from early visits to the UK by the Dead Kennedys and then Black Flag, Minutemen, and Toxic Reasons, hardcore was a relatively obscure genre in the UK in the early eighties. After its introduction mostly through record and tape-trading and the fleet-ing band appearances in the UK, the DIY ethic began to co-opt numerous genres into its aesthetic style. These included metal, hard-core, and thrash having a reciprocal effect on the hardcore and metal genres. All of these changes were to have an effect in terms of the ethical reproduction of the UK DIY punk scene.

28   Mark Andersen and Mark Jenkins, *Dance of Days: Two Decades of Punk in the Nation's Capital* (New York: Soft Skull Press, 2001), 146.
29   Ibid., 180-209.

One of the first hardcore imports into anarcho-punk was Texas band MDC who played fast political music which was up-tempo from its British counterparts but retained a heavy aesthetic link to many of the anarcho-punk bands. For many who were involved in the British anarcho-scene and the wider genres of punk in the 1980s and 1990s such records introduced a whole new genre and style of music that had been eclipsed through the dominance and style of British punk from 1976 onwards. Hardcore has become firmly cemented into the culture since the early 1980s. However, as Rollins[30] notes, the acceptance of the American genre was not easy. Initially British punks were vehemently hostile to the American hardcore band, Black Flag, when they toured the UK in 1980, 1982, and 1984, covering them in spit and verbal abuse. Through Crass licensing the MDC single, *Multi Death Corporations* on their label in 1983, and the associated London anarcho label, Corpus Christi, releasing the debut LP from San Francisco anarcho band, Crucifix, *Dehumanization,* in 1984, the political elements of American hardcore began to reach and influence UK audiences. Sned commented that American hardcore was beginning to circulate via peer tape circulation around 1983. Sned notes:

> A lot of anarcho-punks weren't really into this. I had like a few friends that had like weird tapes of stuff like DRI and Minor Threat and these fast new bands. I was one of the first people to get into DRI and it was absolutely stunning, it was as life-changing as anything in terms of it being fast and political.

Crucifix toured England in 1984 with British anarcho bands Antisect and Dirt. Sned travelled to a Leeds show describing it as a watershed in terms of influence:

> This was 1984, so it was Antisect, Dirt and Crucifix. Antisect and Dirt were pretty good of course but Crucifix, they moved, they ran around and they brought it to life in a lot of ways and it showed us British people how it could be done.

---

30  Henry Rollins, *Get In The Van: On the Road with Black Flag* (Los Angeles: 2.13.61, 1994), 26-35.

Whilst not yet being the mainstay of the British punk scene during this period, the inspiration of hardcore was clearly becoming evident.

Jim and Doug mentioned a key issue that emerged in the mid-1980s. As a result of the influence of American hardcore, the overt politics of anarcho-punk were viewed as unimportant and secondary by these two interviewees. Indeed, when asked about the political influence of music, Doug noted that 'it's not affected me a great deal politically and I am not really motivated by that sort of stuff, but you know it has in personal ways'. These 'personal ways' are identified as an ethical theme generating the personal politics which Doug later became involved in, particularly the 'straight-edge' personal politics of abstinence. Jim articulated this in specific terms in that he reacted against the overt politics of this period and was instead concerned with personal issues:

> The stuff I was into when I first got into hardcore was heavily political. I mean the British bands [were concerned] with animal rights and politics in general. The US at the time, especially the New York bands and the straight edge bands, were more apolitical. It was about looking at yourself and more social issues.

The conduct of personal life can of course be said to be political. What constitutes *the political* is not the exclusive preserve of 'politics in general'. But if there was something of a shift here it involves an aesthetic move from concern with politics in a relatively conventional sense to an ethics of the social in a relatively conventional sense. While this distinction should not be pushed too far, given the overlap involved, the move shifted participants' orientation from punk towards the social politics of hardcore and its associate subgenres of straight-edge. For Jim, the social form of personal politics created a sense of separation from the majority of the punk scene. He noted that he gained a sense of motivation and confidence in his feelings of difference to the majority of the UK Street and anarcho-punk scenes.

Such descriptions of ethical separation within UK anarcho-punk and hardcore etc. leads the chapter firmly into the 1990s and out of the present 1980s remit. Suffice to say that the central point of the chapter is to offer a general, historical discourse detailed via participant interview and primary-source data to identify competing ethical models of anarcho-punk. This in turn has indicated a rhetorical model of punk ethics that is constructed, determined, and informed by a reflexive historical, rhetorical, and political/aesthetic context. Together this account produces a competing set of mixed punk moral compasses evident in the above accounts.

What is outlined above is part and parcel of a small element and a well-trodden discourse of 1980s anarcho-punk ethics. Far more needs to be said of the other aspects of the 1980s scene, gracefully documented by Ian Glasper in *The Day The Country Died: A History of Anarcho Punk: 1980-1984* (2004). That said, the daily stories and accounts of those audience members and anarcho-punks remains to be unveiled. That the UK anarcho-punk scene in terms of its Crass master-narrative went into decline post 1984 is only *part* of the story. More research is urgently required which investigates the participant role of the Somerset, Scottish, Irish, and Northern/Scottish scenes and also thrash metal and its aesthetic germination into the anarcho, hardcore, and punk scenes from 1985 onwards. For example, bands like Sacrilege, Onslaught, and Antisect in addition to the 'britcore' (ENT Heresy and Napalm Death); straight edge (Sorryside, False Face, Step One, and the fan contingent of the Northern Wolfpack) and finally crust subgenres of the late 1980s.[31] Such ethical tales need to be continued and theorised via competing participant and primary source accounts, and certainly *not* via the abstract philosophy of the unrelated and careerist academic commentator.

---

31   See Glasper, *The Day the Country Died*.

MIKE DINES

# LET YOUR SELF-DETERMINATION OVER-RIDE INDOCTRINATION

## DICK LUCAS, CULTURE SHOCK, AND THE ANARCHO OF THE EVERYDAY

**THE RICH, MUSICAL** diversity of anarcho-punk in the 1980s was a reflection of its aptitude and ingenuity to comment on a decade fraught with political complexities. From bands such as Crass and Poison Girls – whose experimentation beyond the 'punk' aesthetic showed influences of the classical, jazz, and experimental – to the more conventional Rudimentary Peni and Anti-System, the musical landscape covered a myriad of self-expression and creativity. Indeed, rather than merely challenging an established 'punk rock' aesthetic, anarcho-punk also challenged the political. As is obvious from its title, anarcho-punk became punk rock's more insurrectionary cousin. Not in the red-topped, headline-grabbing antics of the Pistols, but instead from within an organised political setting, promoting issues as wide-ranging as animal rights, pacifism, feminism, and anti-capitalist action.

Anarcho-punk, therefore, centred upon a manifesto of the radical. Crass sang of 'Bloody Revolutions', Poison Girls of 'Persons Unknown', and Flux of Pink Indians of the irony of 'Progress.' Legion of Parasites sang of a 'Dying World', Anthrax of 'Introduction to War', and Antisect 'The Ghost of Mankind.' The musical object became a platform for the increasingly focussed politics of this emerging scene, and although the umbrella of anarcho-punk encompassed a myriad of musical styles, politics became its unifying characteristic with anti-capitalist and anti-authoritarian principles coming to the fore. Indeed, by its very nature, anarcho-punk became a space for the cross-fertilisation of subculture and radical politics. With a still close relationship with first wave and post-punk movements, the anarcho-scene became a scene where animal-rights met class war anarchism, the ethos of direct action found an ally in pacifist politics, and women's rights found a fellow collaborator in the carnivalesque Stop the City marches. The dynamism and camaraderieship of the radical meant that anarcho-punk became a shelter for a myriad of left-wing, libertarian, and anarchist ideals and thus, in turn, became a scene where punks drew their identity from an intricate assortment of new forms of political, social, and musical awareness.

Although debates continue as to the origins of the definition, politics and musical stylistics of anarcho-punk, there also exists an on-going study surrounding the reflexive and often ambiguous nature of its identity. This chapter aims to be a worthy addition to such a study. By drawing upon the work and ideas of the anarcho-punk band Culture Shock – and in particular its lyricist and lead vocalist Dick Lucas – this chapter will raise questions over the relationship between political/subcultural allegiance and authenticity. Specifically it will look at the way in which this allegiance is played out in the more personal lyrical content of Culture Shock, where the 'everyday' comes into play.

Study of the anarcho-punk scene has almost turned towards a means of justification, of the reification of 'anarcho-punk' beyond its original point of reference, and instead towards a scene which has been re-positioned primarily by political allegiance. It has become a space where expression – predominantly one of protest – is played out in the utterance amid scene and oppressor. There is often little space for the individual, and although the means of production are often discussed (fanzine production, DIY record labels, etc.) there is often little room for the punk, the anarcho-punk, or indeed the anarchist.

Even in Glasper's invaluable *The Day the Country Died: A History of Anarcho-Punk 1980-1984* (2006) the author begins with the anarcho and ends each interview with the political. 'But were we anarchists?' asks Andy Coward from The System, 'well that was our frame of mind, and I don't think it changed really…[But] it was never about freeing ourselves completely from society, more like freeing your mind of all their indoctrination.'[1] Or indeed, in Ruth 'Radish' Elias's words, 'but were [Hagar the Womb] really anarcho-punk? I'm a communist and was at the time…The Anarchy Centre had Stalinists, Trotskyites, apoliticals and even Tories coming along…although I think most people were libertarians of one sort or another.'[2]

In turn, this utterance has become bound up in further complexities. Political and subcultural allegiance – albeit via vegetarianism, anarchist ideals, and other lifestyle choices – became a site of struggle for the authentic. A struggle where, as Elias notes 'those ideals considered as being in tune with being "anarcho," such as vegetarianism, took a strong hold very quickly, but led to elements of righteousness amongst those who adopted them, and hypocrisy amongst those who didn't but didn't want others to know.'[3] Using the work of the French theorist Roland Barthes, the debate around authenticity is further explored below, using his ideas surrounding 'myth' and signification as a 'spatial metaphor'[4] and thus highlighting the ubiquitous nature of authenticity in the scene as a whole.

These abstractions were subsequently played out through the utterance of musical material. Although lyrical subject matter and musical style informed a platform for fresh political debate and a consensus of anti-capitalist and anti-authoritarian opinion, one can observe a predominantly political and social relationship which was brokered on anonymity. Although an element of personal sentiment is offered (via the band member, the hunt sab, the punk) the recipient remains a nameless malefactor: the banker, the hunter, the slaughter-man, or the politician. Indeed, even anti-Thatcherite sentiment became a

---

1 Ian Glasper, *The Day the Country Died: A History of Anarcho-Punk 1980-1984* (London: Cherry Red, 2006), 343.

2 Glasper, *The Day the Country Died*, 156.

3 Ibid.

4 Roland Barthes, *Mythologies*, trans. Annette Lavers (London: Vintage, 2000), 123.

metonym for anti-capitalism and the abuse of State power. 'Who Are
*They* Trying to Con?' sing AOA; '*They* Lie, *We* Die' sing Flux of Pink
Indians (my italics).

There is certainly no question here of political or aesthetic integrity, but instead an exploration of the way in which the anarcho-punk
scene was – and has been – categorised and interrogated. Glasper's
own admission in the introduction of *The Day the Country Died* that
'even trying to label anarcho-punk as "anarcho-punk," you seek to
leech away as much of its power, by stuffing it into a neat pigeonhole,
where, once classified, it can be more easily controlled,' highlights the
definitional problems in writing about this scene. Indeed, his note
that 'the term [anarcho-punk] is one used…for ease of reference only'[5]
is a telling admission to the complexity of labelling the scene.

To add to this debate – and to raise further questions which surround the political and subcultural identity of anarcho-punk – it is
useful to turn to the repertoire of the anarcho-punk band Culture
Shock. Formed in 1986 from the remnants of the Subhumans,
A-Heads and Organised Chaos, Culture Shock remains one of many
British anarcho-punk bands which were aligned with the free festival
circuit and the so-called 'New Age Traveller' movement of the 1980s.
Originating from the southwest of England, and with Stonehenge as a
focal point (in particular the annual Stonehenge Free Festival), bands
such as the Rhythmites, Hippy Slags, and of course Culture Shock became the anarcho-voice of what was commonly termed as the 'Peace
Convoy,' a travelling community which consisted of, amongst others,
'anti-Thatcher town and city kids nurtured on…anarcho-punk.'[6] It
is a movement which is best remembered perhaps for the infamous
Battle of the Beanfield in 1985, when the Peace Convoy was blocked
by police vehicles on their way to the summer solstice celebrations at
Stonehenge, and where 'police attacked vehicles…smashing windows
with truncheons and dragging people through the debris.'[7]

Musically, Culture Shock followed in the footsteps of 'festival
bands' such as Hawkwind, Gong, and Here and Now, bands associated

5    Glasper, *The Day the Country Died*, 6.
6    Andy Worthington, ed., *The Battle of the Beanfield* (Teignmouth: Enabler
     Publications, 2005), 17.
7    Fiona Earle et al., ed., *A Time To Travel? An Introduction to Britain's Newer
     Travellers* (Teignmouth: Enabler Publications, 1994), 18.

more with a psychedelic and extended laid-back 'space rock' repertoire than the short, guitar-driven musical stylistics which are reminiscent of punk. Cultural space was built around a travelling, nomadic community that felt its own subcultural pressures apart from being part of the wider punk scene. Indeed, the travellers' scene highlights the subcultural reflexivity of this time for, although aligned as such, the scene was never 'anarcho' and vice-versa. Sympathies and values were shared, including music, with the fundraising compilation releases of *Travellers Aid Trust* (1988)[8] and *Stonehenge* (1987)[9] being testament of this.

In turn, Culture Shock's lyrics and musical style were reflective instead of aggressive. With a hybrid musical style of dub and punk it allowed lyricist Dick Lucas to explore more subtle subject matters such as interpersonal relationships and subcultural insecurities. Lyrical content moved away from anonymity towards personal experience as Lucas drew upon everyday scenarios inside and outside of the confines of the subcultural. It was also a move away from Lucas's previous band and the noisy, more typical 'punk' repertoire of the Subhumans, as Lucas notes in Martin Sprouse's *Threat by Example: A Documentation of Inspiration* (1990): 'after the mostly angry/cynical style of Subhumans lyrics came the more personal/hopeful style of Culture Shock lyrics – possibly proof that sound influences thought, or that the older you get, the more you experience (or both).'[10]

That said, a brief discussion of the Subhumans is useful to place Lucas's ideas and lyrical style into context. Lucas notes that during his time in the Subhumans, musical animosity 'became specifically directed against tangible forces of control and oppression (media, politicians, police, etc.) as well as further stressing the rights of freedom of speech and action,' a harsh and realistic awareness that 'reflected the political and social nightmare that was Thatcherism.'[11] Yet, it was at this point where Lucas's lyrics delved into a 'new realm of intensified awareness...[where] no one should suffer, yet we are all suffering.'[12]

---

8    *Travellers Aid Trust*, Flicknife Records, 1988

9    *Stonehenge*, Bluurg Records, 1987.

10   Martin Sprouse, *Threat by Example: A Documentation of Inspiration* (San Francisco: Pressure Drop Press, 1990), 18.

11   Ibid., 16.

12   Ibid.

He notes, 'the anger I felt at the way people behaved towards each other presented itself in emotional mirrors held up to myself for anyone to see. All thoughts went to words and their intended effect, that of recreating the feeling experienced when writing the lyrics…All else is peripheral, but still essential: it's the outside view of what you are about.'[13] In terms of subcultural and political integrity then, the personal became as important as the practical. 'Words will not sustain ideas,' he writes, 'if behaviour contradicts them, and the gap between lyrical honestly and empty sloganeering is the gap that proved that for some, punk was an attitude, and for others it was a trend to exploit.'[14]

Through lyrical content, Lucas began to explore the complex relationship between an oppressive capitalist system and the intricate diversity of the individual. If the impetus of the anarcho-punk scene was to criticise the political machinery of government, then lyrically Lucas's work embodied a subtle mixture of subject matter which drew together 'tangible forces of oppression,' and the everyday. With tracks such as 'People Are Scared', which asked the question of why 'nobody says anything on buses', 'Susan,' who 'ends up in a factory', and the nuclear war-driven 'Parasites,' the music of the Subhumans was to move away from expressing the confines of the subcultural towards an aesthetic that depicted the individual, and his or her place in a wider society.

In Culture Shock, Lucas further developed this ethos, steering clear of the anti-capitalist proselytising which was prevalent within the work of many already established anarcho-bands, and instead, through reflective lyrical content and the synthesis between punk, dub, and reggae, provided a lyrical and musical soundscape of the everyday. Of course, there are exceptions. Tracks such as 'Home Economics,' a diatribe against the looming Poll Tax of the late 1980s; 'Four Minutes', a look at the imminent danger of nuclear war; and the self-explanatory 'Northern Ireland' which deals specifically with political situations. But via lyrical reflection and musical style, Culture Shock primarily explored and raised questions of the relationship between the individual and those around them: whether it be the politically charged subculture of punk or through situations by which everyday relationships – meeting those at the bus-stop, observation of

13   Ibid.
14   Ibid.

neighbours, or existing in a bed-sit – are formed beyond the stage-set-ting of the anarcho.

Culture Shock entered the political arena of bands which are now reminiscent of anarcho-punk, but with Lucas instead drawing upon a myriad of social situations and subtle political gesturing to confront some of the insecurities and sources of alienation which were felt within modern capitalism. In 'The Time it Takes' lyrical emphasis is placed on the reconciliation of 'separate people separate lives'; 'Messed Up' is played out against a backdrop of 'social securi-ty, split parent family [and] playground violence'; whilst in 'Joyless', we learn of 'empty eyes without the spark of life', where we 'hide behind [our] anger and [our] pride'. As Sprouse notes, 'I admire Dick Lucas' ability to skilfully address common subjects in a very insightful manner [touching] upon friendships, insecurities, alien-ation and various forms of oppression....His honest emotions and clever prose add depth where others often resort to sloganeering.'[15] As such, Lucas's stance is more observational critique than dogmatic gesturing, with lyrical content drawing upon the personal instead of over-riding political narratives which were seen in many of their anarcho-punk counterparts.

Here, Lucas's social posturing also raises new complexities around the definitional, for perceived from the outside, very few of Culture Shock's tracks were typically 'anarcho'; offering instead an intelligent deliberation of social and political situations which were relevant to those within and outside punk. 'Personal lyrics are based on the prob-ably immodest assumption that the way I feel is likely to be a universal feeling to all people at one time or the other, depending to what depth they feel things,'[16] notes Lucas. There is no proselytising, no specific audience intent, but instead a nod towards a commonality of emotion and sentiment. Furthermore, negativity is turned on it head. With the sparse texture of the idiosyncratic dub-led backbeat, Culture Shock's musical style becomes a rubato-like landscape of lyrical delivery which encompasses subversive and subcultural self-deliberation and, in most cases, celebration.

In a recent interview with the author, Lucas notes that, 'I think it was a lot to do with the music. I'd never sung so much. I'd bordered on

---

15   Ibid., 13.

16   Ibid., 18.

shouting – or actual shouting – all the way through the Subhumans (apart from a couple of slower songs like 'Human Error' or perhaps 'Fade Away') [and] most of the songs were like get it out quite fast, eight syllables a line.'[17] Instead, with the introduction of dub and reggae-like characteristics Lucas was given a new improvisatory lyrical and vocal freedom, where explorative social and political themes and ideas could be played out. 'It was so much freer', adds Lucas, 'I had never sung to that style of music before…and because of that I started to write lyrics that were more about emotional things and the senses and the way people got on with each other, interactions between people rather than factual anger: it wasn't all about war and death and disease…'

This is indeed evident in the track 'Onwards'. 'And rambled and scrambled our heads to rebel,' Lucas sings, 'moaning and groaning but not facing ourselves.' With the freedom of musical stylistic, Lucas had the room to explore new ideas without the rush and urgency of the three-minute punk track. Instead, Onwards's improvisatory outro reflects lyrical subject matter, lasting for approximately half the track time, and is introduced by Lucas's celebratory 'Onwards! Upwards! Forwards! Culture Shock Stylee (sic) – all the time!' The mood is celebratory, upbeat, and positive. On the one hand, he is saying that we need to be more reflective – to look at *ourselves*, and to reflect upon how we treat *each other* – as a means of deciphering the injustices that we see around us; and on the other we should embrace this new perspective, this fresh challenge in looking at ourselves. To remember that change must also come from the individual, the everyday.

This is further explored in the track 'Go Wild (My Son).' Here, Lucas turns to the habitual, subtle practices that encompass the everyday. 'Pinning pictures on the wall,' he begins, 'running when the postman calls/Eating all the chemicals to keep you under.' As in much of Lucas's work, 'you' is translated as 'me' (the listener) but also as 'we' (others around us) whether part of the anarcho-scene or not. The lyrical transcends scene. We *all* run for the postman, we *all* pin up pictures; they are not atypically punk. He continues, 'watch the adverts form your views, get your wages join the queues, see the people

17   Dick Lucas, interview with author, April 4, 2014. All subsequent references are
     to this interview.

just like you it makes you wonder.' Again, lyrical content is neutral and, although non-proselytising presents the listener with a quandary of self-reflection, concluding with the questions 'is your mind a prison?/Is this how you exist?/Afraid to make decisions/Afraid to take the risk.' Lucas's subtle encouragement of a constant re-thinking, of the necessity for self-reflection and the re-working of the personal is evident throughout his work. Here, the idea of 'risk' is paramount, the notion of *our* risks, *our* minds as prisons. It is a communal risk, whilst also drawing upon the personal.

The capacity for reflection meant that lyrical content and musical stylistic also began to provide an observational critique of the anarcho and the wider punk scene. Accompanying this experimentation of musical form and genre there emerged a new form of intelligent critique towards the now maturing punk scene. It is perhaps ironic that a subculture that regularly addressed antiauthoritarian ideas could itself be hierarchical in nature, but of course, this is not just true of anarcho-punk, but also of youth culture *per se*. Moreover, complexities of organisational structures (that can exist within any culture) may also be magnified and exaggerated within the relatively small and restricted arena of the subcultural. From the subjective, or individual – such as the questions of authenticity – and the 'I'm more punk than you' brigade – or to the wider rules which deal with dress code, obvious lifestyle choices, regionalism, and age, 'belonging' and 'fitting in' are concepts and ideas which are bound up in numerous complexities and, perhaps even more so within a culture that confronts and deals with those very ideas.

If Lucas and Culture Shock were trying to highlight these complexities, they were certainly not alone. Others, too, were feeling a sense of personal reflection. Antisect's Pete Lyons notes how the band's 'outright political edge that was there in the earlier years had slowly developed into a much more personal set of values. Just as relevant we felt, but more difficult to put into words.'[18] Or the feeling of pigeonholing and individual restraint in being labelled 'anarcho-punk.' 'Personally, I would avoid such labels,' notes Sean Finnis from Exit-stance, 'why be confined or limit yourself to one form of expression? Surely it's better to experiment and keep things interesting, to keep confronting?'[19]

---

18   Glasper, *The Day the Country Died*, 312-313.
19   Ibid., 321.

Some attempts at confronting an authentic academic anarcho-punk 'identity' or 'definition' have inadvertently built a make-
shift wall between this scene and those around them. The idea/label
of the 'anarcho' has continued to embody a divisive mythology that
has apparently strengthened post-1980s, a practice that has simplified
analytical debate over the relationship of anarcho-punk within the
wider punk scene. Indeed, discussion of anarcho-punk is often centred upon the anarcho being somehow *separate* or indeed *distinct* from
that punk scene. Yet, as well as drawing upon a more organised political approach, the anarcho also drew from the complexities of what is
now 'punk.' It is evident that turntables across the country were playing Crass alongside the Exploited, the Subhumans alongside Charged
GBH, and Amebix alongside Abrasive Wheels: all under the complex
mélange of punk. It is often easier to create divisions where often they
do not exist, to conjure up labels to pigeonhole, and simplify. And,
as the mythology of anarcho-punk has grown over the years, then the
divisive and often detrimental has arisen from its analysis, creating a
'label' that defies dynamism and interplay.

In turn, this mythologising of labels, of analytical emphasis on
lifestyle choices, and the drama between the 'real' and the inauthentic,
also play themselves out on a grassroots level. As the 'anarcho' became
an established label of discourse in the punk fraternity, so those within
that tag also fell prey to the snobbery and condescension of the authentic. Indeed, what had made anarcho-punk so strong – the diversity of political associations and multiplicity of musical styles – also
made it ripe for in-house fighting; but not only in terms of fashion
and subcultural ownership but also in the jostling of the political.
Questions arose over lifestyle decisions and anarcho-membership: is
it possible to eat meat and be an anarcho-punk? Is it possible to vote
and be an anarcho-punk? Indeed, is it okay to *work* within 'the system' and *still* call oneself an anarcho-punk? Self-righteous subcultural
membership – as noted by Elias above – became part and parcel of the
anarcho-punk 'experience.'

Anarcho-punk became, in using the ideas of Roland Barthes and
his seminal work *Mythologies* (2000) 'decorated, adapted to a certain
point of consumption, laden with literary self-indulgence, revolt, images, in short with a type of social *usage*'[20] that denies – nay, *blurs*

20   Barthes, *Mythologies*, 109.

– definition. Authenticity in the scene pervades Barthes's notion of 'myth' and, in particular, his thoughts on 'the quantification of quality,' where 'aesthetic realities…partake of an immaterial essence',[21] and where the indefinable becomes quantifiable through a check list of effects. In Barthes's words, 'a whole circuit of computable appearances establishes a quantitative equality,'[22] where the 'pay no more than' label becomes a sign of anarcho-authenticity and the obligatory anti-war, pro-animal rights tracks become a necessity.

Similarly, Barthes's writing concerning myth and proverb – what he terms as 'statement of fact' – lends itself to the language of the anarcho-punk scene. 'All our popular proverbs thus represent active speech which has gradually solidified into reflexive speech,' he notes, 'but where reflection is curtailed, reduced to a statement of fact, and so to speak timid, prudent and closely hugging experience.'[23] Slogans such as 'Fight War, Not Wars,' 'There Is No Authority But Yourself', and 'No Gods, No Masters' have become synonymous with the anarcho-punk scene, but at the same time stuck-fast, where 'the statement is no longer directed towards a world to be made [but instead overlays] one which is already made.'[24]

The use of Barthes is important here in providing a link between authenticity and subcultural openness. As Lucas notes, there is 'a fine line between suggesting an alternative lifestyle and being dictatorial, so, anyone who didn't like anarcho-punk could always accuse the anarcho-punks of being the latter'.[25] Indeed, Lucas was always a tad uncomfortable with being grouped within the anarcho-punk scene. 'I was still living at home back then, and when I got a car I was obviously buying petrol that was polluting the earth…I was still eating meat until 1983. I didn't think I was 'anarcho' because I wasn't "100% anarcho"…whatever that is.'[26] With hindsight one is able to interrogate stereotypes and labels, to unpack and explore the 'authentic' and to break apart the Barthian essence of myth and proverb, the 'overlaying' the ready-made. Lucas agrees that he has

---

21 Ibid., 153.
22 Ibid., 154.
23 Ibid
24 Ibid
25 Glasper, *The Day the Country Died*, 180.
26 Ibid

'ideas linked to the whole massive canopy of anarchist ideas,' but instead of confining those ideas, he conceived of a celebration of difference, the carousing of diversity as a means of reflection and change; as a suggestive retort towards the often over-authoritarian nature of subculture and the need to accept the underlying etiquette of the organizational.

Indeed, he notes that, 'everyone is different from everyone else, so it is just the case of seeing the uniting factors and the fact that the biggest uniting factor that we've got is that everybody is different to everybody else, and will not readily accept being shoved having labels put on them'. He continues,

> the whole labelling of people is only handy for an instance if you need to know something really quickly about someone...does he like this or that...but there is so much more to discover by checking out people's differences than there is to discover by checking out the stuff that makes you the same as somebody else. Having your own idea of yourself bolstered by meeting people who are similar is nice, but it's not progressive it's just a stabilizing thing – it's good for people to feel that they're part of a crowd, that they're not on their own.

For Lucas, therefore punk rock was a space to unite the disenfranchised:

> to unite people together who felt completely alienated from society because they were being told, "It just goes like this, you grow up, you lose your innocence, you get your exams, you get a job, you get your pension, you marry and have kids in the meantime, you retire, you go on holiday and you die." But what if you're no good at the first one, or the second one? How are you going to progress from really hating being at school and being told what to do, or just not getting it when they tell you it's really easy? And then you try to get on with people around you, and they get it, and they think it's easy, they Lord it over you cos they think

they are progressing it up the social chain, and you're
left struggling trying to find the fucking missing links
– and then music comes along...

This does not mean that Culture Shock were 'anti-label' as such.
Lucas admits that 'the lyrics and attitudes [of the band] became more
anarcho as we found out more and experienced more and saw more
and thought more' but once again he notes the importance of reflection and thoughtfulness, as 'consideration really does open out a lot
more in your own head (it's not what you see so much but how you
react to it that sets these things in motion) so I guess we became more
anarcho-punk as we went on.' What Lucas disliked, however, was the
process of labelling a band/individual as a means of classification. In
other words, a classification 'that sets in motion a whole set of pre-de-
fined norms and values, as the confines of label [which] are in everybody else's head on a singular basis.'

He continues, 'they think "anarchist band, they should be doing
this, they ought to be doing that," and suddenly if you're not doing
this or you're not doing that, then you're a hypocrite or you've sold-
out or whatever.' He concludes, 'you're charging too much for this gig
to get in, if you're an anarchist band why are you playing the 100 Club
– cos they're just money grabbing bastards – all that stuff would occasionally pop up. It's like, well, you know, we're just as anarchist as you
are or we're not as anarchist as you are, and really, stop beating around
the bush and nit-picking. You either like what we do or you don't: if
you don't, do something better, if you do, let us know and we'll carry
on doing it...you don't even set your own rules, the rules are partly set
for you by people who are witnessing what you're doing, and they like
or dislike it and they will put you in a bracket to suit their own taste.'

This is not to say that punk should not re-interpret or appropriate
practices and ideas that provide new insights or creative paths. Indeed,
Elias's noting of the libertarian aspect of punk highlights the porous
nature of the subculture. Furthermore, it should not be surprising
that punk and anarchism should (beside the context of 'chaos') have
much in common with the methodologies and principles of anarchism. As Jesse Cohn so rightly notes, anarchist interpretive practices
lend themselves to be 'theoretical magpies',[27] drawing upon theories

---

27 Robert H. Haworth, eds., *Anarchist Pedagogies: Collective Actions, Theories and*

and ideas that encompass a wide range of libertarian ideologies. In Justin Mueller's words, anarchism 'refers to a cluster of ideologies, movements, and theories that share a family resemblance to each other, rather than to a largely enclosed and holistic system of thought.'[28] Furthermore, 'the wide variety of often conflicting opinions that fall under the label of "anarchism"…should not be termed as simple internal "contradictions" [but rather a representation of] an experimental "plurality of possibilities."'[29]

As a means of 'joining the dots' between the ideas of definition and authenticity it is useful to see punk – and, under its umbrella, anarcho-punk – in terms of this 'plurality of possibilities.' Although it does not altogether solve the tensions within a complex and diverse scene it does, nevertheless, find ways to solve the apparent contradictions which are found in punk. As with the porous nature of 'anarchism,' and the celebration of that fluidity, so 'punk', too, should be seen less as contradiction and more as a unified 'entity.' In terms of anarcho-punk, this also allows for a fresh look at definition. With the amalgamation of two complex entities, a subversive and subcultural space is created where a myriad of ideas are drawn together to provide a fluid and almost transcendental whole. The notion of the 'anarcho' therefore becomes easier to understand by embracing the diversity and contradictions bound up within the 'scene'.

To add to this, Culture Shock shined fresh light on the interpretation of the anarcho-punk scene. They offered a new perspective on unravelling the intricacies and contradictions of the scene, placing emphasis on the individual in the everyday. Proselytizing was thus left to others, with Lucas's lyrical content directed to the individual: evidence of which can be seen in the finale of 'Instinctive Spontaneity Drive', the definitive track from *Onwards and Upwards* (1988). Written overnight 'in the back of a van [whilst] travelling on tour between Toronto and somewhere else in America', it is the track's conclusion that is most indicative of the emotive. Although its reflective beginning is typically Culture Shock, Lucas's lyrical frustration is embedded in the gradual build up of musical texture, structure, and lyrical delivery. The track almost finishes twelve lines early, with Lucas's

*Critical Reflections on Education* (Oakland: PM Press, 2012), 7.

28  Ibid., 15.

29  Ibid

equally dismissive, 'this structure is sick it's even making me ill/It rubs off on me, you can tell by these songs' and referring to Lucas's own lifestyle choices, 'I went the other way, I think it's wrong.' But from here Lucas shows his real frustration. Lyrical delivery turns to recitative, and the flexible nature of Culture Shock's reggae/dub musical style comes to the fore. 'Oh fuck, it's all too much', speaks a worn-out, ranting Lucas, 'It's all out of touch.'

With momentum building again, melody returns, slow at first but building towards the conclusion of the track. 'You're telling me I can hear you, you see/I can see you can hear but you cannot believe/Cos your concept of life lies in envy and greed', continues Lucas. 'But just cos you want something doesn't mean you need/If you can hear and be conscious the rest comes for free'. As the track comes to a close, Lucas completes the reflective circle. 'Now slag this song! Go on tell me I'm wrong/Or tell me I'm right whatever you like/But please don't take so long/Or all the spontaneous thoughts will be gone'. Importance lies not within the aesthetic, nor brokered anonymity. Instead, the individual – whether he/she is a punk, anarcho-punk, or neutral listener – remains.

PETE DALE

# MORE THAN MUSIC?

## CONFUSIONS OF MUSICAL STYLE AND POLITICAL ATTITUDE IN ANARCHO-PUNK FROM CRASS ONWARDS

'MORE THAN MUSIC': it is one of the most long-running conceits in punk. Think of Conflict's proclamation in 'Increase the Pressure': 'it takes more than music, it takes more than words... Power must be tested, it's testing time.'[1] Then there's the *More Than Music Fest* which was held each year from 1993 until 2003 in Columbus, Ohio: the name attempts to signal punk's political importance beyond its aesthetic preferences (at that time, primarily a preference for semi-metal 'hardcore' riffing and screamed vocals, an aesthetic preference which I shall focus upon in this chapter). To a significant extent, the idea that punk isn't just about music goes right back to the 'first wave' UK punks of the 1970s: '"What is this abomination? It's not music." And of course in a way that was the point: it was much better than music – it was something to upset your parents!'[2] This directive – use

---

1    Conflict, *Increase the Pressure*, Mortarhate Records, 1984.

2    Richard Strange of the band Doctors of Madness describing a common response

anti-music to upset your parents, upset the authorities, upset the applecart – has remained a common desire in punk throughout its four decades or so as a subculture. Why, then, is it a 'conceit'?

Again, the Columbus, Ohio *More than Music Fest* is instructive here. My knowledge of this fest is largely based on having headlined the middle day – Saturday night – of the three-day event in 1999, with the band Red Monkey in which I played guitar at the time. The organisers had made a decision to make the event 'womyn-centred' for the first time, in order 'to highlight and appreciate the achievements of womyn in our [punk] communities as well as create an environment that womyn truly feel is theirs.' (Red Monkey had a female vocalist/bassist, thus making us sufficiently 'womyn-centred' for the context.) This positive discrimination was a bold move, given that the festival would normally feature primarily male performers playing a fairly standardised form of US-style hardcore punk, with – accordingly – a largely male audience travelling from all over the United States and beyond for the event: 'A lot of people have questioned our selection process for bands this year,' acknowledged the promoters (several of whom lived at the Legion of Doom punk house in Columbus and were politically active in numerous ways) in advance of the weekend event: 'please don't forget there's more to DIY than bands; our lives are not JUST music,'[3] they requested.

In the event, this plea proved to be largely unheeded: by the time we arrived, on the Saturday afternoon, we were informed by our friends from the Legion of Doom house that there had been consistent and often unpleasant complaints, confrontations, and hostilities. It is not the place of this chapter to offer an auto-ethnographic recollection of a gig that occurred nearly 15 years ago. Perhaps the caption beneath an online photograph of the festival programme, happened upon whilst trawling the internet for others' recollections of *More than Music* 1999, says enough: 'The fest that really killed the whole more than music concept.'[4]

---

to The Sex Pistols at their earliest gigs (*Punk Britannia: Punk 1976-1978*, Dir. Andy Dunn, BBC Four, first broadcast 8/6/12).

3   "More Than Music 1999 Music, D.I.Y, Feminist Politics, Dialogue, Community: What We're Doing (And Why), More Than Music," http://morethanmusic. tripod.com/

4   "SeriouslyGoose: More Than Music 1999," Flickr, http://www.flickr.com/

The question this caption begs is: what *was* the concept in question? For the author of the caption, it is fair to guess that the concept was that the US hardcore punk scene could have an annual event in which like-minded people could get together and enjoy the music. Certainly such appeared to be the core concept behind the 'fest' for many attendees, at least as far as I recall: many regular attendees, who had been coming every year since 1992, were affronted by the musical shift which was necessitated by the programming of 'womyn-centred' bands. This is not to say that the political issues which were promoted at the event were necessarily irrelevant to the average attendee, however. Doubtless issues such as animal rights, the arms trade, and prison reform were of interest to many, for it was highly evident that consciousness with regard to such issues was being promoted by numerous stalls at the event. In the end, however, if the music was not 'hardcore' enough for the bulk of the audience, the festival had been 'killed,' as the caption quoted above indicates. For the festival organisers, or at least the occupants of the Legion of Doom house, by contrast, such was not the case: since 'DIY' is 'not JUST music,' it follows that musical polyvalence was far from a death knoll for the festival. On the contrary, some of these festival organisers appeared to even believe that musical diversity would be a good thing for the punk scene.

A complicating factor in this discussion is that the event under discussion fell in an awkward and particular moment within US punk history: posterior to the 1996 demise of Bikini Kill (which felt, at the time, like the final death of Riot Grrrl, I would argue) but anterior to the rise of the 'Ladyfest' events (which effectively rejuvenated the Riot Grrrl idea in the 21st century). In a way, therefore, the battle as to whether 'womyn' should be allowed to perform, even if their music was not stereotypical hardcore punk, was one which stumbled into this context because, at that moment, there seemed to be nowhere else for punk-affiliated females to explore music making. However, punk's (or, at least, 1990s US hardcore punk's) overwhelmingly rigid musical codification system meant that, in practice, the musical efforts of the female punks found little welcome in the event.

It is not my intention in the present chapter to re-open questions around punk and gender which have already been explored at great length elsewhere. *More than Music Fest* 1999 provides an interesting

photos/teesabrat/2852781142/

case for my present purpose, nevertheless, because the furore which greeted its programming choices was so clearly based upon a tension between music and politics in punk; a tension which has strong roots in anarcho-punk, without doubt. I heard more than one individual joke bitterly, at the time, that – given the furore over the shift in musical content – it should perhaps have been called the *No More than Music Fest* or, even more honestly, just '*Music Fest.*'

Music and politics sit uneasily together in punk and anarcho-punk, then, just as they did when the skifflers, trad-jazzers, and folkies attached themselves to CND in the late 1950s or when the likes of Woody Guthrie and Pete Seeger attempted to marry communism and folksong in the mid-20th century.[5] The rub lies in the friction between action and aesthetics, between consciousness-raising and conscious agency. The nub of the problem, in short, is confusion between making music and making a new society. In punk, though, this problem is particularly marked because, for most punks, the feeling which arises from listening to angry music seems particularly prone to becoming an end in itself; and retaining the power of anger in the music, as a result, often displaces the need for, say, respect for the diverse tastes and preferences of the immediate other (other people, that is, who the punk fan encounters at or beyond the borders of the perceived-to-be-'pure' punk scene).

Punk is an extraordinarily variable subculture, though, and consequently such problems do not always arise so strongly: early punk, for example, featured music as diverse as the avant-garde saxophone bleating of Lora Logic, the electronic blaring of Pere Ubu, and the all-out chaos of the early Slits performances, to name just three examples. Crass and their contemporaries in anarcho-punk would push punk so strongly towards a radical critique of social and political norms that it would seem self evident that something beyond music was in play. As a musicologist, though, I want to add quickly that music *always* has something beyond 'the music itself' going on: this is a fundamental principle behind what is often named 'New Musicology.'[6] So

---

5   For detail as to the relationship between skiffle, the trad jazz boom and the rise of CND in Britain, see McKay (2005), especially Chapter One; for detail of Seeger, Guthrie and other folk singers' involvement in Left wing organising, consult any text on the folk revival or, indeed, the songs themselves.

6   A good introduction to scholarly debates around music and culture is Clayton et al (2003).

Crass isn't 'just music,' granted, but nor – even at its most extreme; 'Nagasaki Nightmare' (1980), say, or the squall of *Yes Sir, I Will* (1983) – is it wholly other than music: people listen to it and, in fact, it is fair to say that for many 'fans' of Crass and anarcho-punk, listening to the music is, politically speaking, as far as they get. Could Crass have chosen to, say, read out texts and display images and thus not to have performed any music whatsoever? Naturally they could, and it is even feasible that expert word-crammer Steve Ignorant would have made a decent public speaker should the band have become something more like a political party or conscious-raising group instead of making music.[7]

What we actually have, though, is music; and 'politics,' yes, but musical products at the core not only of Crass's agency but also at the heart of the punk scene(s) which descended from anarcho-punk across the decades which followed (within which, in case it is not already clear, I would certainly include the *More Than Music Fest* and the US hardcore punk scene from which the 'fest' sprang – and which owed a clear debt to Crass and UK anarcho-punk). The purpose of this chapter, then, is to explore tensions between musical and political content/attitude in anarcho-punk-derived music from the Crass era onwards. In order to explore such a large terrain within the even larger subculture of punk more generally, I shall rely heavily upon three texts by Ian Glasper: *The Day the Country Died: A History of Anarcho Punk 1980-1984* (2006), *Trapped in a Scene: UK Hardcore 1985-1989* (2009), and *Armed with Anger: How UK Punk Survived the Nineties* (2012). As the sub-titles make clear, Glasper covers not only the 'Crass era' of anarcho-punk but also the various related developments thereafter. For my present purposes, Glasper's books provide an excellent resource as the texts are, in effect, an oral history of UK underground/anarcho-punk from the era of Crass onwards.

---

7    If not Steve Ignorant, it is fair to say that Martín Sorrondeguy from 1990s US hardcore group Los Crudos certainly would. Although, to my mind, Los Crudos's on-stage statements between their songs often stand up as political observations in their own right, I would nevertheless argue that it is primarily music, or the combination of the political stance *with* the sonic element (the music, that is), which gives Los Crudos their power; likewise with Crass, I would maintain.

# WAYS OF SEEING 'THE SCENE'

*We always saw our scene as a community and thought there was something more than just music... we saw the festivals that we arranged at [Bradford's epicentre of anarcho-punk] the 1in12 as our contribution to that communal ethos. We also managed to raise money for lots of causes that we were interested in and most importantly we were able to donate hundreds of pounds to the 1 in 12 Club when, at that time [early-to-mid 1990s], it was in a dire financial situation.[8]*

Hardcore punk, as a 1990s continuation from the earlier anarcho-punk era, continued raising money for, and raising consciousness about, causes which gain very little support elsewhere, such as animal rights. According to Sned, of northeast legends Generic and the Flat Earth record label, however, 'It wasn't really a lot more than music, was it? Let's face it.'[9]

The latter quotation can be taken with a grain of salt: those who know Sned (a milieu which includes the present author, it should be acknowledged) know him as, to quote one of his oldest friends, a 'grumpy old bastard.' To suggest that Sned may not have meant quite what he said here is believable enough since, in fact, he has done more than almost anyone else in the UK punk underground – at least in the 1990s – to promote punk's 'political content' (let's leave this troublesome concept largely unpicked for the moment: in short, I mean that Sned's bands and label opposed militarism, major labels, meat eating, and other favoured enemies of the punk scene[10]). Nevertheless, the comment falls in stark contrast to the previous quotation.

---

8    Ian Glasper, *Armed With Anger: How UK Punk Survived the Nineties* (London: Cherry Red, 2012), 694.

9    Ian Glasper, *Trapped in a Scene: UK Hardcore 1985-1989* (London: Cherry Red, 2009), 195.

10   To some extent I am following Street, Inthorn, and Scott here who, echoing a tendency emanating from the Birmingham Centre for Contemporary Cultural Studies (CCCS) in the 1970s, have suggested that 'while politics may indeed be a serious business, it does not follow that it is unconnected to the world of entertainment' (Street, Inthorn and Scott, 2012:339). If popular culture can be configured as involving an element of political engagement, it is fair to add that this is especially so within the punk cultures which have so often actively encouraged direct action of varying kinds.

What is the tension here? Something comparable, perhaps, to the popular query as to whether a glass is half empty or half full: one participant sees 'the scene' as significantly more than music, the other implies that raising money for political causes and suchlike 'wasn't really a lot.' At stake here, probably, is a question as to whether fundraising is as important as, for example, direct action. In the present context, again, space prevents a lengthy engagement with such a question.[11] Perhaps, nevertheless, it is worth cross-referencing this question against some comments from an attendee of the 2002 *More than Music* weekend, some three years after the furore around the 'womyn-centred' fest of 1999:

> I didn't take away much of a 'do-gooder' attitude from the tenth instalment of Columbus, Ohio's More than Music weekend – there were pamphleteers for the pro-choice movement and other lefty causes, and a film celebrating [...] vegan lifestyles and feminist pornograghy, but rock music seemed to be the order of business for most attendees... [T]he kids mostly gravitated towards the merch displays of the bands, labels and distributors associated with the fest.[12]

---

11  Nevertheless, it is probably worth mentioning that, in informal conversation with animal rights activists, I have frequently encountered a firm belief that active involvement in campaigns is always preferable to a financial donation. On the other hand, Susan George, vice president of the French organisation Association for the Taxation of Financial Transactions for the Aid of Citizens (ATTAC), has complained of 'the "black-leather heavy-metal spike-hair" unwashed of [the anti-globalisation protests in] Zurich, whose only goal in life is apparently to riot. Only a qualified psychologist or anthropologist could say whether they have the slightest interest in politics' (quoted in Dupuis-Déri, 2010: 70). We might conclude, then, that opinions differ as to the usefulness of the more extreme end of the direct action spectrum (the 'black-leather heavy-metal spike-hair' protestors probably self-defining as punks, of course) as compared with more conventional forms of political engagement such as raising consciousness and funds.

12  "More Than Music Festival: The Flying Luttenbachers, Rah Bras, Bratmobile, and others," Pop Music Matters, accessed August 20, 2013, http://www.pop-matters.com/pm/review/more-than-music-festival-2002/

PETE DALE

Is such an observation an indictment fit to decry the political value of punk overall? I would suggest otherwise: judging, for example, by Ian Glasper's books on anarcho-punk and the punk scenes which descend from anarcho-punk, punk certainly *has* inspired not only fundraising but, also, various active forms of direct political engagement. According to many of Glasper's informants, furthermore, punk has engendered a feeling that sanity is possible in what many punks perceive as a mad world (punk as self-help activity for the dispossessed, one might say):

> I wanted to promote a state of mind that was free of unwanted conditioning, free from egotism, and free of influences like fashion and racism and sexism – all the negative stuff we have to wrestle with day after day to create some imaginary safety net inside our heads. I was just trying to be accountable to myself, by accepting what my own intuition was telling me, and then play a part with my "brothers and sisters in the scene" in making a better world, a sustainable positive future for everyone... which is why I've always regarded Prophecy of Doom as a DIY punk band, and not part of the death-metal scene that people tried to lump us in with towards the end.[13]

I shall return shortly to the theme which is raised at the end here, namely the tension between 'metal' and punk. Moreover, in any case, it is clear that Glasper's informant used punk (or his involvement in punk) as a self-protecting psychological 'safety net' through which he and his punk comrades could work towards 'a better world.' Perhaps the critical reader (a Marxist, for example) will want to say that this safety net counts for naught unless it leads to action for change: it's worth reiterating, therefore, that Glasper's texts are filled with individuals recording that, through punk, they became involved in hunt sabotage, peace campaigns, alternative ways of living, and other pursuits reasonably described as 'activism.'

That said, there are significant numbers of individuals quoted in Glasper's texts for whom 'the scene' seems to be about little more than

---

13  Glasper, *Trapped in a Scene*, 432.

a (decidedly ritualised) activity with very little in the way of political significance. Consider, for example, the following observation from 1990s Manchester straight-edge hardcore band Area Effect:

> It was always more than music and it always will be…We were 19 year old kids who could roll up in a town 300 miles away in a van and jump around for 20 minutes and thrash our instruments to a bunch of like-minded kids who wanted to jump on each other's heads. I mean, how many people can say they could do that?[14]

Not many, one assumes, but a useful antidote to Area Effect's comments is offered by Joe Deacons of Glasgow group Disaffect: 'It seems we're all about "respect and unity" in the punk scene… until the music starts and then we start knocking the shite out of people.'[15] There are tensions, then, between the ways of seeing 'the scene' amongst those who perceive themselves to be within it. For some, the political content is decidedly vague: 'The lyrics were all about different forms of violence… Everything from being angry at someone and wanting to hurt them, to general violence in the world, like wars and shit.'[16] For others, the 'safety net inside our heads' (see above) appears to be at risk of dissolving into ignoring rather than confronting the status quo: 'I would like to think that people got to engage in a bit of escapism when they came to an Imbalance gig,'[17] notes Andy from the band Imbalance.[18]

In *Armed with Anger*, Glasper's text on punk in the 1990s, meanwhile, several individuals express a desire to avoid the explicit (and, by then, felt to be clichéd) targets and topics of earlier traditions of anarcho-punk: 'I tried to make [the lyrics] more poetic than political,'[19]

---

14  Glasper, *Armed With Anger*, 147.

15  Ibid., 578.

16  Ibid., 23.

17  Ibid., 126.

18  To be fair, Andy also emphasises that he wanted the audience to 'think' and 'do it themselves' which *are* important core principles of punk; 'escapism' is an odd word here, though, and possibly a revealing one.

19  Glasper, *Armed With Anger*, 132.

remarks Phil from Withdrawn, for example. 'We wanted to be on Sony and sell lots of records,'[20] the Apocalypse Babys state baldly; fair enough, perhaps, but a far cry from the old anarcho-punk ideals, surely. Kito's vocalist Rob Hallowes states that they wanted to steer clear of 'humdrum rants about vegetarianism or whatever.'[21] Anth from Middlesbrough band Embittered echoes this desire to avoid the clichés of anarcho-punk-related music: the band were active in animal rights activities and sabotaging hunts yet they wanted to take their political attitude away from the 'stereotypical grind mindset.'[22]

It would seem, then, that the 1990s scene(s) which descended from anarcho-punk saw punk's political requirements and bases somewhat differently from the way it had been perceived previously. Anth from Embittered again: 'For me personally it was the essence of taking the elements I'd held on to from the early-to-mid-Eighties anarcho-punk scene to where I was an individual by the early 1990s. By then I had become [questioning] of a subculture that was entrenched in always assuming that we were right and everyone else was wrong.'[23] Of course, any political pressure group must do this to some extent; yet the complaint is interesting and should not be dismissed too quickly. A good cross reference, indeed, is Knuckledust's problematic statement that in the early 1990s London hardcore scene, 'everyone at those shows hated everyone that was outside of those shows': for those of us who *were* 'outside of those shows,'[24] receiving hatred for our supposed error is somewhat hard to take.

Probably, here, we have a cornerstone problem in punk culture, not only in musical but also in political terms: has there ever been a subculture which more firmly believed that you *can* judge a book by its cover? Consider, with regards to this, the following comments from Rob of Throw Bricks at Coppers:

---

20   Ibid., 207.

21   Ibid., 90. Hallowes, it should be noted, is or at least was a vegan: the 'humdrum' comment, therefore, is certainly not made on account of some personal antipathy but, rather, comes from a desire to move forward from the direct and simple statements one could hear ten or fifteen years earlier from the likes of Conflict.

22   Ibid., 94.

23   Ibid., 99.

24   Ibid., 412.

> I find that the ability to question all things includ-
> ing oneself and the political intelligentsia as well as to
> experiment with various musical styles and original art-
> work forms to achieve something new has all but been
> eradicated within the punk scene by an unquestioning
> acceptance of uniformity and peer-group conformity.[25]

It seems, then, that there are several different ways of seeing 'the scene' within punk, with the 1990s era drifting quite far, in several ways, from the earlier period of anarcho-punk. For some bands and individuals, there was a wholesale rejection of politics in favour of music in the 1990s (something which is not noticeable in Glasper's books on earlier periods of punk): 'We weren't ever not serious about the music, but it was never about trying to change the world or spreading a message',[26] notes Mark from Freebase; 'I'm not sure what the real goal of the band was, to be honest [but] for me, it was to play music'[27] notes Karl from Canvas. In other cases, specific political affiliations seem to have sat uneasily alongside the anarchistic allegiances of the bulk of the punk scene yet musical affiliation *would* appear to have been in play, including Jase of Ironside; 'I didn't feel that my [communist/socialist] values ... sat well in Ironside... although musically it was exactly where I wanted to be.'[28] Matt from Kito, meanwhile, effectively takes the opposite view, emphasising 'anti-corporate' dissent over and above any musical or presentational preference:

> To many of the people involved in the DIY network,
> the term 'punk' had never been purely representative of
> an image or a sound, but rather a way of doing things,
> an act of dissension against corporate greed, a passion
> for maintaining a strong sense of ethics and equality,
> of a collective conscience and a development of more
> proactive, positive, meaningful forms of dissent.[29]

---

25  Ibid., 385.
26  Ibid., 212.
27  Ibid., 65.
28  Ibid., 26.
29  Ibid., 92.

PETE DALE

In summary, if the reader will forgive the use of an old expression, 'one man's beef is another man's beer': when it comes to seeing the punk scene as 'more than music' or otherwise, a wild range of opinions can be discerned within Ian Glasper's books on punk, with the 1990s appearing to have been a period in which divergence between political and musical motivations became particularly strong. I would like to return, in the following section, to a particular issue which was raised above, namely the increasing predominance of heavy metal styling in punk from the late 1980s onwards. With regard to metal, some 1990s bands such as Canvas from Leeds are honest enough to admit that they came to punk after firstly being into heavy metal; without question, many more besides these made the same progression even if they choose not to mention it in Glasper's book. What, then, is the significance of this drift in terms of punk's claim to be 'more than music'? Could, for example, the kind of political aspirations of the likes of Crass translate effectively into such a musical style?

## TOO METAL FOR PUNK, TOO PUNK FOR METAL

The first thing to say, on this topic, is that to at least some extent punk's diversification into metal supports the idea that 'the scene' could be about more than music. This is so to the extent that metal, in the early 1980s at least, was very much felt to be a separate genre from punk. For punk bands to diversify towards metal therefore implies that the 'politics of punk' – the allegiance to 'DiY' principles, for example – could translate, in theory at least, to differing musical styles and retain significance.[30] A quote from Rob Miller of Amebix – a crucial group within punk's shift towards metal, judging at least from Glasper's *The Day the Country Died* – indicates that a *rapprochement* between punk and metal could have some positive aspects: 'One guy even said [on an internet forum] that it helped him and his brother relate when they didn't have a relationship at all! One liked punk, one liked heavy metal... And then along came Amebix!'[31] Miller remarks, touchingly, that for him to hear

---

30  To my knowledge, this possibility remains at the level of theory: I am not aware, that is, of any actual punk-inspired ground swell of DIY within heavy metal; not, at least, with the kind of ideological impetus found in DIY punk.

31  Glasper, *The Day the Country Died: A History of Anarcho Punk 1980-1984* (London: Cherry Red 2006), 208.

this was 'really nice.'[32] Martyn from VDG, meanwhile, remarks that his band thought metal 'pretty much sucked' except for one band member who 'always had a wider taste in music.'[33]

Doubtless there are elements of classic subcultural antagonism in the tension between punk and metal: Martin of Salad From Atlantis, for example, describes violence flaring up between punks and 'metal-core' fans at a gig in Germany in 1989.[34] The shift towards metal, which Glasper's books would suggest arose strongly in the late 1980s, would seem to have even managed to win some support from those who were instinctively mistrustful of an influence from beyond punk's normal stylistic parameters: '"Crusties" were just hippies to me, and metal a big no-no, but I liked the attitude of Doom, Sore Throat, Electro Hippies, and early Napalm Death; they were younger, fresher kids, unburdened by past expectations and the weight of history,' notes Mike from Decadent Few.[35]

Punk's shift towards metal reflects at least some element of musical diversification, then. This noted, it remains clear that within the punk scene there has been significant querying of the legitimacy of metal. Dean Beddis of Cowboy Killers, for example, remarks that punk is/ was 'something that stays with you all your life; you don't just dance to it, or head-bang to it – not all metal's like that – but punk and hardcore had something more to it than just that.'[36] Beddis goes on to clarify something of what this 'something more' consists of: 'All those songs about religion, racism, fascism, sexism and animal rights... they made us think, and that was the best thing about punk and hardcore, it made people think.'[37]

It is fair to say, overall, that the metal-influenced UK hardcore sound of the late 1980s entailed a shift away from this desire to 'make

---

32  The remark is touching because Amebix's music, described by Glasper as 'like standing before the open door of a blast furnace and melting into the white-hot miasma of pagan savagery' (Glasper, *The Day the Country Died*, 198), would not naturally lead one to assume its vocalist to be capable of such enthusiasm for fraternal peace-making.

33  Glasper, *Trapped in a Scene*, 385.

34  Ibid., 371.

35  Ibid., 349.

36  Ibid., 450.

37  Ibid.

people think.' It is also the case, indeed, that this musical development coincided – although perhaps not in the sense of 'coincidence' as that word is normally understood – with a movement away from core DIY principles such as the separation of punk from major labels. Dig from Earache records: 'I was also acutely aware of a kind of social barrier between the hardcore punk scenesters and the underground metal scenesters; they simply did not mix at the time [mid-to-late 1980s], but I developed a chameleon-like tendency to befriend both camps, so I spent ages evangelising about HC punk bands to met-allers, and vice versa.'[38] For Dig, UK punk bands were 'crippled' by a lack of ambition and an obsession with being 'more punk than you.'[39] For the pro-DIY punks, that said, Dig's 'chameleon-like' striking of business relationship with Sony from 1993 onwards would be better described as 'snake-like,' perhaps.

Certainly many from the punk scene would seem to have believed that metal-style punk entailed a problematic move towards music industry norms: 'I have always hated metal and never liked Slayer and their ilk, or the rock star pretensions that seem to accompany so many metal bands'[40] says Simon from Suicidal Supermarket Trolleys. By the late 1990s, a band such as Withdrawn who felt themselves to be 'in the SXE [straight-edge] niche' would seem to have felt it necessary to attempt to 'take on the pure metal kids' by changing their name to the less punky/angsty-sounding Evanesce. 'I don't think vegan SXE was ever going to be sexy enough for a metal crowd,' reflects guitarist Danny, due to the 'fake-ass cock-rock attitude' he associates with metal.[41]

In Glasper's *Armed With Anger*, the sense that a *musical* shift towards metal encouraged a sense of some form of *political* betrayal within the 1990s punk scene is overwhelming: '"Too metal for punk and too punk for metal" has always followed us around and there's always been someone waiting to shoot us down for whatever reason or other – tossers!' Interestingly, this seems to have occurred even though the band, Hellkrusher, remained operationally 'true to the DIY ethic we were brought up on'[42] notes Skotty from Hellkrusher. Similarly

---

38 Ibid., 501.

39 Ibid., 502.

40 Ibid., 379.

41 Ibid., 133.

42 Glasper, *Armed With Anger*, 77.

Rectify complain that 'we were too metal for the punks and too punk for the metallers.'[43]

In an interesting twist on this theme, Four Letter Word summarise that they were 'too pop for the punks and too punk for the pop punks.'[44] Perhaps, then, a large part of the antipathy towards metal (where it existed; it is worth emphasising that many punk-affiliated groups and individuals have no truck with metal at all, as is reflected elsewhere within Glasper's books) actually amounts to no more than the classic subcultural tensions mentioned above: within one micro-cosm of the larger punk subculture ('the pop punks,' for example, who listened to the likes of Screeching Weasel and Green Day at a time when the latter were still identifiable as part of the punk un-derground), stylistic allegiances have been codified and, thus, music which falls even slightly outside of the stylistic code is to be denigrat-ed. That said, it would appear that – in some cases, at least – punk audiences may have based musical preferences upon political criteria. Consider, for example, the following allegation which was made by Eddie of Slum Gang: 'We were also becoming disillusioned with such a supposedly open-minded scene where people all dressed the same and just wanted to see Discharge clones all singing the same old lyrics. It was as if because we were melodic we weren't allowed to sing about politics or have any opinions.'[45]

If Eddie is correct, his band – who held faith in 'punk as a lifestyle, not just a haircut,' it is worth adding – were unable to gain much support from 'the scene' *not* because of their political affiliation but, rather, because of their *music*. 'More than music'? How *much* more, that is the question. Before attempting any conclusive response to it, though, it is probably worth exploring one more particular case, in order to further explore what response is provoked when punk is provoked by musical sounds beyond its normal palette.

## 'PROPER PUNK' VERSUS THE 'PRETENTIOUS KIND'

In this section I want to focus on a milieu of bands which associat-ed with legendary early 1990s hardcore band Dead Wrong. By their own account, Dead Wrong attempted to fuse 'the best of American

---

43    Ibid., 554.

44    Ibid., 527.

45    Ibid., 194.

hardcore with crusty UK punk influences.'[46] The latter influence is specified as deriving from Doom, ENT, and Heresy, groups with a clear lineage from anarcho-punk.[47] That said, the group consciously went against perceived norms: 'We didn't fit the straightedge, crust or generic hardcore punk mould and I think we wanted to kick against those stereotypes in the scene. We didn't have Mohicans or dreads and we didn't felt-tip Xs on our hands. We didn't wear the "uniform" basically.'[48]

In brief, Dead Wrong 'could probably have been the biggest metalcore band ever from the UK,'[49] according to Ian Glasper. Instead, however, they disintegrated with very little in the way of recorded output. Some ex-members reformed under the name Des Man DeAblo, and attempted to diversify somewhat, musically speaking; sadly though, as we have seen above, the idea that punk could be 'more than music' often stalls in practice: 'People were eager to see what most of Dead Wrong had become, but I think Des Man surprised a few of them as it was quite different; a few proper punks that used to like DW came to the first few shows, but that quickly stopped.'[50]

For the 'proper punks,' then, there would seem to be a tightly policed limit to acceptable musical content, with 'quite different' music being quite unacceptable. Of particular interest for our purposes, though, is a strongly-voiced musical disapproval in turn from the ex-members of Dead Wrong directed towards one individual who did not join Des Man DeAblo: 'One guitarist… started hanging around in Leeds 6 too much with some guys who were into playing a more pretentious kind of hardcore that involved "jazz-stylings."'[51]

---

46  Ibid., 136.

47  Entries on these three bands in Glasper's *Trapped in a Scene* indicate inspiration deriving from the likes of Crass, Chaos UK, and such like. Overall, the book makes an inheritance from Crass and anarcho-punk overwhelmingly clear, just as the influence in turn of the kinds of bands covered in *Trapped in a Scene* is unmistakeable within *Armed With Anger*.

48  Glasper, *Armed With Anger*, 138. The felt-tipped X on the hand is a well-known signifier of allegiance to the 'straightedge' principle: no drugs, no alcohol and, according to some, no sex.

49  Ibid., 135.

50  Ibid., 142.

51  Ibid., 140.

What *is* the 'pretension' here: that music other than punk could be worth playing or listening to? One can reasonably object that there is more pretending involved in trying to argue that you could have had punk rock, or indeed rock music at all, without first having the music known as jazz. In truth, though, the commentator probably doesn't really *mean* the word pretentious: rather, he means that his ex-guitarist was making music that just wasn't punk enough, it is fair to guess; rather than pretentious he might have said non-conformist.

The band with 'jazz-stylings' in question is Baby Harp Seal. Elsewhere in *Armed With Anger* Glasper refers to them as 'emo lady boys.'[52] Presumably, again, this is because their music isn't straightforwardly 'punk' enough, although it is arguable – given his inexcusable wording – that a base homophobia/chauvinism is the larger cause of Glasper's ire. In any case, it is relevant to note that, in fact, Baby Harp Seal had a drummer and bass player who were almost certainly the best players in the UK punk scene of the 1990s: outstanding musicians whose interest in jazz, I would argue, is simply a facet of a more general interest in music.[53] Maybe punk *is* about music, then: but one kind only, it seems, with very little space for variation, at least in the 1990s 'post-anarcho' scene(s) under discussion here.

The disappointing thing, for those who would encourage faith in the idea that punk is about 'more than music,' is that Baby Harp Seal were in fact very much in favour of punk's principles over and above its music. During an interview I conducted with them in early 1996, for example, it was 'the ideology and its potential' which the band were keen to emphasise: 'Obviously it's cool if, like, you see a band that's just DIY and it's really good, but even if they're really shit at least they're trying to do it themselves instead of going through the usual bullshit channels.'[54]

---

52   Ibid., 30.

53   Ex-Baby Harp Seal drummer Neil Turpin has been hired in recent years by composer Yann Tiersen as well as being invited to play solo in Madrid on a bill also featuring Seb Rochford. See http://sightsoundrhythm.tumblr.com/post/40622821818/neilturps for details. The band's ex-bassist Seth Bennett, meanwhile, has since played in orchestras, jazz bands, folk groups and more, http://tommyevansmusic.com/friends/seth-bennett.

54   Interview with author, 1996. Published in *Fast Connection* fanzine, issue #2, eds., Pete Dale and Rachel Holborow (Newcastle upon Tyne, UK, 1996), 5.

## CONCLUSION

Early 1980s anarcho-punk was extraordinarily politically charged; that much is overwhelmingly clear from Ian Glasper's *The Day the Country Died* alongside all other accounts. The music, however, was not terribly varied. Over time, though, musical variety – including a marked shift towards heavy metal – was accompanied by a lessening of political conviction. Over thirty years since Crass released their early records, it has become possible for a player from the 1990s post-anarcho hardcore scene to reflect, risibly, that 'It was never an act with us… we loved wearing shorts.'[55] This rather lacks the bite of The Sex Pistols 'we mean it, maaan,' let alone the invective of Crass and their ilk.

Why, though, should musical diversification have led to political dilution? The data which is assembled in this chapter does not prove any necessary link in this sense: indeed, several voices which were quoted above seem to suggest that it was precisely the narrowness of the permitted musical content which rendered the anarcho-punk scene as politically dubious, on one level at least. It is worth remembering, though, that punk has always also encouraged instability: in the words of Dave from Cress [sic], 'it's always good to challenge people's ideas of what they believe punk to be about!'[56] Perhaps taking this suggestion to its logical conclusion involves, in the last instance, risking the ground of punk disappearing entirely.

With regard to the Columbus, Ohio *More Than Music Fest*, it may be that precisely such a disappearance occurred: according to the attendee of the 2002 event quoted above, 'It did feel grassrootsy and DIY, but for all the networking going on (I came away with a sack full of promotional booty), it may as well have been a much larger festival, like CMJ or even Sundance.'[57] This, as noted already, was some three years after the 1999 'womyn-centred' *More Than Music* event; perhaps, then, it was precisely the musical diversity (which, it seems, the inclusion of more women had entailed) that led to this shift towards *More Than Music* becoming a more conventional festival? For

55  Glasper, *Armed With Anger*, 148.

56  Ibid., 161.

57  "More Than Music Festival: The Flying Luttenbachers, Rah Bras, Bratmobile, and others," Pop Music Matters, http://www.popmatters.com/pm/review/more-than-music-festival-2002/

the sake of argument, let us suppose that such is the case: what, then, is gained when post-anarcho-punk is conceived as a principle or set of principles (the encouragement of the DIY *modus operandi*, say, and/or the promotion of left-wing causes) which can be divorced from punk/hardcore/anarcho-punk/whatever as *music*? What is gained but, also, what is lost?

The gain, I would suggest, is fairly obvious: punk, when it stops worrying about 'sounding punk' and defines itself instead as an operational tendency, can promote its political principles more widely and have greater justification in core claims such as the idea that 'anyone can do it' (even if, for example, they enjoy 'jazz stylings').[58] Not everyone is going to want to listen to, say, the clattering clashes of Crass or the grinding sludge of Doom, and yet – *despite* the music – many would identify strongly with the ideals and the message of such bands. If punk could 'challenge people's ideas of what they believe punk to be about!' (to re-quote Dave from Cress) to the extent that punk no longer had *any* central musical identity, perhaps the operational and polemical politics of 'the scene' could then break out of its confines and have a far wider impact.

Something about this idea, however, is deeply unsatisfactory. Punk without music: what's left? A few slogans – 'fight war, not wars' and such like – and the principle that anyone can 'do it yourself'; not much more, I would suggest. In the twenty first century, the idea of making your own music and offering it up to a public audience is as radical as MySpace, though; and if 'fight war, not wars' is a good slogan – which I would contend it is – a Crass fan will always hear, in their 'minds eye,' a sonic picture, if you like: a whole assemblage of associations, in other words, a large bulk of which is tied up with sonic experience (music, by any other name).

More than music? Of course, yes; but punk *is* music, primarily: to pretend otherwise is, as I said at the outset, something of a conceit. What the epithet conceals is that punk songs are what punks like to listen to; obviously so, sure, so why pretend otherwise? This is not to say that the kind of musically-based prejudices and exclusions of 'the scene' which have been discussed here are nothing to be concerned

---

58   For a detailed account of punk's operational tendencies see Pete Dale, *Anyone Can Do It: Empowerment, Tradition and the Punk Underground* (Aldershot: Ashgate, 2012), 25-31.

about. On the contrary, the present author has a personal investment in not only punk but also in music and politics more generally and, therefore, I am acutely aware of the frequently disappointing musical and political conservatism which the scene(s) that descend from anarcho-punk have often tended towards. To suggest that punk should become musically polymorphous to the extent that it is just about the message and no longer at all about the music, however, seems to me a curious wish, at least for a person – such as myself – who has taken immense pleasure from listening to all kinds of anarchistic punk music (as well as a good deal more besides, for the record).

Punk is interesting, politically, and anarcho-punk especially so; and for the attuned ear, it is worth listening to. As to those whose ears are not attuned to such music, punks would do well to bear their opinion in mind. It does not necessarily follow, however, that punk should be ashamed of what, in essence, it is: angry music for angry people. There are many important emotions beyond anger, granted; empathy, for example, and joy. Anarcho-punk and the music(s) that derive from it can sometimes be lacking in such emotions, certainly. However, to risk using a bland and popular phrase, 'It is what it is': the things about punk which are supposedly 'more than music' paradoxically *are* the music to a certain extent, or at least are part of the music. To pretend otherwise is to wish away the heart of the matter.

MATTHEW WORLEY

# THE END RESULT

## AN INTERVIEW WITH STEVE IGNORANT

**FOR MANY, *THE*** *Feeding of the Five Thousand* (1978) remains *the* seminal punk record. Crass's debut release, which was wrapped in Gee Vaucher's distinctive sleeve, marked a step-change in punk's evolution. The implicit politics of The Sex Pistols's 'Anarchy in the UK' were here taken seriously; The Clash's commitment to engage with the world around them found expression beyond the point of description. The appropriation of punk, so blatant and brazen as 1977 became awash with day-glow vinyl, new boots and contracts, was buried beneath the invective of a band which was committed to attack from the outside. If punk was dead … then long live punk.

Standing stage front, howling at the moon, was Steve Ignorant. Crass's lyrics came from multiple sources; Crass songs had multiple voices. But Steve Ignorant shouldered much of the burden. Where Penny Rimbaud exuded a cutting intellect, Steve embodied punk's instinctive rebellion; a guttural 'fuck you' that he captured in 'Do They Owe Us a Living', a freeform rant cut from Arthur Seaton's cloth. Indeed, as Steve makes clear below, his fury was fuelled from the same sense of injustice that underpinned the classic kitchen-sink dramas of the 1950s and 1960s, his 'anarchy' born not of Bakunin but of a commitment to rub against the grain.

As is well known, Crass proved contentious. Their open commitment to countercultural influences that pre-dated punk challenged the sense of purge that came with the Pistols. Their residing in Dial House appeared at odds with the urbanity of punk's first wave, seeming to dilute the guttersnipe stance of punk social realism. The fact that their politics refused to fit into boxes which were prepared by both the left and right led to confusion and animosity – a fact compounded by Crass's objective to smash any such political binaries. Even within the anarchist milieu that Crass helped to forge, the minutiae of the band's ideas became bones of contention – their lyrics picked over and discussed by would-be disciples and proudly pious heretics.

Ultimately, however, Crass left a legacy that transcended such petty squabbles. They provided a very real alternative to both the mainstream music industry and the conceits which were peddled by a London-centric music press. As importantly, Crass injected punk with a point and a purpose that spread into the provinces to establish a vital network of bands, labels, fanzines, and people. As the 1980s crumbled beneath the heel of Thatcher's neoliberal boot, so Crass led the resistance, refuting the dull uniformity of a life which was framed by a coercive system geared towards profit, self-interest, and perennial conflict. No longer were they a symbol of 'endless, hopeless, fruitless, aimless games', but a cultural force of their own making. Proof, if it were needed, that there is no authority but yourself.

**MATTHEW WORLEY (MW):** *What did 'punk' mean to you when you first became aware of it? How did you understand it?*

**STEVE IGNORANT (SI):** Purely and simply it was just a two's up to everything I'd known. It was funny because, on the one hand, the fucking Sex Pistols were brilliant, you know, because that's the first introduction I got. Not the Bill Grundy interview, but the one they did with Janet Street-Porter – and I thought 'oh fantastic', and then I suddenly thought, 'well why didn't I think of that?' And I think a load of people thought that as well, but it took someone like John Lydon or The Sex Pistols to [do it]. I don't think it was all about Malcolm McLaren; I don't think it needed him to suddenly bring it about. It was just something I'd been waiting for, ever since the skinhead thing ran-out. In between we went through the doldrums of the Bay City Shovellers. David Bowie, and the Glam Rock thing were okay, but then we hit the doldrums. Plus I'd found an FS1 Yamaha, so I was trying to be a bit of a biker! But suddenly it came back; it felt like the terraces; it felt like 'yes, this is my thing now; this is my time'. I had no idea of politics or anything like that to begin with, I don't think anyone gave a shit about that at the time. It was just pissing people off by dressing a bit weird and getting your head kicked-in for it.

**MW:** *So you felt an affinity for people like Lydon and you saw The Clash didn't you, early on?*

**SI:** I saw The Clash, yeah, I definitely had an affinity with them. I couldn't understand what they were saying on stage, obviously because it was a shit PA, you know. I came to learn later on, when I bought the album and I heard the words and I was like 'fuck me, this is definitely it – definitely it'.

**MW:** *What about Penny Rimbaud? I know it's difficult to speak for someone else – but I just wondered to what extent Penny's take on punk was the same as yours?*

**SI:** I think Pen's take on it was a bit different. He'd been through, if I can call it this, 'revolutions' before; he'd been through the Mod thing and he'd been into Elvis. He'd been through the avant-garde thing, so I think his approach was different to mine in that he immediately saw punk as a way of doing something himself – DIY. That's what Exit had been doing, you know, an avant-garde band. Plus, the sort of stuff he was writing at the time, which became 'Christ's Reality Asylum', just kind of fitted in under the umbrella of punk. Lots of people, like Ian Dury, had been on the circuit for years, doing pubs and clubs and things. Then, suddenly, punk came along and they were in. Not that I'd necessarily call Ian Dury or the avant-garde stuff Pen was doing 'punk', but – in a funny way, you know – I wouldn't necessarily call Crass 'punk'. That sounds really odd, I know. I mean, we fitted in alright. But like Genesis P-Orridge, who was close to punk in that punks would listen to it [Throbbing Gristle] ... I mean, what was punk? You get confused, you know.

**MW:** Do you mean Crass did something different to what had become recognisably 'punk'?

**SI:** Well, we certainly weren't going to try and break America like The Clash. We did go, but lost money [laughs]. Gee was out there, Freddie Laker's thing was going on at the time, so it was like £50 a ticket. We played to about twenty people a night or something, but I felt punk had lost something when I came back from America; when sat back in the Dog and Duck in Basildon or something … oh great [laughs]. So I never had qualms about it, but I felt that a lot of bands, like The Sex Pistols (that dreadful tour) and The Clash, who I felt just fucked off to America and came back as a rock band … that really upset me. Not because of America, but because they then made a record that was all about America. Well, I can't relate to that. If they were writing about, God help me, Barking – you know, Billy Bragg – I could relate to it. Or the Cockney Rejects; I could instantly relate to that. But I couldn't relate to 'hey guys, I saw Deanna Durbin walk into a bar on Broadway …' What does that fucking mean to me?

**MW:** *So, do you think it important for punk to have some discernible link to everyday life?*

**SI:** Yeah, I can read books about people in America, but to relate to something then it has to be what I know.

**MW:** *Is that why Crass never travelled too far after the States? Why you mainly toured round Britain?*

**SI:** I think we were sort of alright to tour Europe. People got it; they'd read the lyrics and stuff. But we did a tour of Holland and then went on to Dusseldorf in Germany. For some reason we turned up late. It was pissing down with rain and the punks were all standing outside a club that refused to open its doors. So the local police turned up and told everyone to get out of it. The punks refused, and we arrived just as they turned the car over and set fire to it [laughs]. So the police then came and said they were stopping the gig, to which we said: 'well, if you stop the gig, you're going to have to deal with that lot'. We did the gig. But there was a big discussion in the Crass kitchen afterwards: do we know enough about European Law to help people out? In England we knew what the law was. If you get in trouble with the police, then you don't say anything until you get a solicitor, etc. etc. These are your rights; remember those little leaflets we gave out? But we didn't know how all this worked in Europe, so we wondered if we should be going to places like Europe, promoting all this stuff, but then not being able to take responsibility if we saw someone getting nicked in front of us. That's why we only did Britain after that, which did make sense and worked. We started playing anywhere, which then helped us set up that network of, like, Subhumans, Conflict, Flux, Rubella, and all those bands, playing places like Winsford in Cheshire. Where the fuck is that? Or we'd go to the Lake District, you know Cumbria, places where no-one played; Wales, you know, Cornwall, or Fife.

**MW:** *Off the beaten track?*

**SI:** Yeah, yeah, yeah … and, meanwhile, all the so-called first wave, your Billy Idols and all that, were heading for Los Angeles or sticking to the same old circuit, just doing big halls. We went to small places; got in schtum for it, but we did it.

**MW:** *Crass are associated with developing punk's relationship to anarchy, though you seemed to forge your own version of it, a kind of 'DIY anarchy'. Where did Crass's ideas come from? What do you think helped inform how Crass saw the world; what were you reading about, thinking about, talking about to inform Crass's worldview?*

**SI:** Well, I know that Penny's idea was pacifist, like the Gandhi effect. He, obviously, had come through the sixties thing; Gee as well. For me, I'd come up through football and all the usual working-class stuff. For me, anarchy comes … I mean, I didn't really understand the anarchist books. I tried to read Bakunin but found it boring; it made no sense. I'd never been to Russia and am probably never going to go. So, my anarchy – or my sense of anarchy – came from the sense of injustice that I had from being a kid. I didn't know it, but I was always into black and white sixties films like *Taste of Honey*, *The Loneliness of the Long Distance Runner*. Again, stuff I could relate to. *Up the Junction*, a great film that is heavily underrated. That was what I was on about; that injustice, you know, that's what I wanted to change and remains the way I approach the things I do to this day. You know, I can be beaten on an academic level, but I will not be beaten on a pure and simple thing like injustice. And that was what anarchism was to me. But then I stopped calling myself an anarchist because it all split into factions: anarcho-syndicalists, anarcho-this-that-and-the-other. If you had milk in your fucking tea, you weren't a proper veggie – all that stuff. In the end I thought, 'you can shove your fucking anarchism up your arse mate, because all I want to be is me'.

**MW:** *Did those tensions play out in Crass? Were they discussed at Dial House?*

**SI:** Yeah, absolutely, oh agonising debates. I mean, we used to be up until three or four in the morning just trying to work it out. What the fuck were we on about? And somehow it all got taken up and out of our control. I think I can actually remember when it happened, when we sort of became a *political* thing. It was when these people from Sicily came over from an anarchist group and wanted Crass to go and play there. Not all of us went. I think Phil Free and Pete Wright did; like a sort of delegation thing. After that it all became more highly political; the fun fuck-off stuff like 'Owe Us A Living' sort of went out the window as these supposedly more meaningful songs came in. That's when I lost it a bit, you know. I just thought: 'well, the only thing I can do is talk to people at the bar and talk on their level', which is what I did. So, you see, we didn't deliberately set out to be anarchists or anything. But that's what we suddenly found ourselves being.

**MW:** *The usual story, which I know Pen has told before, was of trying to find somewhere beyond the left and right divisions of the time; to differentiate yourself from all that.*

**SI:** Yeah, because you can't just stand there and say 'I am not an anarchist'. I'm an ex-skinhead, from when I was twelve or something, then glam, then punk. That's what I am; I'm that sort of 'ist'. A fashion-ista ha ha – course I fucking am [laughing].

**MW:** *What about setting up your own label. That was important for so many reasons. How did Crass Records actually work in practice; were all of the band equally involved in it?*

**SI:** Well, it meant that we could do and say whatever we liked. And if we got into trouble for it, then we were the only ones responsible. That's why all the Crass stuff says 'written and performed by Crass'. If we ever got taken to Court, they couldn't pin it on one person; we'd be a group rather than an individual. You know, strength in numbers, that sort of thing. And we certainly didn't want to get anyone like Pete Stennett from Small Wonder into any trouble. We could choose who we wanted to go on the label; we could offer them whatever and we could just put out a record and lose money on it because we were the ones who were losing. It wasn't EMI, who we obviously didn't want to be involved with anyway – says Steve, thinking about the motorbikes and the chip shop he could have had [laughs]. So it was important to be wholly independent. Again, we didn't set out to do it in a predetermined way. It just seemed the natural thing to do. We put on the 'pay no more than …' and hoped other people would do the same, which they did.

You know, my idea – or Crass's idea – of what a punk rocker was, was some kid with spiked hair living on a council estate in Barnsley with ten woodbines and only one left in the packet, his gas fire going out. That was the sort of people we were approaching. Fuck the London lot, with all their brothel creepers and all that. The people who came to Crass gigs couldn't afford all the clothes. I couldn't!! So we weren't on the inside. We were out there, with the misfits and the scruffs; they were the people that we talked to and that was the most important thing. It's why Crass worked and several of the bands that came along with and after Crass worked too. Like the Subhumans, from the west country.

**MW:** *The Bullshit Detector compilations were a great thing. They were much maligned at the time in the mainstream music press – but they seemed very much in line with what Crass was all about …*

**SI:** Loads of cassette tapes, we'd get sent tape after tape. And we'd listen through them and do the famous 'five second listen' thing. If you went 'ooh, that sounds ok', then you'd give it another go: then, that's a definite, that's a possible, blah blah blah. We used to just literally sit there and listen to them going 'yeah, that one', hence getting Andy T, the Chumbas, etc., providing an opportunity to get on a record. They didn't get paid for it you know, but fucking hell…

**MW:** *Is there a Crass record that really captures what you were all about?*

**SI:** Yeah, *Feeding of the Five Thousand*. Definitely, it's gotta be. It's so raw; it was straight, you know.

**MW:** *We were talking earlier about how bands, particularly punk bands, often seem to make their first record the best. Maybe it's a product of that moment 'before', when all the disaffection or whatever is built up to be released.*

**SI:** Or you find out what works in the studio – Penny gets his producing earhole on and starts getting a bit arty [laughs]. Maybe the sound gets softer, less raw. Obviously you can't do it all the time like that. But, you know, listen to the early Cockney Rejects stuff and Stinky Turner's voice is just … he's really going for it, you know, like I used to. On *Feeding …*, all the songs say absolutely what it was about at that time.

**MW:** *Crass linked up to other activist movements, CND being the most obvious one. How did that come about? Were members of the band active in CND prior to Crass?*

**SI:** No, I don't think so. But we had all this stuff going on. The left wing was after us; the right wing was after us. And we said no. Tell you what, we're anarchists. Of course, most people's idea of an anarchist back then was like that poster of a bearded bloke with sunglasses throwing a bomb. So we were like, fucking hell, we've got to do something. So Penny and, I think, Eve Libertine went round to the offices of CND in London – Gray's Inn Road I think, tiny little office somewhere. They picked up some leaflets and offered to hand them out at gigs, which was when we started putting the Peace, CND symbol up. You have to remember this was all pre-internet. So it was a way of communicating with the young punks. First it was nuclear, then cruise missiles, then Greenham Common.

**MW:** *So just as the Cold War began to reignite?*

**SI:** Yeah, absolutely. It all fitted in and that was where the CND symbol came in; to this day you still see the peace and CND symbols.

We got heavily involved with them, the shop in King's Cross and *Peace News*. We used to hand out stuff at our gigs; it was like information, information to read. Christ knows how much we spent on paper and badges with the CND thing, just to give it out and spread the information.

**MW:** *What kind of other movements were you involved in, I mean the animal rights stuff was more Conflict wasn't it?*

**SI:** Yeah, we didn't really get involved in that. We did a few benefits, as we'd do benefits for everyone. But we didn't really get too linked to the animal rights or vegetarian side of it. People say 'oh it's Crass', but I don't think we even wrote a song about it – except the one saying I hope it fucking chokes ya [laughs]. We equated the flesh on the plate with the flesh on the battlefields, as a metaphor. But we didn't write a song about not eating meat. Flux of Pink Indians and then Conflict really got onto that – meat means murder. Then Morrissey, taking up the mantle. I am a vegetarian, and I did write 'Berkshire Cunt', so …

**MW:** *What about the Stop the City Campaign? There is a piece in the book about Stop the City. Crass didn't organise it, but to what extent were you involved?*

**SI:** Mick Duffield filmed it. I didn't go the first one, for some reason. I went to the second, but not the third – I didn't bother, because the police had already sort of sussed it out by the second, so the third was just a farce. Our role was to support it really. I remember a few phone calls and stuff like that, guarded phone calls and letters. But, personally, I didn't get involved in it. By that time I was already thinking that it had got a bit too political for me; it's not my style. As an individual, I'd like to be involved – but I didn't want to have to go to something like that because 'I am Steve Ignorant out of Crass'. It began to feel like if you were in Crass then you *had* to go on whatever fucking march it was. You *had* to be there, you know. And I got fed up with that.

**MW:** *A sense of obligation?*

**SI:** Yeah, and it spoils it; it stops it being fun. Because you have to make sure you are, so someone can say 'I saw Steve Ig there'. Thank fuck for that, now let's go home ...

**MW:** *The term 'anarcho' seems to have been applied retrospectively to you and the bands inspired by Crass. What are your feelings on that? When did you see a kind of movement coming out of what Crass were doing?*

**SI:** Pretty quick. The funny thing is though, Matt, I didn't really feel a part of it. You know, it felt like something that was nothing to do with me. Alright, I was in Crass and shouting down a microphone; I was the front man if you like – even though we tried to avoid it. But I didn't really involve myself in the organised political thing; I wasn't interested and didn't really get it half the time. I would rather – and this sounds dreadful ... but, you know, if I was watching a black and white film like *A Taste of Honey*, then I got it. I knew that's why I was doing what I was doing. But I didn't always see why I was supporting whoever, except with the miners' strike. That, of course, you had to. We were all out there, guns blazing – and I still talk to blokes today from the miners' strike. But I left the others to it. They were all talking that language, and I didn't understand it. There'd be punks coming, or people looking a bit sort of punk, you know, to do with the Wapping Centre, and they'd come up and talk to you. But I'd lose interest and want to go down the pub to talk football and how stupid it was for rival factions of football hooligans to be fighting. Then Class War came along telling me stuff about football matches, thinking they could get all the fucking hoolies together to rise up. It didn't quite work that way ... but Class War I sort of understood, although I didn't totally buy in to it. I could understand it, you know. It was real; it was in front of me.

**MW:** *When I think of Crass, I always put you, first, with the Poison Girls and, later, with Conflict. Were they the two groups you felt closest to at certain times?*

**SI:** We felt close to lots of other bands: Dirt, Subhumans, all of them. I mean, Crass never played with Subhumans. I wish we had, because that would have been a nice little fucking thing. But, then, on the other hand, they were doing what they were doing very well, so they didn't need us and we didn't need them. It was a bit like you kept an eye on each other and, now, when I talk to Dick Lucas, it's like 'fucking hell, we should have done this and we should have done that'. But there you go; everyone was doing their own thing. And it's funny because everyone goes 'oh Crass, Crass, Crass', but there were people out there doing just as much as we were. Maybe they just didn't have as smart a symbol or whatever [laughs].

**MW:** *You were the pioneers I guess. And pioneers always get the flack!*

**SI:** Yeah, and we sure did get loads of flack for it, but there you go…

**MW:** *Which I guess leads on to how punk become so factionalised, be it 'anarcho', 'Oi!' or whatever. Did you find that frustrating at the time?*

**SI:** Oh yeah. I would have loved to have been able to go down the Bridge House. I would have loved to have gone and seen The Business, even just to check it out beyond the media talk. But I didn't feel I could because I would've got my fucking head kicked in. Not by the bands, but by the lunatic fringe that followed them around. You know, fucking bands like The Exploited didn't help: fuck a mod, sex and violence, Crass are wankers – all that. Fuck off: we've just spent years trying to get people to start thinking about stuff and you take it back five years. Same as when the American thing came over, the skate punk. We'd just got everyone taking things seriously and it's suddenly 'one, two three, four, skate!'

**MW:** *Crass were interesting as you did try and mend some bridges: playing the Bridge House for example, playing with The Exploited.*

**SI:** Yeah, we did do the Bridge House and the 100 Club. And, fair play to Wattie, it was he who phoned up, got in touch with us via Annie Anxiety, who he was going out with or something. But I would have loved to have played with the Rejects. When I met Garry Bushell recently, we just said how stupid it all was. His excuse was that we were young, but he still made it hard with what he was saying back then. All that hippie, middle-class stuff. See, I am working class and I am not ashamed of it and I'm not fucking proud of it. It's just where I am from. What am I now? Working? Fucking middle? Upper middle? I don't know what the fuck I am. But at that time I was trying to lose that sense of being trapped. You know, it wasn't about football. Punk, to me, it was about losing all the bullshit we had been through and getting into rows about. It was about getting on with your mates and I always thought, stupidly as it turned out, that if you was a punk and you saw another punk, then you'd instantly know what you both thought about things. But no, you don't. I remember being really disappointed when we went to play in Wigan and the Wigan lot were all waiting for the Preston punks to come down. And I'm, like, saying 'c'mon, we're all punks aren't we'. But, no, not the fucking Preston lot apparently. I don't see it; I don't get it.

**MW:** *Final question: what are you most proud of; what is Crass's legacy?*

**SI:** I think the fact that I can be standing in a pub in Norfolk, in Sea Palling, and someone will come up to me. Like this guy Liv, an ex-miner from Derbyshire, and Mel from Cheshire, and we can crack on about what a bitch Thatcher was. Mel told me he was up in Chesterfield just a couple of weeks ago, wearing a Crass polo shirt, and a load of people talked to him about Crass and he was able to get on, you know. There's, like, a network – that's the word – a network of people for whom Crass is a symbol. It's a symbol that will start a conversation and, nine times out of ten, the person wearing that symbol will be an alright person. You know, Matt, it's certainly never been about money or anything. I'm actually making more money now than I did when I was in Crass. But here's the thing: I can basically go anywhere in the world, and if I'm wearing the Crass symbol, then somebody is going to come and talk to me about it.

**MW:** *It struck me when Thatcher died last year, and the press all got so sycophantic over her life and legacy, that history needs to show just how many people actually loathed and objected to what she did. And I think Crass articulated and embodied that opposition better than anybody.*

**SI:** Yeah, I'm really proud to have been a part of it. That's my proudest thing; that a spotty little oik from Dagenham actually stood up, knees trembling as he avoided the ash trays being thrown at him, and still fucking did it.

# THE KIDS WAS JUST CRASS

**IT'S THE FINAL** scene of *Trainspotting*. Renton, the book's main protagonist, creeps out of a hotel room with a bag full of money and flees to Amsterdam. Having completed a drug deal with his childhood friends, he's now ripping them off. But this is no simple tale of avarice. It's the act of betrayal that motivates Renton, much more than the money. By ensuring that his psycho-mate Begbie will kill him if he ever returns to Edinburgh, Renton is trying to engineer a clean break with his junky past: "There, he could not be anything more than he was. Now, free from them all, for good, he could be what he wanted to be." In reality a break is never clean. We always bring a remainder with us, whether familiar modes of acting or habitual patterns of thought. But at least by breaking with his old haunts and his junky associates, Renton has increased his chances of self-reinvention.

A similar tale is told in Julian Temple's documentary *Joe Strummer: The Future is Unwritten*. A key moment in the film comes when Strummer's band, The 101ers, support The Sex Pistols. At the time The 101ers were the more successful of the two but Joe immediately knew his group were over. They had been a close-knit group named after the squat they lived in at 101 Walterton Road. Yet Strummer not only broke up the band but also cut his former housemates dead. The film contains poignant testimony of the hurt and bewilderment the ex-101ers felt when Strummer refused to acknowledge them. Over the next few weeks Strummer altered his look, changed his sensibilities and joined The Clash. Punk was a Year Zero for Strummer. He felt he had to break from his hippy friends if he was to explore the new potential.

It's a truism of course that while punk produced a feeling of rupture, it was actually a continuation of much of the counterculture of the 1960s and 1970s. Many of the people who helped shape punk in its early days were themselves countercultural veterans: Malcolm McLaren and Jamie Reid worked on The Sex Pistols, while Caroline Coon and Bernie Rhodes both managed The Clash. On a more fundamental level London's large, politicised squatting scene was a key part of the material infrastructure that made punk possible. So while punk felt like a clean break with the past, it's better understood as a reconfiguration of that past, closing off some paths of sub-cultural development and opening up others. New antecedents were (re)discovered, while others were 'forgotten'. This resetting, however, is never a one-time deal. There's a pattern to events of this kind: once the initial explosion of possibility begins to contract, then the battle over the event's meaning – and therefore its future and past – gets reignited. At this point veterans of past events can play a vital role offering past experience as a guide to the future.

We can place Crass here, within the secondary battle over punk's direction. As a band they were the foremost proponents of the idea that punk was a continuation of the counterculture that had gone before. They prominently rejected punk's declaration of a Year Zero. Recently Penny Rimbaud has gone further, appearing to deny that punk was a moment of rupture at all: "Certainly the first wave of punk (Pistols, The Clash, etc,) was little but an extension of Tin Pan Alley culture, but what followed (led, I believe, by Crass) was a radical and often life changing movement that changed many lives and had deep effects within mainstream culture."[1] This claim seems contradic-

---

1   Quoted in Jeremy Allen (2016) "Punk was Rubbish and it Changed Nothing". Available at: http://noisey.vice.com/blog/punk-was-rubbish-and-it-didnt-change-anything-an-investigation

tory to us. If early punk was "little more than music business hype", why did it have such a profound effect on the people who would go on to form Crass? In fact, punk was an event that opened up a whole new set of – partly contradictory – ideas and problems. It took more than a decade to work through them.

The members of Crass were reconfigured by the event of punk just as Crass reconfigured punk's future. The result was the anarcho-punk scene of the 1980s. Much less celebrated than the counterculture of the 1960s, it was probably much more widespread, finding its way into even Britain's smallest towns. In turn, anarcho-punk's popularity helped regenerate the UK's moribund anarchist movement. It reshaped both anarchism and radical politics in ways that are still detectable in today's social movements. For this reason alone it deserves to be revisited. But in writing this chapter, we also have personal reasons to disinter this arcane history. The Free Association first met as friends during the early 1990s, in a political scene desperate to escape anarcho-punk's limitations. That was another time of attempted clean breaks and personal reinventions. While we're using this chapter as a kind of settling of accounts, there are wider lessons to be drawn about moments of rupture, the formation of generations and the handling of inheritance.

## BLOODY REVOLUTIONS

*I was 13 in the school playground when The Beatles happened, I was 18 and went to university when the revolution in drugs happened, and I was 26 and a TV presenter with my own show when punk happened. And then it was when I was 38 that acid house happened. Because it's a 13 year cycle: 1950, 1963, 1976 and 1989. I was too young for the Teddy Boys in 1950. My big ambition is to be around for 2002 when the next thing happens. – Tony Wilson*[2]

The year 2002 must have disappointed Tony Wilson. There was no pop-cultural revolution. Tony died in 2007 and so missed the similar non-event of 2015. And today it looks as if that 13-year pop-cultural cycle of rupture, rebirth and exhaustion has definitely ended. Of course you could argue that, if the cycle only revolved four times, it

2    David Nolan, *Tony Wilson – You're Entitled to an Opinion....* (London: John Blake Publishing Ltd., 2010)

may never have existed at all. Perhaps we are just seeing false patterns in random data. The difficulty is that such dynamics can't be seen directly, and are only detectable by their effects. They become concrete when the expectation of a cycle's return feeds back upon itself to structure experience, almost as if a rupture can be willed into existence.[3] This idea of a Year Zero was a powerful and constant theme in punk, just as it had been in previous pop-cultural revolutions.

We can add some depth to the idea of a subcultural cycle by placing it within Mark Fisher's concept of 'popular modernism'. While modernism's drive to discover the new is usually associated with art, architecture and literature, popular modernism is about the way avant-garde ideas and practices were reworked, extended and circulated through popular culture. By rethinking post-war popular culture in this way it's possible to identify a trajectory in pop that takes its model from Mod (the original modernists) and reaches its apogee with post-punk. This idea of a modernist strain in pop fits nicely with both the accelerated innovation of a pop subcultural cycle and the desire for a clean break with the past. The popular modernist dynamic contains an oscillation between two modes of the popular; the first is popular identification with music and icons but at times this leads to a second mode, popular participation in cultural production. We find this model interesting because it closely mirrors the structuring problem of radical politics (how to popularise unpopular ideas). But it's also important in its own right. It was this pattern that allowed working (and middle) class kids unprecedented control over their culture for a period of forty years.

It's tempting to situate Crass within a British pastoralist tradition, if only because they lived at Dial House, a farmhouse in the Essex countryside. But we think it might be more useful to fit them into a popular modernist lineage. This is most obvious when we think about Gee Vaucher and Penny Rimbaud's stint at art school. These

---

3    This certainly seemed to be the case in the mid-1980s when the expectation of a new pop-cultural event was so strong that it provoked several false starts. The band Sigue Sigue Sputnik, for instance, hyped themselves relentlessly as the pioneers of pop's fifth generation. They were – thank fuck – quite wrong but just three years later the cycle was confirmed in a place no one was looking. The rise of Acid House in 1989 took everyone by surprise and turned everything upside down.

institutions played a central role in propagating a modernist feel to post-war pop, allowing smart working class kids like Gee to encounter avant-garde ideas. It also provided them with enough free time to incorporate these ideas into the problems of their own lives. The influence of modernist artists seems self-evident in Gee Vaucher's gouaches and collages for Crass, not least the anti-fascist and communist pieces by John Heartfield and John Hamilton's 1956 collage, *Just What is it that Makes Today's Homes so Different, so Appealing?* Other elements of Crass's practice also bear a modernist mark: there are echoes of Jasper Johns in their extensive use of stencilled graffiti; Gee has herself highlighted the influence of the Fluxus movement and the Situationists, saying "We were affected by street theatre – by the idea of taking something out of our four walls and off the canvas"; and there is a Dadaist/ Situationist flavour to Crass's use of stunts and pranks.[4] Finally, the Crass symbol and all the elements of Crass's live performance also fit the mould – from the banners to the uniforms to Mick Duffield's films, the techniques of both the avant-garde and mass communication were thrown into the mix. All combined these extra-musical activities gave Crass an air of mystery and ambiguity that either made you want to walk away or delve deeper to work it out.[5]

The example of Crass reveals how popular modernism contains its own internal dynamic with an accelerated sense of progression offering a series of Year Zeros. Each subcultural cycle was, in part, a working-through of particular problems within that dynamic, but they were also structured by the wider socio-economic situation of the time.

Of course, situating punk within the crises of the 1970s is nothing new. In fact it's a story that's all too easily mobilised to justify the

4    The 'Thatchergate' tapes, an infamous faked conversation between Thatcher and Reagan cut together by the band and released to the press, were thought by MI5 to have been put together by the KGB. Crass also sneaked an anti-marriage song onto a flexidisc given away by the unsuspecting *Loving* magazine.

5    On the other hand it's obvious that Crass weren't ever part of popular culture in the way that, for example, The Jam were. The DIY ethic of the anarcho-punk scene reflected a willful embrace of marginality that became a major problematic in 1980s anarchism. All the same, there's something compelling about the way Crass melded avant-garde practices with mass communication techniques; it's almost as if they had all the attributes to be huge but deliberately held back.

neoliberal turn: early punk is placed alongside images of the winter of discontent to symbolise a country in terminal collapse. Instead we find it more useful to overlay the notion of longer economic waves onto the pattern of popular modernism. The period of popular modernist subcultural cycles is co-extensive with the period of welfarist, social democratic capitalism and its effects – from the birth of Rock 'n' Roll in the 1950s to the Acid House revolution in the late 1980s.[6] By 2002 the effects of neoliberal hegemony had altered everyday life too much for the cycle to continue.[7] It's evident from this that widespread creativity and innovation depends on a bedrock of material security.

The mid-1970s, far from being a low point of hardship for young people, were the highpoint of material equality in the UK and, by many measures, a time of unprecedented freedom for working and middle class youth.[8] We should also remember that 1976, the year of The Sex Pistols' emergence, saw the IMF impose austerity and neoliberal policies on Jim Callaghan's Labour government. The turn towards neoliberalism was already under way by the time of Thatcher's election. In this light punk can be freed from the tale of neoliberal inevitability and recast as a popular modernist expression of the first indications that the space of freedom was closing down.[9]

---

6     You could question our periodisation here because Acid House emerged several years into Thatcher's reign. We argue that at that time there were still enough gaps in the neoliberal order, and indeed enough residual material support, to allow the cycle to continue. It was only as the 1990s wore on that neoliberal globalisation gained enough hegemony to eclipse other possibilities.

7     Of course, changes in the technology of music distribution have also played a role in this but neoliberalism's effect on material conditions has been decisive. Material inequality has increased dramatically while wages have stagnated. The lack of affordable housing, alongside the crackdown on squatting and the day-to-day state interference that now goes along with claiming benefits, has eliminated the space of freedom upon which youth culture relied.

8     This claim should be tempered by an acknowledgment that other types of oppression were prevalent at the time. Expressions of sexism, racism and homophobia, for instance, were much more routine and explicit than now.

9     As Deleuze and Guattari remind us, music is the most deterritorialised and fluid of all art forms. This allows it a predictive role, anticipating and prefiguring trends that have yet to crystallise.

## BUY NOW PAY AS YOU GO

The Conservative (monetarist) analysis of the 1970s crisis saw too much money in the economy, with inflation driven by high wage demands. To bring this under control interest rates were trebled in the early 1980s with the aim of provoking a recession and stimulating unemployment. The expansion of youth unemployment was the cutting edge of the neoliberal attack on working class confidence. Yet the welfare state, still at that time designed for an economy of nearly full employment, placed few conditions on unemployment and housing benefit. The anarcho-punk scene exploited this for its material infrastructure and played an important role in collectivising and politicising the experience of unemployment into a potential space of freedom. It acted as the cutting edge of a wider dole culture, building a lifestyle based on thrifty enjoyment. Crass introduced the practice of printing the words 'pay no more than...' on their record sleeves to hold down the price of records, and the scene revolved around cheap gigs in unconventional venues.[10] The squatting scene was revitalised with an expansion of squatted houses in many cities and even squatted social centres in some. A youth dole-culture that sought to engineer the time of unemployment into a space of freedom undermined the unemployed's economic role as a reserve army of labour. It was in this sense an effective means of resisting the attack on wages.

We might call this a strategy of exodus – one that, on its own, would never be sufficient to defeat the neoliberal offensive. The promise of anarcho-punk was for dole culture to also be the basis for wider political activism. It's here that the influence of Crass became a mixed blessing. With their roots in hippy counterculture they introduced elements of a New Age-inflected individualism that cut against the collectivism found in anarcho-punk's reproductive practice. In Penny Rimbaud's words, "Anarchists believe that if each individual can learn to act out of conscience, rather than greed the machinery of power will collapse."[11] This attempt to have a 'revolution in your head' not only underestimated the influence material circumstances have on the ideas in our head but its focus on

---

10  In many ways this focus on 'the look' and 'the attitude' still followed the model set by Mod, although now consumption had to be conspicuously thrifty.

11  Penny Rimbaud, 'The Last of the Hippies' in *A Series of Shock Slogans and Mindless Token Tantrums* (Essex: Exitstencil Press), 1982)

individual conscience led away from the collective political strategies needed to effect material change.

While Crass set the initial flavour of anarchism in the scene, the general 'structure of feeling' of the times also influenced the direction of the politics. The threat of nuclear war loomed large and anti-nuclear protests and peace camps became the main political manifestation of anarcho-punk. Peace activism created a dynamic that led to the Stop the City demonstrations of 1983 and 1984 while a variety of other issues also became a focus for different elements of the scene, from animal rights to feminism. It was an admirable breadth of concerns but it also reflected the idea of politics as a personal, moral choice. At times the ideology of anarcho-punk fell into a kind of militant liberalism with increasingly stringent, although opaque, rules of moral conduct used for one-upmanship and policing of the scene. As the Bash Street Kids declared, "For most anarchism remained a 'look' and attitude first, and a set of political ideas second (if at all)."[12] Of course, it was precisely the looseness with which the ideas were held that allowed them to spread so far; this in turn provided a larger pool from which political activists could be drawn. It's another iteration of the popular modernist dynamic between popular identification and popular participation. This looseness, however, was a real hindrance to the ability to think strategically about what was changing and how to respond to it.

As the decade wore on, two transformations began to break up the anarcho-punk scene. The first was an intensification of class struggle and the defeat of the miners and printers. The miners' strike, in particular, was an event that forced people to recompose their politics in relation to a battle where lines had been so clearly drawn. Most anarcho-punks recognised what side they were on and supported the miners, often practically, but this only increased the pressure on subculture-based politics. To effect the change they wanted to see, the punks needed the support of 'ordinary people' ("the very Mums and Dads you spiked your hair up to piss off in the first place", as the Bash Street Kids put it). It produced a trajectory that was further boosted by the second transformation, the credit-fuelled boom of the second half of the 1980s and the availability of jobs that came with it. This,

---

12   Bash Street Kids, 'Nostalgia in the UK', *Smash Hits* 3, October 1998. Available at: http://www.uncarved.org/music/apunk/nostalgia.html

along with increased conditionality on benefits, undermined the material basis of the entire scene.

As a result, the trend within anarchism was towards its class struggle varieties. In particular, the group Class War used a punk aesthetic to lead the scene towards class politics. Often, however, those politics seemed based on a concept of class as a kind of socio-economic identity. The *Beasts of Burden* pamphlet offers a neat summary of the period:

> Haircuts, clothes and diets changed rapidly as people rushed to adopt the dead end 'working class identity' that they had earlier tried so hard to escape from... With hindsight, the most that can be said about developments of the 1980s was that it represented a step sideways from one confused set of ideas to another. People were no more or less working class when they adopted their patronising 'prolecult' lifestyle than when they were punks. Being working class has got nothing to do with what you wear, eat or how you talk – it's about being subjected to a life dominated by work (this applies not just to people in waged work, but the unemployed whose conditions of existence are determined by their relation to the labour market).[13]

Crass had already broken up as a group in 1984, and by the start of the 1990s the anarcho-punk scene they had helped spawn was defunct. If we can find fault with the way both Crass and the class struggle anarchists handled their inheritance from earlier generations, then what might a better mode of inheritance look like? To think this through we need to briefly consider what we mean by a generation.

## END RESULT

When people talk about generations they usually have some sort of age cohort in mind – 'Baby-boomers', 'Generation X', 'Millennials' and so on. Sometimes these categorisations relate to a specific demographic change (the Baby-boomers, for instance, are named after the

---

13 Anonymous, *Beasts of Burden: Capitalism-Animals-Communism* (London: Antagonism, 1999). Available at: http://libcom.org/library/beasts-burden-antagonism-practical-history

post-war growth in population) but this is not usually the case. In fact, political generations are formed through shared experience of disruptive events. Although these events affect people of any age, they tend to leave a disproportionate mark on those in their late teens to mid-twenties.

We need to make a distinction here between two different types of events. The first kind are those that are received passively, apparently coming from a realm beyond human control. The second kind of event are experienced as the product of the active participation of those involved. We've called these second types of events 'moments of excess', by which we mean moments which exceed the pre-existing sense of social, political and cultural possibility.[14] These two types of events generate very different kinds of generations. Let's look at some recent events to explore the distinction. The global economic crisis of 2008 is an example of the first kind of event. For most it felt like a natural disaster, as their lives were buffeted by forces they could neither understand nor control. That experience reconfigured people's material circumstances and tended to undermine belief in the naturalness of the current system. But crucially it wasn't able to offer a way out of the crisis. It took the active events of 2011, the moments of excess produced by the protests, movements and revolutions of that year, to form a 'political' generation that could move in a common direction.[15]

At this point we need to be clear about what happens in these moments of excess. Despite the claims of each pop-cultural revolution, there is no wiping out of the past: instead, moments of excess open up the future precisely by reconfiguring the past, unclogging history and opening up new lines of continuity.[16] This recalibration draws new vectors which smash through the present and fly outwards to different futures. This is exactly what happened to Joe Strummer after The Sex Pistols gig: "Yesterday I thought I was a crud. Then I saw The

---

14   The Free Association, *Moments of Excess* (Oakland: PM Press, 2011)

15   We are now seeing the effects of this combination of events in representational politics. There have been, for example, unexpected levels of youth support for Bernie Sanders and Jeremy Corbyn – although the example of the Ukraine after Euromaidan shows that these kinds of events can also produce a far-right generation.

16   As Faulkner puts it, "The past is never dead. It's not even past."

Sex Pistols and I became a king and decided to move into the future." And it seems clear that punk triggered the same affective response in the founder members of Crass.

Of course, punk is just one example of a particular subset of moments of excess. Indeed, each popular modernist subcultural cycle represents the working through of the new possibilities revealed by a moment of excess. Just as we can distinguish different types of cycle (subcultural, socio-economic, etc.), so we can also distinguish between the different kinds of generations they produce, not least because each kind of cycle has its own temporality. In fact, we might reverse this and say that the concept of a generation is simply the way we talk about the collective experiential affects of cycles. There are, or have been, distinct political generations just as there have been generational distinctions in cultural tastes and attitudes. These different generational distinctions overlap and interfere with each other. Popular modernism, for instance, sped up innovations in culture so that it cycled faster than the formation of political generations. This is how we can understand the continuities between hippy and punk. The most powerful moments occur when socio-economic, political and cultural generational cycles fall into sync and amplify one another.

The production of generations by events also raises another prospect, that veterans of one generation can find themselves regenerated by participating in subsequent moments of excess. This is not an easy task to accomplish. It's common for one political generation to experience new events as mere repetitions of the one they lived through (which is why generals always prepare to fight the last war). The mode of providing inheritance that we've been looking for is one that can bring past generational knowledge to bear upon subsequent events while retaining the ability to see what's new in the new situation. In a sense, veterans must find a way to rediscover the openness of their youth. The older participants who joined Crass seemed able to do this: they were regenerated by punk, accepting its new problems and challenges without having to renounce all of their past. When that cycle came to a close, unfortunately they didn't seem able to do it again.

Of course this task may have been easier in the accelerated generational flux of popular modernism: as Tony Wilson knew, you only had to wait a few years for the Next Big Thing to happen. If we're right in suggesting that those cycles of pop-cultural revolution are no longer possible, then the longer economic waves present a more difficult problem. In the dark days of the mid-1990s Fredric Jameson talked of "one of the fundamental peculiarities of human history, namely that human time, individual time, is out of synch with socioeconomic time, and in particular with the rhythms or cycles – the so-called Kondratiev waves – of the capitalist mode of production itself, with its brief windows of opportunity that open onto collective praxis, and its incomprehensible inhuman periods of fatality and insurmountable misery."[17]

Those of us who hope for future regeneration need to develop the means to survive the "inhuman periods of fatality" without losing our openness to the influence of events-to-come. As a hat tip to Steve Ignorant, we might call these mechanisms 'lifeboats'. They are forms of organisation that can maintain collective political purpose while being buffeted by generational waves that might otherwise make us lose coherence. Dial House acted as a lifeboat. It allowed the participants a collective project of alternative living while its open door policy allowed new influences to filter in. Penny originally hoped that Dial House would act as an example and spur a network of open houses across the country. This didn't come to pass: as the alternative culture they were a part of diminished and the outward facing project of Crass broke up, Dial House found itself too far adrift from the shores of 'ordinary' life to dock at future events erupting there.

So what model can we find to allow those in their lifeboats to present their inheritance to future generations? What role can they play in subsequent moments of excess? Perhaps, to quote Pignarre and Stengers, it's the role of the sounders of the depths, who "stay at the front of a ship, but… do not look into the distance. They cannot announce directions nor choose them. Their concern, their responsibility, the reason for the equipment they use is the rapids where one can be smashed to pieces, the rocks that one can hit, the sandbanks where one can run aground. Their knowledge stems from the experience of a past that tells of the dangers of rivers, of their deceptive currents, of their seductive eddying."[18]

17  Frederic Jameson, 'Actually Existing Marxism' in Casarino, Cesare et al (eds) *Marxism Beyond Marxism* (New York: Routledge, 1996)

18  Philippe Pignarre and Isabelle Stengers, *Capitalist Sorcery: Breaking the Spell* (Basingstoke: Palgrave Macmillan, 2011)

# CONTRIBUTORS

**RUSS BESTLEY** is Reader at the London College of Communication, University of the Arts, London, where he is currently Course Director for MA Graphic Design. He has co-authored and designed a number of publications, including *Visual Research: An Introduction to Research Methodologies in Graphic Design* (2004, revised 2nd edition 2011), *Up Against the Wall: International Poster Design* (2002) and *Experimental Layout* (2001), and has contributed articles to publications including *Eye*, *Zed*, *Emigré*, *The National Grid* and the *Oxford Encyclopaedia of the Modern World*. His most recent book, *The Art of Punk*, was published by Omnibus Press (UK), Voyageur (North America), Hannibal Verlag Gmbh (Germany) and Hugo et Compagnie (France) in 2012. His PhD thesis, entitled *Hitsville UK: Punk Rock and Graphic Design in the Faraway Towns, 1976-84*, was completed in 2008 and led to several publications, a website, and exhibitions in London, Southampton, Blackpool and Leeds. He is also an Associate Editor of the academic journal *Punk and Post Punk*, published by Intellect Ltd.

**RICH CROSS** researches, presents and writes about different aspects of first wave British anarcho-punk. His work has appeared in *Socialist History*, *Music and Politics*, *Punk & Post-Punk* journal and *Freedom* anarchist newspaper. He continues to work on a full-length study of British anarchist punk. He edits the *The Hippies Now Wear Black* blog (through which the full-text of many of his works are accessible: http://thehippiesnowwearblack.org.uk), and has written, performed and recorded with Nottingham punk band Pointy Boss since 1999. For info, contact info@thehippiesnowwearblack.org.uk

**PETE DALE** is Senior Lecturer in Popular Music at Manchester Metropolitan University. His monograph *Anyone Can Do It: Empowerment, Tradition and the Punk Underground* (2012) explored the source of political power which appeared to arise with each re-arrival of punk subsequent to its first wave. A new monograph, *Popular Music and the Politics of Novelty* (2016), examines related themes around empowerment and the importance to the Left of 'the new' (or perceived to be new). He has also published on music education and, prior to his academic career, worked as a school music teacher, musician, record label co-ordinator and bookseller.

**MIKE DINES** is Programme Leader for BMus (Hons) Popular Music Performance at the Institute of Contemporary Music Performance. He is co-founder of the Punk Scholars Network, obtaining a PhD in anarcho-punk from the University of Salford in 2005. Other publications include 'Learning Through Resistance: Contextualisation, Creation and Incorporation of a "Punk Pedagogy"', *Journal of Pedagogic Development* (2015), 'The Sacralization of Straightedge Punk: Nada Brahma and the Divine Embodiment of Krishnacore', *Musicological Annual* (2014) and the co-edited *Tales From the Punkside* (2014). His research areas include punk pedagogy, popular musicology and Krishnacore.

**THE FREE ASSOCIATION** is an ongoing experiment in collective writing and production. They're loosely based in Leeds–Leicester–London, in England, although they find themselves at home nowhere (and everywhere). David Harvie, Brian Layng and Keir Milburn freely associated to write this article. Further writing can be found at: http://freelyassociating.org.

**ALASTAIR 'GORDS' GORDON** is Senior Lecturer in Media and Communications at Leicester De Montfort University. His current research is based around genre authenticity and hierarchy across international networks of DIY punk with specific focus on Japan and Europe. He researches in and runs modules on paranormal media. In 2012, Gords co-founded the Punk Scholars Network with Mike Dines and records and tours internationally with his two bands, Geriatric Unit and Endless Grinning Skulls. Gords hates Tories, neoliberals and collects old socks.

**MATT GRIMES** is a Senior Lecturer in Music Industries and Radio at Birmingham City University. He is a member of the Punk Scholars Network and the Birmingham Centre for Media and Cultural Research where he is currently undertaking PhD research into 1980s British anarcho-punk, its impact on the subsequent lives of its participants and popular/ cultural memory and nostalgia. Other research interests and publications include British anarcho-punk 'zines, radio and marginalised communities and the use of radio as a tool for change

**GEORGE MCKAY** is a British academic with a longstanding research interest in alternative cultures and living practices, festivals and gardens, participatory arts and media, music, protest, peace, disability, and social movements. He was a teenage punk, and first saw Crass and Poison Girls in 1979; he first wrote about Crass in 1992. He is Professor of Media Studies at the University of East Anglia, and an Arts and Humanities Research Council Leadership Fellow for its Connected Communities Programme (2012–18). Among George's books are *Senseless Acts of Beauty: Cultures of Resistance since the Sixties* (1996), ed. *DIY Culture: Party & Protest in Nineties Britain* (1998), *Glastonbury: A Very English Fair* (2000), co-ed. with Pete Moser *Community Music: A Handbook* (2004), *Circular Breathing: The Cultural Politics of Jazz in Britain* (2005), *Radical Gardening: Politics, Idealism & Rebellion in the Garden* (2011), *Shakin' All Over: Popular Music and Disability* (2013), and ed. *The Pop Festival: History, Media, Music, Culture* (Bloomsbury, 2015). His website is georgemckay.org.

**MICHAEL MARY MURPHY** grew up in suburban Dublin during the punk and post-punk era. As a member of the city's DIY music community he worked in his local independent record shop and contributed to Irish fanzines. He performed in and managed bands before emigrating in the 1980s. Later he was employed by major labels in London and New York as an A&R person and worked with the Rollins Band, amongst others. He then founded a music management company and guided a number of acts to gold and platinum disc status. Murphy's primary area of research is entrepreneurial activity in the music scene and the music industry. He recently completed a PhD in Trinity College Dublin where his topic was 'A Social History of the Irish Music Industry: 1920-1985'. Michael teaches in Dublin and works with a not-for-profit collective which provides advice and support to up-and-coming as well as established artists.

**ANA RAPOSO** is a graphic designer, an educator and design researcher. Her PhD thesis entitled '30 Years of Agitprop: The Representation of 'Extreme' Politics in Punk and Post-Punk Music Graphics in the United Kingdom from 1978 to 2008' was completed in 2012 at

Central Saint Martin's College of Art and Design of the University of Arts London. She has worked as a design practitioner since 2001, as a lecturer at ESAD since 2004, and as a researcher for the Mott Collection in London.

**HELEN REDDINGTON.** While attending Brighton Art College in 1976 she became waylaid by punk. A stint in the worst band in Brighton and numerous political demonstrations later, she formed The Chefs, who left Brighton for London and recorded several BBC sessions for John Peel, as did her later band Helen and the Horns. After touring for seven years she burned out and started working on estates in South London as a song writing facilitator, before joining the new Commercial Music BA at the University of Westminster as a lecturer. That is where she completed a PhD, which became her book *The Lost Women of Rock Music: female musicians of the punk era* (2007/2012). She also contributed chapters to *The Post Subcultures Reader* and *Music, Power and Politics*. She is currently researching other punk-related subjects and also female producers and engineers in the UK, as well as performing/recording solo under the name Helen McCookerybook. Lastly, she work as an illustrator and has contributed work to *Let's Start a Pussy Riot* (eds. Emily Neu, Jade French and Pussy Riot, 2013) and *Punkademics* (ed. Zack Furness, 2012).

**DAVID SOLOMONS** is a musician and writer about music. He is a regular contributor to 'Freq', one of the longest-standing and most respected online music magazines, and an occasional contributor to music documentaries such as 'Afro Beat Rebellion' (about the life of Fela Kuti) and 'Morning and Night' (an overview of Indian classical music). He is currently writing an alternative history of Punk Rock entitled 'Ain't It Fun?'

**PETER WEBB** is a writer, lecturer and musician who specialises in research into popular and contemporary music, subcultures, globalisation, new media technology, politics, cultural and social theory. He is a Senior Lecturer in the Department of Sociology at the University of the West of England. He has previously worked at Cambridge University, Goldsmiths College, University of Birmingham, was a fellow at Fitzwilliam College and was a Research Assistant on an ESRC project on E-commerce and the music, fashion and financial services industries in the department of geographic sciences at the University of Bristol. His PhD was on the Sociology of networks of musicians and their negotiations with the music industry. He has published a book on these networks; *Exploring the Networked worlds of Popular Music: Milieu Cultures* (2010). Webb has also worked within an independent record label from 1996–2002 as an artist and tour manager and is a published musician (member of the PRS and PPL) with three albums, various singles and remixes under the names of Statik and Statik Sound System. As a musician he has worked with the physical theatre companies Blast Theory and Intimate Strangers and the film company Parallax Pictures. He currently plays with the `post-punk' band Idiot Strength. He has recently set up the DIY publishing company PC-Press whose first publication is a book on Test Dept called *Total State Machine* (2015).

**MATTHEW WORLEY** is professor of modern history at the University of Reading. He has written widely on twentieth century British politics and is currently researching a project on the link between youth culture and politics in Britain during the late 1970s and early 1980s. He is a co-editor of *Twentieth Century Communism* and member of the Subcultures Network steering committee, whose *Fight Back: Punk Politics and Resistance* was published in 2015. His articles on punk have been published in *History Workshop Journal, Twentieth Century British History, Contemporary British History, Punk & Post-Punk* and the *Journal for the Study of Radicalism.* He is currently completing a history of British punk from 1976 to 1984.

# MINOR COMPOSITIONS

As well as a multitude to come…

CPSIA information can be obtained
at www.ICGtesting.com
Printed in the USA
BVHW030235040422
633160BV00006B/149